ORANGE COUNTY PUBLIC LIBRARY
ORANGE, CALIFORNIA
21

ORANGE COUNTY PUBLIC LIBRARY

A14922 545812

S0-BZC-372

DISCARD

THE CONFIRMATION OF OTHERNESS

THE CONFIRMATION OF OTHERNESS

IN FAMILY, COMMUNITY, AND SOCIETY

Maurice Friedman

THE PILGRIM PRESS
NEW YORK

PROPERTY OF:
ORANGE CO PUBLIC LIB
DISCARD DRIVE SOUTH
ORANGE 92668

21

COPYRIGHT © 1983 BY THE PILGRIM PRESS
ALL RIGHTS RESERVED

NO PART OF THIS PUBLICATION MAY BE REPRODUCED, STORED IN A
RETRIEVAL SYSTEM, OR TRANSMITTED IN ANY FORM OR BY ANY MEANS,
ELECTRONIC, MECHANICAL, PHOTOCOPYING, RECORDING, OR OTHER-
WISE (BRIEF QUOTATIONS USED IN MAGAZINES OR NEWSPAPER REVIEWS
EXCEPTED), WITHOUT THE PRIOR PERMISSION OF THE PUBLISHER.

LIBRARY OF CONGRESS CATALOGING IN PUBLICATION DATA .

FRIEDMAN, MAURICE S.
  THE CONFIRMATION OF OTHERNESS, IN FAMILY, COMMUNITY,
  AND SOCIETY.

  INCLUDES BIBLIOGRAPHICAL REFERENCES.
  1. INTERPERSONAL RELATIONS.   2. OTHER MINDS
(THEORY OF KNOWLEDGE)   3. FAMILY.   4. COMMUNITY LIFE.
I. TITLE.
HM132.F7   1983   158'.2   83-5648
ISBN 0-8298-0651-2

ACKNOWLEDGMENTS APPEAR ON PAGES 299–301.

THE PILGRIM PRESS, 132 WEST 31 STREET, NEW YORK, N.Y. 10001

TO
DAN WILSON'S PENDLE HILL

CONTENTS

Part IV
CONFIRMATION OF OTHERNESS IN COMMUNITY

Part V
CONFIRMATION OF OTHERNESS IN SOCIETY

Part VI
TOWARD A COMMUNITY OF COMMUNITIES

This person is other, essentially other than myself, and this otherness of his is what I mean, because I mean him; I confirm it; I wish his otherness to exist, because I wish his particular being to exist. That is the basic principle of marriage and from this basis it leads, if it is real marriage, to insight into the right and the legitimacy of otherness and to that vital acknowledgment of many-faced otherness—even in the contradiction and conflict with it—from which dealings with the body politic receive their religious ethos. That the men with whom I am bound up in the body politic and with whom I have directly or indirectly to do, are essentially other than myself, that this one or that one does not have merely a different mind, or way of thinking or feeling, or a different conviction or attitude, but has also a different perception of the world, a different recognition and order of meaning, a different touch from the regions of existence, a different faith, a different soil: to affirm all this . . . in the midst of the hard situations of conflict, without relaxing their real seriousness, is the way . . . from which alone we are from time to time permitted to touch . . . on the other's "truth" or "untruth," "justice" or "injustice."

MARTIN BUBER
BETWEEN MAN AND MAN

PREFACE

THE CONFIRMATION OF OTHERNESS transcends the bounds of the intrapsychic—the traditional province of psychology—in its concern with the realm of the "between." It is with this realm of the "between" that *The Confirmation of Otherness* begins, laying a philosophical foundation for the very concrete and specific areas of concern that are pointed to in the subtitle, *In Family, Community, and Society*, to each of which one part of this book is devoted. Though there are more chapters under the heading of "The Confirmation of Society" than under the other two headings, this area, because of its vastness and complexity, is the one most sketchily covered. I have made no attempt to offer an overall theory of society, much less detailed political, economic, and sociological studies. Rather, I have pointed as best I could to what the unfolding of the confirmation of otherness and the "community of otherness" might mean. In all three areas—family, community, and society—I have brought in what I have made my own, either as an outgrowth of earlier writings and present concerns or because I have been specifically asked to turn my attention to one or another topic (such as the role of the father in the family, aging, transcultural nursing, and un- and underemployment).

The Confirmation of Otherness is not only concerned with the sphere of the "between" but also with "confirmation." Many years ago I met my old Harvard professor Carl Friedrichs and told him that I had just finished a doctoral dissertation on Martin Buber. "Buber is a seminal thinker," Friedrichs said to me. One of Buber's seminal ideas which has interested me for many years is that of "confirmation"—the confirming of one person by another through the first person's making the other present, *meaning* him or her in his or her uniqueness, and inducing this other's inmost self-becoming. Some of Buber's seminal ideas, such as dialogue and the I-Thou relationship, he himself developed fully. Confirmation and, in particular, the confirmation of otherness (to which the motto at the head of this book so vividly points) he left mostly in seed. By trying to bring this seed to flower through exploring the implications of confirmation, I feel that I am carrying on a dialogue with Buber after his death. This feeling was given vivid expression a few weeks ago in a dream in which I found myself sitting across the table from Buber who was now ninety-one (in fact, he died at the age of eighty-seven) and engaging in an intensive dialogue on his thought.

I used to say that if I gained the wisdom and experience, I should like to write a book on confirmation. I have recognized since that if I waited until then, I should never write the book. So I have chosen instead to say what it is I can say on the basis of the limited wisdom and experience that I now possess. In my book *Healing Through Meeting: Dialogue and Psychotherapy* I devote a whole section of four chapters to confirmation. In this sense, *Healing Through Meeting* overlaps with *The Confirmation of Otherness*. Since this overlapping does not mean a repetition, the reader of this present book may find it fruitful to read Part Four of *Healing Through Meeting*—"Confirmation and the Dialogue of Touchstones."

No one has invented new words that have solved the problem of gender to my satisfaction, and I am not content to always use "he" and ask the reader to assume I also mean "she" or to always use "she" and ask the reader to assume I also mean "he." I know no better way to show my equal respect and concern for both women and men than inconsistency. Therefore, sometimes I write "he," sometimes "she," sometimes "one," and sometimes "s/he." The same applies to "her" and "his" and "him." Wherever possible I use "person" or "human" instead of "man," but the reader will probably find occasions in which I use "man" in the generic sense, as in "the problem of man" or even "the image of man" (usually I say the "human image" or "the image of the human").

I wish to express my thanks to my student and friend David Zucker for his critical comments on the chapters "The Learning Community" and "Dialogue in Mentoring and Research," which helped me in reformulating them.

I also must express my deep gratitude to Eugenia Friedman, my wife and partner since 1947, who shared with me most of the experiences that I have used as illustrations in this book and who has given me invaluable advice as to which of the most personal ones to retain and which to delete.

Maurice Friedman
Solana Beach, California
July 1981

Part I

CONFIRMATION AND THE ONTOLOGY OF THE "BETWEEN"

Chapter 1

THE PHILOSOPHY OF THE INTERHUMAN

ONTOLOGY IS the study of being or, as Paul Tillich would say, the "really real." To speak of something as "really real" is not to suggest that everything else is unreal. It is to imply that other things stand in a secondary or derivative relation to the really real. They are "real" too, but their reality comes through the reality of the really real. Accordingly, the "ontology of the between" does not suggest that individual persons are less than fully real, but it does claim that they find their reality again and again through meeting, through the between. The psychological by this reading is not something delusory, but neither is it the touchstone of reality. It is the accompaniment and by-product of the "between." "Psychologism" means to make the by-product the essential and remove the events that happen between persons into feelings or occurrences within the psyche.

The ontology of the between is implicit in those "existentialists of dialogue," such as Gabriel Marcel, Karl Jaspers, Franz Rosenzweig, Albert Camus, and, to a lesser extent, Maurice Merleau-Ponty, whose touchstone of reality is not the self taken by itself but the self in its relationship to other selves. But it was Martin Buber who made it explicit—in his first book on philosophical anthropology, *What Is Man?*—and who systematically developed its implications into the philosophy of the interhuman in *The*

Knowledge of Man. The sphere in which person meets person has been ignored because it possesses no smooth continuity. Its experience has been annexed to the soul and to the world, so that what happens to an individual can be distributed between outer and inner impressions. But when two individuals "happen" to each other, there is an essential remainder which is common to them but which reaches out beyond the special sphere of each. That remainder is the basic reality, the "sphere of the between."

In an essential relation the barriers of individual being are breached and "the other becomes present not merely in the imagination or feeling but in the depths of one's substance, so that one experiences the mystery of the other being in the mystery of one's own." The two persons participate in one another's lives not merely psychologically, as images or feelings in one another's psyches, but ontologically as a manifest, even if not continuous reality of the between. For such a relationship to be possible, each must be a real person in his or her own right. A *great* relation not only breaches the barriers of solitude of each of these persons, claims Buber, but is stronger than death: it "throws a bridge from self-being to self-being across the abyss of dread of the universe."

In man something takes place which takes place nowhere else in nature. One person turns to another as this particular being in order to communicate with the other in that sphere of the between that reaches out beyond the special sphere of each. In that sphere what happens cannot be exactly distributed between an "outer" event and an "inner" impression. This realm of the between exists on the far side of the subjective and on this side of the objective "on the narrow ridge where *I* and *Thou* meet." This sphere of the interhuman is where the human comes into being, and it is man's contact with the really real:

> Human life touches on absoluteness in virtue of its dialogical character, for in spite of his uniqueness man can never find, when he plunges to the depth of his life, a being that is whole in itself and as such touches on the absolute. Man can become whole not in virtue of a relation to himself but only in virtue of a relation to another self. This other self may be just as limited and conditioned as he is; in being together the unlimited and the unconditioned is experienced.[1]

It is essential not to confuse Buber's ontology of the between with Martin Heidegger's ontology of Being, as some philosophers and psychologists have done. For Heidegger, human existence takes place primarily in the relation between individual man and Being per se and only secondarily and correlatively in the relationship between person and person. Heidegger's interpretation of Heraclitus's *logos* as the speechless Word through which man brings Being to unconcealment contrasts in the strongest possible fashion with Buber's interpretation of it as the "speech-with-meaning" through which persons build together the common cosmos of the Essential We. From Buber's standpoint Heidegger's claim that man can relate directly to Being as the unique, not-to-be-outstripped potentiality of nonrelational man means taking one's stand in the realm of monologue and turning one's back on the life of dialogue. As Buber himself writes in "What Is Man?":

> Heidegger, influenced by Hölderlin, the great poet of this mystery, has undoubtedly had a profound experience of the mystery of being which is dimly apparent through all that is; but he has not experienced it as one which steps before us and challenges us to yield the last thing, so hard fought for, the being at rest in oneself, to breach the barriers of the self and to come out from ourselves to meet with essential otherness.[2]

In *The Knowledge of Man*, the last and decisive stage of his philosophical anthropology, Buber found it necessary to deepen the ontology of the between by discovering the two basic movements from which the twofold principle of human life (I-Thou and I-It) is derived. The first of these two movements Buber calls the "primal setting at a distance," the second "entering into relation." The first movement is the presupposition for the second; for we can enter into relation only with being that has been set at a distance from us and thereby has become an independent opposite. Only through this act of setting at a distance does man have a "world"—an unbroken continuum which includes not merely all that he and other men know and experience, but all that is knowable now and in the future. But that "synthesizing apperception" through which being is perceived as a whole and as a unity takes place not only through setting at a distance, but also through entering into relation.

In human life together, it is the fact that man sets man at a distance and makes him independent that enables him to enter into relation, as an individual self, with those like himself. Through this "interhuman" relation men confirm each other, becoming a self with the other. The inmost growth of the self is not induced by man's relation to himself, "as people like to suppose today," but by the confirmation in which one person knows himself to be "made present" in his uniqueness by the other. "Self-realization," that vague shibboleth which occupies so large a place in our popular culture, is not the *goal* but the *by-product*. The goal is completing distance by relation, and relation here means cooperation, genuine dialogue, and mutual confirmation.

Buber distinguishes the "interhuman" from the "social" in general, a distinction of great significance in an intellectual climate in which the importance of "interpersonal relations" and the "social self" are increasingly recognized and at the same time are indiscriminately confused with "dialogue" and the "I-Thou" relationship. The "social" includes the I-It relation as well as the I-Thou: many interpersonal relations are really characterized by one person's treating the other as an object to be known and used. Most interpersonal relationships are, in fact, a mixture of I-Thou and I-It and some are almost purely I-It. Both George Herbert Mead and Harry Stack Sullivan include something of what Buber calls the "interhuman" in their treatment of the social self and the interpersonal, but, unlike Buber, neither man singles out the interhuman as a separate dimension, qualitatively different and essentially significant.

The unfolding of the sphere of the between Buber calls the "dialogical." The psychological, that which happens within the soul of each, is only the secret accompaniment to the dialogue. The meaning of this dialogue is found in neither one nor the other of the partners, nor in both added together, but in their interchange. This distinction between the "dialogical" and the "psychological" constitutes a radical attack on the psychologism of our age. It makes manifest the fundamental ambiguity of those modern psychologists who affirm the dialogue between person and person, but who are unclear as to whether this dialogue is of value in itself or is merely a function of the individual's self-acceptance and self-realization. "Individuation is only the indispensable personal stamp of all realization of human existence," writes Buber in *The Knowledge of Man*. "The self as such is not ultimately the essential, but the meaning of human existence given in creation again and again fulfills itself as self."

By pointing to dialogue as the intrinsic value, and self-realization as only the corollary and by-product rather than the goal, Buber also separates himself from those existential psychotherapists like Binswanger and May who tend to make the I-Thou relationship just another dimension of the self, along with one's relation to oneself and to one's environment.

We have in common with every thing the ability to become an object of observation, writes Buber in *The Knowledge of Man*, but it is the privilege of man, through the hidden action of his being, to be able to impose an insurmountable limit to his objectification. Only as a partner can man be perceived as an existing wholeness. To become aware of a man means to perceive his wholeness as person defined by spirit: to perceive the dynamic center which stamps on all his utterances, actions, and attitudes the recognizable sign of uniqueness. Such an awareness is impossible if, and so long as, the other is for me the detached object of my observation; for he will not thus yield his wholeness and its center. It is possible only when he becomes present for me.

The essential problematic of the sphere of the between, writes Buber, is the duality of being and seeming. The person dominated by being gives himself to the other spontaneously without thinking about the image of himself awakened in the beholder. The seeming person, in contrast, is primarily concerned with what the other thinks of him, and produces a look calculated to make himself appear "spontaneous," "sincere," or whatever he thinks will win the other's approval. This seeming destroys the authenticity of the life between one human being and another and thus the authenticity of human existence in general. The tendency toward seeming originates in man's need for confirmation and in his desire to be confirmed falsely rather than not to be confirmed at all. To give in to this tendency is the real cowardice of man, writes Buber; to withstand it is his real courage.

Mutual confirmation is essential to becoming a self—a person who realizes his uniqueness precisely through his relation to other selves whose distance from him is completed by his distance from them. True confirmation means that I confirm my partner as this existing being even while I oppose him. I legitimize him over against me as the one with whom I have to do in real dialogue. This mutual confirmation of men is most fully realized in what Buber calls "making present," an event which happens partially wherever men come together, but in its essential structure only rarely. Making the other present means to "imagine the real," to imagine quite concretely what another person is wishing, feeling, perceiving, and thinking. This is no empathy or intuitive perception, but a bold swinging into the other which demands the intensest action of one's being in order to make the other present in his wholeness, unity, and uniqueness. One can do this only as a partner, standing in a common situation with the other, and even then one's address to the other may remain unanswered and the dialogue may die in seed.

The "between" is an ontological category, the "interhuman" a philosophical-anthropological one. The two are linked through the ontological significance implicit in all philosophical anthropology and explicit in Buber's philosophy of the interhuman:

> Every anthropology of a subject touches on its ontology, hence every investigation of a subject in its conditioning by the manner, the nature, the attitude of man leads us toward this subject's place in being and its function in meaning. Thus to the degree that we fathom the relation of a circle of reality to us, we are always referred to its still unfathomed relation to being and meaning.[3]

Chapter 2

DIALOGUE AND THE UNIQUE

SO FAR from being opposites, as is commonly thought, dialogue and the unique are necessary corollaries within the philosophy of the interhuman.

By the unique I do not mean difference. Uniqueness is what makes a person or thing of value in itself, that which is unrepeatable and for which no other value can be substituted, that which is not a matter of usefulness or function but, however much it may exist in relation to others, is a center in itself. Uniqueness is the necessary first step toward the philosophy of the interhuman. The true meaning of the relation of the person to the reality that he encounters can neither be understood nor approached except by way of this concept.

Though William James and John Dewey are both central figures in the stream of American pragmatism, their attitudes toward the unique are diametrically opposed. James says of pragmatism that she is willing "to count the humblest and most personal experiences." "She will count mystical experiences if they have practical consequences. She will take a God who lives in the very dirt of private fact—if that should seem a likely place to find Him."[1] Dewey's instrumentalism, in contrast, excludes not only mysticism and God, but also James's willingness to "count the humblest and most personal experiences"—"the very dirt of private

9

fact." Dewey sees "the primary significance of the unique and morally ultimate character of the concrete situation" as transferring "the weight and burden of morality to intelligence," and he defines the part played by intelligence, not as entering into the response to the unique or pointing back to it, but as abstracting from its concreteness, destroying its wholeness, blurring its vividness, discounting its more insistent traits.[2]

A similar contrast in attitude toward the unique may be found within phenomenology, if the term is used broadly enough to include the two different fountainheads of the movement—the historian, psychologist, and philosopher Wilhelm Dilthey and the philosopher who founded the philosophical school of phenomenology, Edmund Husserl. For Dilthey the suspension of conclusions and the approach to investigations in terms of typologies also included a type of I-Thou participation of the knower in what is known and with it the possibility of apprehending the unique in whatever phenomenon is dealt with as well as its place in relation to ideal types. For Husserl, in contrast, the task of unfolding the universal egology, in which the transcendental Ego brackets all assumptions about the independent existence of what it deals with and about natural-scientific causes and effects, is accompanied by an eidetic insight into structural essences which leaves no real room for the unique. Hence when Husserl tries to correct Descartes' solipsism in his *Cartesian Meditations* by establishing a world of intersubjectivity, he still sees one person as knowing another only as the "not-me," the person "over there" in relation to my "being here," or knowing his anger by analogy with my anger.

Another contrast, this one within psychiatry, might be offered between Harry Stack Sullivan, whose therapy was based on the faith that we are all much more simply the same than we are unique, and his one-time student and disciple Leslie H. Farber who, precisely in rejecting all the models of psychotherapy as based on psychopathology and for that reason being more "humanoid" than human, points us in the direction of the unique. There is more real humanity in one page of Dostoevsky, says Farber, than in all the laborious definitions of man offered by the conflicting schools of psychoanalysis.

Ordinary usage to the contrary, the unique is not the different nor is it the individual. Both of these are known only in comparison and contrast while the unique is known only in and for itself.

As applied to the human person, moreover, the unique is not purely descriptive—Where could we hope to isolate and identify it?—and still less purely normative—It is the enemy of every general ideal that looks away from the concrete situation from which one starts. The unique is a concrete life-event, of value in itself. It is the inmost meaning of the "person" as distinct from the "individual."

In his doctrine of "entelechy" Aristotle saw each individual person as having a *telos*, or end, that draws him to its fulfillment and that is at the same time part of the process whereby all things are drawn to the Good. The Hebrew Bible speaks in terms of man being created in the image of the imageless God and each person, therefore, having a unique value and a unique created task that no other person has. This notion of created uniqueness was expanded and developed in Hasidism, the popular communal Jewish mysticism of eighteenth- and nineteenth-century Eastern Europe:

> God never does the same thing twice, said Rabbi Nachman of Bratzlav.
>
> That which exists is unique, and it happens but once. New and without a past, it emerges from the flood of returnings, takes place, and plunges back into it, unrepeatable. . . . It is because things happen but once that the individual partakes in eternity. For the individual with his inextinguishable uniqueness is engraved in the heart of the all and lies for ever in the lap of the timeless as he who is constituted thus and not otherwise.
>
> Uniqueness is the essential good of man that is given him to unfold.[3]

It might appear that one's uniqueness is identical with what is today called "self-realization." This is so only if self-realization takes place, not as an end in itself or a form of being preoccupied with oneself, but as the by-product of one's response to the unique created task which one is called to perform. We need the freedom for self-realization; yet uniqueness is not identical with human potentialities or even the realization of such potentialities. It is, rather, what governs the difference between meaningful and nonmeaningful realization of potentialities; for potentialities are essentially neutral, and their realization is not necessarily of value in itself. Realizing "human potentialities" is not the same as becoming the unique person one is called to become in dialogue with the world that calls one. On the contrary, the concern with the realization of potentialities—whether one's I.Q. or one's "musical talent"—can prevent one's hearing the address of the event or person that calls one to respond and to become himself through his response.

The unique is not an embodied Platonic idea or Aristotelian form. It is no *a priori* essence or destiny or mere chance. It is the movement of the person through time, the response of the person to situation, the interaction of the person with event. It is not "to become what you are" but to be what you are called to become. As such its realization takes place through knowing and being known—in that reciprocal contact in which Adam "knew" Eve—through calling and being called, through the courage to address and the courage to respond. It is *our* uniqueness yet it is not *in* us. It comes into being *between* us and what is not ourselves. We cannot possess it or claim it as an attribute of our nature or being. Yet it and it alone makes us unmistakably ourselves.

The unique is known only through dialogue. Only in genuine dialogue do I relate and respond to the other for himself and for the sake of our relationship and not as a function of knowledge and use, comparison and contrast, reflection and analysis, education and exploitation. But the converse is also true. Every genuine dialogue is unique. An ever-renewed presentness and presence can be fully concrete and meaningful only insofar as it is unique. There is no essence of dialogue that can thread its way through the world of particulars as some ideal universal. The proper understanding of dialogue includes uniqueness; for it is only in uniqueness that there is real mutuality, presentness, and presence. Dialogue means a mutual sharing in reciprocal presentness of the unique. The unique implies otherness but otherness capable of entering into communion.

In the presentness of meeting are included all those things which we see in their uniqueness and for their own selves, and not as already filtered through our mental categories for purposes of knowledge or use. In this presentness it is no longer true (as it obviously is in the "having become" world of active subject and passive subject) that the existing beings over against us cannot in some sense move to meet us as we them. Because these existing beings are real, we can feel the impact of their active reality even though we cannot know them as they are in themselves or describe that impact apart from our relation to it. This "impact" is not that which can be objectively observed by any subject; for in objective observation the activity of the object is usually thought of as part of a causal order in which nothing is really active of itself. It is rather the "impact" of the relationship in the present moment between the human I and that human or nonhuman existing being which has become real for him as "Thou." This impact makes manifest the only true uniqueness; for that inexhaustible difference between objects which we loosely call "uniqueness" is really nothing other than a product of our comparison of one object with another and is nothing that exists in the object in itself.

There is, at the same time, a decisive difference between the revelation in dialogue of the uniqueness of a human and a nonhuman existing being. The latter, whether it be a tree or a flower, will not hide itself from us by any conscious act of will. Man, in contrast, cannot and will not allow another to "see into his soul" if he senses that that other comes merely as objective observer, scientifically curious analyst, or prying manipulator. I can only become aware of another as I perceive him in his wholeness as a person, and that means to perceive that dynamic center which stamps on all his utterances, actions, and attitudes the tangible sign of uniqueness. As long as the other is for me the detached object of my contemplation or observation, he will not yield his wholeness and its center to me, and I shall not be aware of him as a person, only as an individual. Only when I step into elemental relationship with the other, only when he becomes present to me as I to him, only when I risk and reveal myself as he risks and reveals himself will I grasp his uniqueness as he mine.

The uniqueness of each of the partners of the dialogue is made up of, created, or formed by the uniqueness of this particular relationship, the uniqueness of which, in turn, is made up of, created, or formed by the uniqueness of the particular, present event of meeting. Yet each past event may become present again when it is taken up in its concrete uniqueness into a new present event. The new event is not identical with the old, but it carries it into reborn presentness. Because this is so, we may also say that the uniqueness of each of the partners of dialogue is included and revealed in the uniqueness of this particular relationship and the uniqueness of this particular relationship is included and revealed in the uniqueness of the particular, present event.

The word "person" bridges over and unites three separate

realities of personal existence. On the one hand, we speak of the mysterious imprint of uniqueness on an incessantly changing, varying process which would have no essential unity as an "I" were it not for this imprint. Second, however, the person finds his full reality in the present, and personality exists in actualized form only in the present. When we speak, as we must, of personality extending over time, it is the alternation between actual and potential personality that we mean. The existence of the person in time is not a smooth process but an alternation between moments of real presentness and other moments—of sleep, of semiconsciousness, of distraction, inner division, illness—when a person falls from actualized presentness into mere subsistence, or potentiality.

Third, a person finds himself as person through going out to meet the other, through responding to the address of the other. He does not lose his center, his personal core, in an amorphous meeting with the other. If he sees through the eyes of the other and experiences the other's side, he does not cease to see through his own eyes and experience the relationship from his own side. We do not experience the other through empathy or analogy. We do not know his anger because of our anger; for he may be angry in an entirely different way from us. But we can glimpse something of his side of the relationship. That too is what it means to be a real person. A real person does not remain shut within himself or use his relations with others as a means to his own self-realization. He realizes himself as an "I," a person, through going out again and again to meet the "Thou." To do this, however, he must have the courage to address and the courage to respond.

We have in us the potentiality of response which can be awakened. But *we* must do the responding. No one can handle our side of the dialogue, even from the beginning. There is an irreducible uniqueness that has to do with the fact that each person, even identical twins, has a very personal way of responding that can be discerned at six months and even earlier. Responsibility means to respond, and genuine response is response of the whole person. Yet we ought not think of the question of how to be a whole person but only of how, in any given situation, to respond more wholly rather than less so. We never become "whole persons" as a state of being, attained once and for all. In every situation we are asked to respond in a unique way. Therefore, our wholeness in that situation is unique, too. Each moment of personal wholeness is unique even though we become more and more "ourselves" through such response and, hence, more and more recognizable by others in a personal uniqueness that extends beyond the moment. Abraham Lincoln responded with greatness to a unique historical situation and became the unique person that he was. We only really exist when we exist in a situation, and we become ourself in responding to that situation.

We are all persons, to a certain extent, by courtesy of one another. We call each other back into being persons when sleepiness, sickness, or malaise have divested us of our person-hood. What makes us persons is the stamp of uniqueness, of personal wholeness, and this is not anything that can ever be looked at or grasped as an object. This stamp of uniqueness is not something we can know directly in ourselves. We know it of each other as we enter into dialogue, but we know it of ourselves only in that dim awareness that has to do with becoming more and more uniquely ourselves in responding to what is not ourselves. The whole self is not what I am aware of when I am simply selfconscious. For then I am turning myself into an object and losing my intuitive grasp of the person that I am. The intuitive awareness that comes in responding is not incompatible with objectivity, analysis, or psychoanalysis. But it *is* incompatible with making these the final court of appeal as to what is real.

Our wholeness is most there when we have forgotten ourselves in responding fully to what is not ourselves. Any genuine whole-hearted response—"When the music is heard so deeply that you are the music while the music lasts"—can bring us to this immediacy. Our selfconsciousness returns when we go back, as we must, from immediacy to mediacy. Yet it need not get in the way as much as we usually suppose. The fact that we are reflective can be handled lightly instead of heavily, especially if we do not make the mistake of identifying our "I" with that reflective consciousness and regarding the rest as just the object that the "I" looks at.

Chapter 3

TRUSTWORTHINESS AND THE LIFE OF DIALOGUE

The motto of life is "Give and take." Everyone must be both a giver and a receiver. He who is not both is as a barren tree.

Hasidic master

A sound man's heart is not shut within itself
But is open to other people's hearts:
I find good people good,
And I find bad people good
If I am good enough;
I trust men of their word,
And I trust liars
If I am true enough;
I feel the heart-beats of others
Above my own
If I am enough of a father,
Enough of a son.

Laotzu

Once when I was standing in the room of my master and teacher, the rabbi of Kotzk, I understood the meaning of what is written in Proverbs: "But a trustworthy man who can find?" This does not mean that you can find only one in a thousand. It means that a trustworthy man, that is to say a man who can really be trusted, cannot be found at all, for he is well hidden—you may stand right in front of him and yet you will not find him.

Hasidic master

THE REASON we cannot find a trustworthy man is not only that the *zaddik*, the righteous and trustworthy person on whom the world stands, is often hidden, but also because trustworthiness is not something that inheres in a person like a quality or virtue, the Boy Scout's creed to the contrary notwithstanding, but something that is found only in give and take, in the openness of the heart between person and person, in the "life of the dialogue."

About five years after the publication in 1955 of my book *Martin Buber: The Life of Dialogue*, I wrote to Martin Buber saying that if I were to write it again I would write a conclusion showing "existential trust" to be the real heart of Buber's teaching. Buber replied that I was right, that existential trust was indeed the heart of the attitude underlying his life and thought. The existential trust that stands at the center of the life of dialogue is the "holy insecurity" which is willing to go out to meet the unique present, rather than to take refuge in orientation and knowing one's way about. The person of "know how" wants to master the situation. The person of existential trust is able to accept the unique which is present in each new situation, despite all resemblance to the past. Real presentness means presence—being open to what the present brings by bringing oneself to the present, allowing the future to come as it comes, rather than attempting to turn it into a predictable replica of the past. The life of dialogue realizes the unity of the contraries in meeting others *and* in holding one's ground when one meets them. This is the existential trust that "all real living is meeting," that meaning is open and accessible in the lived concrete, that our true concern is not the unraveling of mysteries but the way of the human being in partnership with creation.

Real, uncurtailed, personal existence begins not when one says to the other, "I am you," but when one says, "I accept you as you are," in your otherness and uniqueness. The typical mark of the inauthentic person of today is that s/he does not really *hear*, s/he does not really *listen* to another. In so doing, s/he becomes guilty not just to the other but to the common world that we are all building together, to the common We. "In our age," writes Buber, "in which the true meaning of every word is encompassed by delusion and falsehood and the original intention of the human glance is stifled by tenacious mistrust, it is of decisive importance to find again the genuineness of speech and existence as We."

Existence as We can never mean that the individual merely conforms to society or subordinates his or her own self to the collectivity. It means that each contributes to the common order from where and from what he or she is. Buber sees marriage as the exemplary bond; for marriage means that I can share in Present Being only if I take seriously the fact that the other *is*, answering her address and answering for her as one entrusted to me. Through marriage, I enter into relation with otherness, "and the basic structure of otherness, in many ways uncanny but never quite unholy or incapable of being hallowed, in which I and the others who meet me in my life are inwoven, is the body politic." Real marriage leads to "vital acknowledgment of many-faced otherness—even in the contradiction and conflict with it."

> That the men with whom I am bound up in the body politic . . . are essentially other than myself, that this one or that one does not have merely a different mind, or way of thinking or feeling, or a different conviction or attitude, but has also a different perception of the world, a different recognition and order of meaning, a different touch from the regions of existence, a different faith, a different soil: to affirm all this, to affirm it in the way of a creature, in the midst of the hard situations of conflict, without relaxing their real seriousness, is the way by which we may officiate as helpers in this wide realm entrusted to us as well, and from which alone we are from time to time permitted to touch in our doubts, in humility and upright investigation, on the other's "truth" or "untruth," "justice" or "injustice." But to this we are led by marriage, if it is real, with a power for which there is scarcely a substitute . . . by its crises and the overcoming of them which rises out of the organic depths.[1]

Buber carries this experiencing of the otherness in marriage into the sexual act itself. In love, "imagining the real" takes place not as some Emersonian meeting of soul and soul but with the whole body-soul person:

> A man caresses a woman, who lets herself be caressed. Then let us assume that he feels the contact from two sides—with the palm of his hand still, and also with the woman's skin. The twofold nature of the gesture, as one that takes place between two persons, thrills through the depth of enjoyment in his heart and stirs it. If he does not deafen his heart he will have—not to renounce the enjoyment but—to love.

I do not in the least mean that the man who has had such an experience would from then on have this two-sided sensation in every such meeting—that would perhaps destroy his instinct. But the one extreme experience makes the other person present to him for all time. A transfusion has taken place after which a mere elaboration of subjectivity is never again possible or tolerable to him.[2]

True lovers have a bipolar experience, a contemporaneity at rest. They receive the common event from both sides at once "and thus for the first time understand in a bodily way what an event is." This is the otherness of the other who lives with me as Thou, who faces me as partner, who affirms and contends with me, but vows me faithfully to being as I vow her.

In the relations between parent and child and teacher and student, it is again the recognition of otherness, of the uniqueness that has its own right and must grow in its own way, which informs the mutual contact and the mutual trust.

Trust, trust in the world, because this human being exists—that is the most inward achievement of the relation in education. Because this human being exists, meaninglessness, however hard pressed you are by it, cannot be the real truth. Because this human being exists, in the darkness the light lies hidden, in fear salvation, and in the callousness of one's fellow-men the great Love.[3]

For this trust to exist, the teacher or parent must be really there, really facing the child, not merely there in spirit. To be there she need possess none of the perfections which the child imagines, but she "must have gathered the child's presence" into her own store "as one of the bearers" of her "communion with the world, one of the focuses of" her "responsibilities for the world." She does not have to be concerned with the child at every moment, but she must have gathered the child into her life in such a way "that steady potential presence of the one to the other is established and endures."

The catastrophe for the child comes not if the parent or teacher turns out to be less than perfect, but if she is trying to *seem* to be a certain type of person in order to win the approval or dependence of the child. The essential problem of the sphere of the inter-human, as we have seen, is this duality of being and seeming.

The person who lives from his or her being may wish to influence others, but s/he does not concern him or herself with how s/he appears to others, or try to appear in a certain way in order to gain confirmation from the other. The seeming person produces a look which is meant to appear to be spontaneous but is actually only concerned with the effect it produces. In the interhuman realm, "truth" does not mean saying whatever comes to mind, but letting no *seeming* creep between oneself and the other. It does not mean letting go before another but granting that person a share in one's being.

If the perception of the other's wholeness, unity, and uniqueness is only possible when I step into an elemental relation with her and make her present as a person, then by the same token the analytical, reductive, and deriving look that predominates between person and person today stands in the way of this perception:

> This look is a reductive one, because it tries to contract the manifold person, who is nourished by the microcosmic richness of the possible, to some schematically surveyable and recurrent structures. And this look is a deriving one, because it supposes it can grasp what a man has become, or even is becoming, in genetic formulae, and it thinks that even the dynamic central principle of the individual in this becoming can be represented by a general concept. An effort is being made today radically to destroy the mystery between man and man. The personal life, the ever-near mystery, once the source of the stillest enthusiasms, is leveled down.[4]

This critique of the modern "look" applies not only to the "look" of Sartre that makes the other into an object but also to that of Freud—a synthetic combination of analytical subcategories which systematically excludes from its view the wholeness and uniqueness of the person. In isolating the conflicts of superego and id, Freud misses the real context in which this dualism of repression and sublimation takes place—namely, the sickness of modern man that is produced by the decay of organic community and the crisis of confidence, or trust, that accompanies it:

> Where confidence reigns man must often, indeed, adapt his wishes to the commands of his community; but he must not repress them to such an extent that the repression acquires a

dominating significance for his life. . . . Only if the organic community disintegrates from within and mistrust becomes life's basic note does the repression acquire its dominating importance. The unaffectedness of wishing is stifled by mistrust, everything around is hostile or can become hostile, agreement between one's own and the other's desire ceases, for there is no true coalescence or reconciliation with what is necessary to a sustaining community, and the dulled wishes creep hopelessly into the recesses of the soul. . . . Now there is no longer a human wholeness with the force and the courage to manifest itself. . . . The divorce between spirit and instincts is here, as often, the consequence of the divorce between man and man.[5]

"Basic trust" lies in the integral relationship between existential trust and what I call the "community of otherness."[6] Existential trust grows out of the "partnership of existence" and expresses itself in "the courage to address and the courage to respond." Trustworthiness in the partnership of existence means, among other things, recognizing that other people do not possess fixed character—good or evil, honest or dishonest—but that the way in which we approach them, the way in which we allow life to flow between us and them, frees them to possibilities of goodness, trust, and openness, just as our mistrust and categorizing make it difficult for them to break out of habitual modes of dishonesty and mistrust. "Bad people" and "liars" are not bad and dishonest the way a table is a table or a chair a chair. Approached with openness and trust, they may be able to respond in kind. Approached with hatred and distrust, they will be confirmed in the mold in which their earlier interactions have already fixed them.

Existential mistrust quickly becomes reciprocal. If we reflect suspicion on someone else, it is reflected back on us until we find the very evidence we are looking for: the other also mistrusts us and acts in ways to confirm our worst fears about him. The typical behavior of large groups and societies in relation to one another is exactly what we would call paranoid if we encountered it in individuals. Each group has a shut in, closed world, sealed off from seeing in the way that the other sees. Each interprets the motives of the other in terms of its own world of defenses, fears, and suspicions.

True confirmation means that I confirm my partner as this existing being while I oppose him as the person that I am. To meet others and to hold our ground when we meet them is one of the most difficult tasks in the world. We tend, as a result, to alternate between two opposite forms of not meeting: "meeting" others through leaving our ground—taking on other people's thoughts and feelings while losing our own—and "protecting" our own ground through closing ourselves off and holding others at arm's length.

We do not help another if we bring anything but ourselves. Our seeming compliance with the other's demands is really a deception which injures the relationship as much as anything he may do. When we break out of our self-repression, we usually lay *all* the blame on the person whom we have allowed to dominate us, not recognizing that our submission is also a form of domination and manipulation. What the other really needs and asks of us is ourselves, even if that means that we oppose him or her. Often, schizophrenics have grown up in homes where no conflict is allowed to become manifest, as family psychiatrist Lyman Wynne has noted. They have not been able to become persons through coming up against real opposition. They have always been smothered in the miasma of pseudoharmony, pseudomutuality, and pseudoconfirmation.

We cannot know the other's side of our mutual relationship without standing our ground because we can only know the other *as a person* in a relationship in which his or her uniqueness becomes manifest in coming up against our uniqueness. Some people would be halfway decent if we gave them a chance by demanding that they start with us. One reason people do not have the courage to show themselves to others as they are is that they think thereby to avoid conflict. The truth is the exact opposite. The only way we can *avoid* coming into conflict with the other is by standing our ground, imagining the other's side of the relationship but also letting the other see our side. Otherwise, we are moment by moment making a false, deceitful contract in which we are letting the other think that we are going along with him or her freely and gladly while underneath, in fact, the resentment builds up. Then it is inevitable that conflict will come; for we are not affirming and responding as a whole person.

Trust accepts the fact that a genuine relationship is two-sided and therefore beyond the control of our will. What can be known in this situation can be known only by taking the risk of entering the relationship. This is a real risk, without guarantees of any sort, for we may find a response and we may not. Therefore, trust must never be understood as trust that in this particular occasion we know there will be a response. Genuine trust is a readiness to go forth on this occasion with such resources as we have and, if we do not receive any response, to be ready another time to go out to the meeting. Many people imagine that they are justified in a settled mistrust or even despair because once or twice they ventured forth and encountered a stone wall or a cold shoulder. After this they anticipate rejection and even bring it about, or they protect themselves from it by never risking themselves.

The courage to address and the courage to respond must include the recognition that there are no formulae as to when and how to address and when and how to respond. They also include the courage *not* to speak out and *not* to respond when we cannot do so in this situation as a whole person in a meaningful way. Our response ought not be triggered—that is merely a reaction. We ought not to respond to what we know somewhere in our being is not a true address to *us*. But it is equally essential not to withhold ourselves. One of the forms we have of withholding ourselves is that protective silence which makes us feel we never have to speak out, that we are merely observers in the family or group, that nothing is demanded of us. Another of the forms of withholding ourselves, however, is that anxious verbosity that overwhelms the situation so that we are not truly present and we do not allow anyone else to be present either. Still another form of withholding ourselves is substituting technique for trust.

We address others not by conscious mind or will but by what we are. We address them with more than we know, and they respond—if they really respond—with more than they know. Address and response can never be identified merely with conscious intent or even with "intentionality." When we truly respond, we respond not to the way the other is regarding and treating *us* but to the other—to that in her which calls out to us even when *she* does not speak to us. She may be asking us for help without knowing that she is doing so. If we refer her existence only back to ourselves and how she regards us, we shall fail to hear the question that she puts, we shall fail to answer the real need that she has. It is possible to ask ourselves whether, over and above what upsets us in others and we find so threatening, there is something they are trying to tell us, something to which we are called to respond. This applies even to those who are unjust to us. If someone upbraids and accuses us falsely and with great passion, that very excess and unfairness suggests that there is some hurt in this person that is expressing itself in this distorted way. In the depths the other may be asking for understanding and reassurance from us. Listening and responding at a great depth is the direction away from a specious individualism to the reality of the partnership of existence.

Chapter 4

CONFIRMATION AND THE "ESSENTIAL WE"

CONFIRMATION, AS we have seen, is an integral part of the life of dialogue. Dialogue may be silent and monologue spoken. What really matters in genuine dialogue is my acceptance of the "otherness" of the other person, my willingness to listen to her and respond to her address. In monologue, in contrast, I only allow the other to exist as a content of my experience. Not only do I see her primarily in terms of her social class, her color, her religion, her IQ, or character neurosis; I do not leave myself open to her as a person at all. The life of dialogue is not one in which we have much to do with others, but one in which we really have to do with those with whom we have to do. And it is only when I "really have to do" with the other that I can really be responsible to her. "The idea of responsibility is to be brought back from the province of specialized ethics," writes Buber, "of an 'ought' that swings free in the air, into that of lived life. Genuine responsibility exists only where there is real responding."[1]

Responsibility means the response of the whole person to what addresses her in the "lived concrete"—her full concrete situation. No abstract code is valid in advance of particular situations. None has universal validity because value does not exist in the universal at all, but in the particular, the concrete, the interhuman. This

27

does not mean that moral codes are of no use if they are recognized as what they are—abstractions, generalizations, rules of thumb that may be helpful in pointing us back to the concrete values that persons have discovered in real meeting. But they cannot take the place of our discovering for ourselves, each time anew, what is the right direction in a particular situation. The movement of values, therefore, is from the concrete situation and the deep-seated attitudes which one brings to that situation to the response and decision that produces the moral action.

> No responsible person remains a stranger to norms. But the command inherent in a genuine norm never becomes a maxim and the fulfillment of it never a habit. Any command that a great character takes to himself in the course of his development . . . remains latent in a basic layer of his substance until it reveals itself to him in a concrete way. . . . Whenever a situation arises which demands of him a solution of which till then he had perhaps no idea. Even the most universal norm will at times be recognized only in a very special situation. . . . In moments like these the command addresses us really in the second person, and the Thou in it is no one else but one's own self. Maxims command only the third person, the each and the none.[2]

The "ought" which arises in the concrete situation is not the pure "I-Thou," but the *quantum satis*—the sufficient amount of what one can do in that hour and in that situation. Just because real values arise in the concrete situation and in terms of the particular person confronted with that situation, the "ought" must include and be based on the real concrete person and all the limitations and resources that she brings with her into the situation.

This is not a question of free will versus determinism. Everyone is subject to all kinds of conditioning that one brings with one into the new situation; yet everyone has some measure of freedom of response which is more than mere conditioned reaction. The real problem is discovering what is the actual point and moment of freedom in any particular situation, what is the real possibility of awareness and response. But this can never be done by advance assessment, no matter how thorough one's knowledge of oneself or another. Except in general terms and overall predictions, one's resources are only known in the situation itself. This is because one's resources, one's potentialities, do not simply inhere in one as a part of one's makeup, but are called out of one in response to what meets and demands one in this hour.

The fundamental fact of human existence is human being with human being, the genuine dialogue between person and person. The psychological, the psychic stream of happenings within each person, is only the accompaniment of the dialogical. It is not itself the reality and goal of human existence. "All real living is meeting." Individuation is not the goal, only the indispensable way to the goal. Many psychotherapists and psychologists who today recognize the essential importance of mutual relations between persons still see these relations largely as the function of the individual's becoming and the means to that end. As long as dialogue is entered *merely* as a means to the end of health, maturity, integration, self-expression, creativity, "peace of mind," "positive thinking," and richness of experience, it will not even produce those things. It will no longer be true dialogue, and it will afford no real meeting with the other.

Real meeting is based on the double movement of distancing and relating. Distance given, man is able to enter into relation with other beings ("I-Thou") or to enlarge, develop, accentuate, and shape the distance itself, turning what is over against him into his object ("I-It"). An animal cannot set its companions apart from their common life, nor ascribe to the enemy any existence beyond his hostility. Man sets man at a distance and makes him independent. He is, therefore, able to enter into relation, in his own individual status, with those like himself. But to enter relation is possible only through that mutual confirmation in which each person recognizes the other in his or her uniqueness:

> The basis of man's life with man is twofold, and it is one—the wish of every man to be confirmed as what he is, even as what he can become, by men; and the innate capacity in man to confirm his fellow men in this way. That this capacity lies so immeasurably fallow constitutes the real weakness and questionableness of the human race: actual humanity exists only where this capacity unfolds. On the other hand, of course, an empty claim for confirmation, without devotion for being and becoming, again and again mars the truth of the life between man and man.[3]

This mutual confirmation of persons is only realized, as we have seen, in making the other present, or imagining the real.

The particular pain I inflict on another surges up in myself until, paradoxically, we are embraced in a common situation. It is through this making present that we grasp another as a self, an event which is only complete when the other knows himself made present by me. An animal does not need confirmation because it is what it is unquestionably. The tiger cub grows up to be a tiger. A human being needs confirmation because s/he exists as a self, at once separate and in relation, with unique potentialities that can only be realized if s/he is confirmed in his or her uniqueness.

> Sent forth from the natural domain of species into the hazard of the solitary category, surrounded by the air of a chaos which came into being with him, secretly and bashfully he watches for a Yes which allows him to be and which can come to him only from one human person to another. It is from one man to another that the heavenly bread of self-being is passed.[4]

"Imagining the real" is crucial for genuine ethical responsibility, in which one's response is not to subjective interest or to an objective moral code, but to the person one meets. It is also essential for friendship and love, marriage and family life, in which each member of the relationship is made present by the other in her concrete wholeness and uniqueness. But imagining the real is essential too for all the helping relationships—pastor and congregant, teacher and student, therapist and patient, parent and child. If we overlook the real "otherness" of the other person, we shall not be able to help her. We shall see her in our own image or in terms of our ready-made categories and not as she really is in her concrete uniqueness. But if we allow her to be different and still accept and confirm her, then we shall have helped her realize herself as she could not have without us. No amount of knowledge on the part of the teacher and no amount of scientific technique on the part of the doctor and the psychotherapist can make up for the failure to experience the relationship from the side of the other as well as our own.

The relation between persons takes place not only in the "I-Thou" of direct meeting but also in the "We" of family and community. As the "primitive Thou" precedes the consciousness of individual separateness, whereas the "essential Thou" follows and grows out of this consciousness, so the "primitive We" pre-

cedes true individuality and independence, whereas the "essential We" only comes about when independent people have come
together in essential relation and directness. The essential We
includes the Thou potentiality; for "only men who are capable of
truly saying *Thou* to one another can truly say *We* with one
another." This We is not of secondary or merely instrumental
importance; it is basic to human existence. "One should follow
the common," Buber quotes Heraclitus, i.e., join with others in
building a common world of speech and a common order of being.

> Man has always had his experiences as I, his experiences with
> others, and with himself; but it is as We, ever again as We, that
> he has constructed and developed a world out of his experi-
> ences. . . . Man has always thought his thoughts as I, and as I he
> has transplanted his ideas into the firmament of the spirit, but as
> We he has ever raised them into being itself, in just that mode of
> existence that I call "the between" or "betweenness." . . . It is to
> this that the seventh Platonic epistle points when it hints at the
> existence of a teaching which attains to effective reality not
> otherwise than in manifold togetherness and living with one
> another, as a light is kindled from leaping fire. Leaping fire is
> indeed the right image for the dynamic between persons in We.[5]

Thus amid the changes of world image, "the human cosmos is
preserved, guarded by its moulder, the human speech-with-
meaning, the common logos."

The importance of this concept of the common world as built by
the common speech-with-meaning can hardly be overestimated.
Speech, from this point of view, is no mere function or tool, but is
itself of the stuff of reality, able to create or destroy it. Speech may
be falsehood and conventionality, but it is also the great pledge of
truth. Whether one takes refuge in individualism or collectivism,
the person who flees answering for the genuineness of his existence is marked by the fact that he can no longer really listen to
the voice of another. The other is now only an object that he
observes. But true dialogue, as Franz Rosenzweig pointed out,
means that the other has not only ears but a mouth. S/He can say
something that will surprise one, something new, unique, and
unrepeatable for which the only adequate reply is the spontaneous response of the whole being and nothing that can be prepared beforehand. Only if real listening as well as real talking

takes place will the full possibility of mutual confirmation be present in family, community, and society. Only thus, and not through any mere *feeling* of group unity, will the full potentiality of the group as a group be realized.

It is not only the fate of smaller and larger groups that depends upon the common speech-with-meaning. If man does not recover the genuineness of existence as We, he may cease to exist at all.

> In our age, in which the true meaning of every word is encompassed by delusion and falsehood, and the original intention of the human glance is stifled by tenacious mistrust, it is of decisive importance to find again the genuineness of speech and existence as We. This is no longer a matter which concerns the small circles that have been so important in the essential history of man; this is a matter of leavening the human race in all places with genuine We-ness. Man will not persist in existence if he does not learn anew to persist in it as a genuine We.[6]

Buber's teaching of the essential We and of the common reality of human existence that one "ought" to follow is the foundation for his distinction between "groundless" neurotic guilt—a subjective feeling within a person, usually unconscious and repressed—and "existential guilt"—an ontic, interhuman reality in which the person dwells in the truest sense of the term. True guilt does not reside in the human person but in his failure to respond to the legitimate claim and address of the world. Similarly, the repression of guilt and the neuroses which result from this repression are not merely psychological phenomena but events between persons. Existential guilt is the "guilt that a person has taken on himself as a person and in a personal situation," an objective dialogical guilt that transcends the realm of inner feelings and of the self's relation to itself. Existential guilt is the corollary of the answerability and responsibility of the self in the concrete dialogical situation. It is failure to respond and, by the same token, failure to authenticate one's existence. "Existential guilt occurs when someone injures an order of the human world whose foundations he knows and recognizes [in some level of his being] as those of his own existence and of all common human existence." This "order of the human world" is not an objective absolute existing apart from the human world: it is the interhuman itself, the genuine We, the common logos and cosmos. The person who suffers from existential guilt can reenter the dialogue with otherness that has been broken off by his action through walking the road of illuminating that guilt, persevering in his identification of himself as the person who took on that guilt, and, insofar as his situation makes possible, restoring "the order of being injured by him through the relation of an active devotion to the world."[7]

Part II

THE PROBLEMATIC OF CONFIRMATION

Chapter 5

CONFIRMATION AND THE EMERGENCE OF THE SELF

CONFIRMATION IS central to human existence, but human existence is itself problematic, and the heart of its problematic is that of confirmation. This problematic can be grasped most clearly if we look at what we ordinarily take as a self-evident reality and as the foundation of our personal existence—our "I." The "I" is not an object or a thing. Indeed, it escapes all attempts to objectify it. But even as a subjective reality, it is not something continuous, secure, or easily discernible. It is elusive and insubstantial, paradoxical and perplexing to the point of illusion or even downright delusion. It cannot be understood as something taken by itself, outside of all relationship, but neither is it a part of a whole. It rests on the reality of the "between," the interhuman. I cannot regard my "I" as merely a product of social forces and influences, for then it is no longer an "I." There has to be that in me which can respond if I am going to talk about any true personal uniqueness. Therefore, I cannot say with George Herbert Mead, "The self is an eddy in the social current." I cannot turn the self into a mere confluence of social and psychological streams.

On the other hand, if I speak of the "I" as an "essence," that is misleading because it suggests something substantive that is within us as a vein of gold within a mountain waiting to be mined. Our uniqueness is our personal vocation, our life's calling that is discovered when we are called out by life and become "ourselves" in responding. We must respond to this call from where we are, and where we are is never merely social nor merely individual but uniquely personal. We need to be confirmed by others. Our very sense of ourselves only comes in our meeting with others. Yet through this confirmation we can grow to the strength of Socrates, who said, "I respect you, Athenians. But I will obey the god and not you." Socrates made his contribution to the common order of speech-with-meaning—he expressed his responsibility to his fellow Athenians precisely in opposing them. But if Socrates had not had seventy years in Athens in which he was part, first of his family of origin and then of his own family of wife and children, and if he had not been confirmed by the Athenian youth with whom he met in daily discussion, confirmed even when they opposed him, he would not have been able to stand alone.

The religious person sometimes imagines that one can be confirmed by God without any confirmation from one's fellow human beings. This is possible for a Jesus or a Buddha when they are adults. We are really set in existence, and existence is social existence. Once you have had real dialogue with human beings, you may then leave them for a desert island where you relate only to the chameleon, the Gila monster, or the waves lapping on the shore. But if you had no such relationship to begin with, you would not become a self. Or if you had such relations but were not confirmed or were even disconfirmed as an infant and young child, then your self will exist only in that impairment with which we are familiar in the schizophrenic, the paranoid, or the severe neurotic.

One of the paradoxes of confirmation is that, essential as it is to our and to all human existence, we cannot *will* to be confirmed. We cannot even *will* to confirm. When we do so we fall into what Leslie Farber has called willfulness, that sickness of the disordered will that seeks an illusory wholeness through trying to handle both sides of the dialogue. Kierkegaard understands this paradox very well when he says in *Fear and Trembling*, "I spend all my efforts executing the movements of the knight of infinite resignation and have nothing left over for anything else." In *Fear and Trembling*, Abraham, the "knight of faith" whom Kierkegaard admires so much, achieves what he does not through any act of will but through understanding and accepting the two-sidedness of the dialogue. Abraham was able to give up his son Isaac and still believe by virtue of the absurd that he would get him back. If Abraham *knew* that he would get his son back, then the seeming dialogue would become merely a monologue of manipulation and magic tricks. Abraham's faith was not a certainty of any sort but merely a trust in what might come from the other side in his dialogue with God. The same is true in our human relationships. Hence the futility and frustration of the lovelorn and the jealous who try to give up the beloved in order to receive her back and only make things worse in doing so. A large part of the pain of unrequited love as of jealousy comes from just this fact—that we cannot control others, that we must leave them really free to handle their side of the dialogue, to respond freely to our address rather than react as the effect of which *we* are the cause.

If we cannot *will* what the other side will give us, we *can* will not to receive. This is the other side of the coin. In a saying that Martin Buber has entitled "Give and Take," one Hasidic master says: "Everyone must be both a giver and a receiver. He who is not both is like a barren tree." There are people who so habitually see themselves and are seen by others in the role of helper, responsible person, or giver, that they have never learned how to accept and still less how to ask for what they need. Once Rabbi Mendel sat motionless at his plate when everyone else at the Sabbath dinner was eating soup. "Mendel, why do you not eat?" asked Rabbi Elimelekh. "Because I do not have a spoon," Mendel replied. "Look," said Rabbi Elimelekh, "you must learn to ask for a spoon and if need be for a plate too." Rabbi Mendel took the words of his teacher to heart, and from that time on his fortunes mended.

I have always been deeply moved by St. Francis' prayer, which for many years I said every night before going to sleep:

> *O Lord,*
> *Make me an instrument of Thy peace.*
> *Where there is hatred, let me sow love;*
> *Where there is despair, hope;*
> *Where there is darkness, light;*
> *Where there is sadness, joy.*
>
> *O Divine Master*
> *Grant that I may not so much seek*

To be understood as to understand,
To be consoled as to console,
To be loved as to love.
For it is in giving that we receive,
It is in pardoning that we are pardoned,
And it is in dying that we are born into eternal life.

However, I have come increasingly to recognize that this prayer presents only one aspect of reality. A person has also to allow himself to be understood, to be consoled, to be loved. Toward the end of his life, St. Francis said, "I was too hard on Brother Ass," by which he meant his own body. Even by medieval standards, his asceticism was unbelievably harsh. St. Francis loved every person and every thing, but he did not love himself quite enough. There is a compassion for oneself which is the opposite of self-pity and self-indulgence because it arises from a distancing from oneself rather than from a wallowing in subjective emotions. Such compassion is a form of humility whereas being too hard on oneself is a form of pride. "Everyone must have two pockets to use as the occasion demands," said Rabbi Bunam. "In one pocket should be the words: 'For my sake the world was created,' and in the other, 'I am dust and ashes.'"

To exist as human beings we must, as long as we live, enter ever anew into the flowing interchange of confirming and being confirmed, of addressing and responding. This means that we must have that courage to address and that courage to respond which rests on, embodies, and makes manifest existential trust. It also means a new and deeper understanding of responsibility and of its relation to confirmation. Responsibility means to respond, and genuine response is response of the whole person. In every situation we are asked to respond in a unique way. Therefore, our wholeness in that situation is unique too, even though we become more and more ourselves through such response—hence, more and more recognizable by others in a personal uniqueness that extends beyond the moment.

Because confirmation is a reality of the between, no one can offer another a blanket of unconditional confirmation, regardless of what that other says, does, or is. We can only give what we have, and what we have, first of all, is not a technique of confirmation but our personal selves—selves which can make another present and "imagine the real" but selves which also respond from where we are. Further, because confirmation means a confirmation of our uniqueness, a blanket confirmation would be valueless. We need to be confirmed in our uniqueness as what we are, what we *can* become, and what we are called to become, and this can only be known in the give and take of living dialogue. Therefore, as Martin Buber stressed in his 1957 dialogue with Carl Rogers, that affirmation which says "I accept you as you are" is only the beginning of dialogue and must be distinguished from that confirmation which has to do with the development of the person over time. Rogers emphasized an unqualified acceptance of the person being helped, whereas Buber emphasized a confirmation which, while it accepts the other as a person, may also wrestle *with* him against himself. Rogers spoke of acceptance as a warm regard for the other and a respect for him as a person of unconditional worth, and that means "an acceptance of and regard for his attitudes of the moment, no matter how much they may contradict other attitudes he has held in the past." Buber, in response, said:

> I not only accept the other as he is, but I confirm him, in myself, and then in him, in relation to this potentiality that is meant by him and it can now be developed, it can evolve, it can answer the reality of life. . . . Let's take, for example, man and wife. He says, not expressly, but just by his whole relation to her, "I accept you as you are." But this does not mean, "I don't want you to change." But it says, "I discover in you just by my accepting love, I discover in you what you are meant to become."

To Rogers' statement that complete acceptance of the person as he is is the strongest factor making for change, Buber countered with the problematic type of person with which he necessarily had to do. By this Buber meant the person whose very existence had run aground on the problematic of confirmation, a person whom simple acceptance could not help:

> There are cases when I must help him against himself. He wants my help against himself. . . . The first thing of all is that he trusts me. . . . What he wants is a being not only whom he can trust as a man trusts another, but a being that gives him now the certitude that "there *is* a soil, there *is* an existence." And if this is reached, now I can help this man even in his struggle against himself. And this I can only do if I distinguish between accepting and confirming.[1]

As babies we are really at the mercy of "significant others." Some people in their early years do not receive enough confirmation to enable them to be human. It is even possible that a nursery-school teacher could make all the difference for a deprived child's capacity to grow up human. Although once we are grown we imagine ourselves as independent "I"'s, as babies and little children we are totally dependent upon being called into existence as persons. Our notion of ourselves as separate consciousnesses that then enter into relation is an error produced by the individuation that we experience later. When we grow up, we think of ourselves as first and foremost "I" and imagine that we enter into relationship with others as one nation might send out ambassadors to foreign countries. Actually, as John Donne said, "No man is an island, entire of itself; every man is a piece of the continent," a continent that is based on the distancing and relating of our person-to-person relationships and of the "essential We" of family, group, community, and society.

To say that all men are created equal means, if anything, that each person may be and deserves to be related to as Thou. It does not mean, however, that this actually happens. There is a fundamental *inequality* insofar as the actual confirmation that each person receives is concerned. No one can ever change the fact of being an older brother or sister or a younger one or, for that matter, of being born with a gold, silver, lead, or copper spoon in his mouth. In every social group there is a sense of status, and in every social group there are those who have come out on the short end of the stick as far as confirmation is concerned.

What makes the emergence of the self still more problematic is that even where confirmation is given and given lavishly, it is usually with strings attached. It takes the form of an unspoken, invisible contract which reads: "If you are a good boy or girl, student, churchgoer, citizen, or soldier, we shall confirm you as lovable. If you are not, not only will you not be confirmed but you will have to live with the [introjected] knowledge that you are fundamentally unlovable." This is a contract that most of us buy, more or less, and there is no human way to be wholly free of it. This means that most confirmation is *not* unconditional, however much it may be "positive." As we grow older, this problematic is complicated still further by the need people have to fix each other in social roles. This is, if you like, a tragedy, but it is a well-nigh universal one. There are people who are made so anxious by not being able to put you in a given cubbyhole that they will never accept you. How many parents love their child but love him or her only as "my child" and will never allow that child to grow up—to become a person with a ground of his or her own. There is little that can be done about that at the time of childhood, and even if an Ellen West should be so fortunate as to go to therapy with a Carl Rogers, as the latter fantasizes, I seriously question whether this situation could be basically changed.

This does not mean that there is no hope in therapy. What it does mean is that the therapist must work with the given of the person who comes before him and that it is truly a matter of grace if that person is able to receive and accept the confirmation that the therapist with "unconditional positive regard" has to offer. There is a distinction that must be made between a basic confirmation that gives us our ticket to exist and the confirmation along the road which has to do with the way in which we exist. If we are so fortunate as to have been confirmed in our right to exist, that does not mean that the confirmation then extends to everything we do. If, on the other hand, we have not been confirmed in our existence itself, then all the later confirmation we receive is not likely to fill the vacuum within.

Other people fix us in their images of us, and we in turn internalize those images and fix ourselves in them. Why is it so important to a child who goes to college not to be called by the nickname which his or her family and friends used when s/he was at home? It is because the young person wants to feel "I am growing up now." When such a young person goes home for vacation and the family calls him or her by the nickname he or she feels s/he has outgrown, they are imprisoning that young person in an image of him- or herself which has power over his or her self. It leads one to limit one's sense of what one can do. It gets in the way. Eventually, of course, one reaches the strength to say, "I am not this," and the still greater strength of standing one's own ground without being made anxious, defensive, or upset. If it remains a conflict situation, one can accept the tragedy for what it is. Unfortunately, some people never attain this courage and strength and, even if they succeed in getting their families to call them by different names, they remain bound to the roles in which their family has cast them.

Chapter 6

THE LIMITS OF CONFIRMATION

OUR DISTINCTION between accepting and confirming already implies one important limit to confirmation and so does our recognition that even the therapist can only confirm the client as the person he is with the resources that he has at any one time. Asked whether the therapist should try to appear concerned about a patient even when he is not, Sidney Jourard replied, "Why should you impersonate somebody who is thinking about this patient 40 hours a week, when in point of fact you not only are not but cannot? . . . He is consulting you as you are with your limitations, and he is entitled to that." Jourard also raises the question of how much of the therapist's attention the client can take. "Sometimes too much attention destroys the thread of relationship that you have."[1]

Ronald Laing raises a still more serious problem of the limits of confirmation when he writes: "There are sudden, apparently inexplicable suicides that must be understood as the dawn of a hope so horrible and harrowing that it is unendurable."[2] But the most important problem of limits of confirmation for our purposes is raised by Ivan Boszormenyi-Nagy's positive statement about the basic trust and loyalty that ideally arises in earliest childhood:

> Ideally, what is being learned and developed in this earliest phase in the relationship between parents and children is a ca-

45

pacity for mutual trust and loyalty commitments based on the laws of reciprocity and fairness. This can evolve only when parents have also experienced trust in their earliest object relationships, which comes as a result of having their physical and emotional survival needs adequately gratified.[3]

What about those all-too-frequent cases that fall short of the ideal? If the parents have not experienced trust in their own early relationships with their parents and remain unconfirmed, then they cannot confirm their children.

When basic trust is lacking, it cannot easily be replaced. Yet we do not have so much ground for mistrust as we usually think. We cut the ground from beneath our feet by a self-fulfilling prophecy. We were confirmed so little as children, perhaps, that we are used to living with just the crumbs from the table and are unwilling to eat a full meal when it is offered to us. We already know in advance that nothing really joyful can happen to us, and we make sure that nothing joyful does happen. We impoverish our lives a great deal more than they need to be because we live on a scarcity economy in which we exclude *a priori* much of the grace that is waiting to come to us if we are really open, and we imagine our resources to be far less than they are. We are not able, we are not even *willing*, to imagine that new resources come to us all the time as we move into the situation that awaits us.

Our desire for security leads some of us to see ourselves as forsaken simply because life does not comport itself as we think it should. We wish to prescribe to life what will come to us and, like Kafka's mole, construct a burrow that will make it sure that nothing reaches us except what we want to reach us. Our views of existence are based upon our disappointments, upon the shattering of trust that every child experiences no matter how confirming his parents are. Every child experiences separation and betrayal. On growing up and first entering into romantic relations with the opposite sex, he is already expecting rejection and hurt—the repetition of his early experiences. Time and time again we think that we have "had it," yet at another moment we are able, like a character in Samuel Beckett's novels, to get up and go on.

Yet there are real limits that we discover in the work of healing the atrophied personal center in those who come for therapy— not theoretical ones but practical ones that grow out of the limitations of resources in this particular situation. There are tragedies of miscommunication and mismeeting and tragedies of crystallized opposition where each is as he is and there are not enough resources to turn that opposition into fruitful dialogue. Obviously a healer, to some extent, can have a role in making up for the disconfirmation, the lack of confirmation suffered by the "sick" person (the person with malaise) who is before him. But I do not believe that it is possible, even in the most ideal therapy, to make up for this nonconfirmation entirely.

To take two extremes, there are some people who have been given the sense that they have a right to exist because they are *persons* and other people who feel they have a right to exist only insofar as they justify that right at every moment by producing, accomplishing, playing the guitar, singing, or being charming. Most of us fall somewhere in between these two extremes. I do not think that therapy can ever make up totally for the lack of early confirmation *as a person.* Yet I think it can have to do with this lack in a very serious way.

To deal with this lack, the therapist has to remember that there are limits to *willing* confirmation—either willing to confirm another or willing to be confirmed. Confirmation is not a matter of will alone; for that would be what Farber calls willfulness. Existential trust and "existential grace," to use my own term, go together. We have to remember the two-sidedness of the event. If healing takes place in meeting, so does confirming. It is something that the therapist may "facilitate," but he cannot cause it to be.

All the phony attempts at confirmation that pervade so much of the healing and helping professions and the human potential movement, not to mention the "faith healers" and the downright quacks, have done a lot to promote existential mistrust in our culture today and with it the loss of faith in words. Often we cannot really accept the other's attempt to confirm us because we think that he is either selling us a line or is trying out on us the latest therapeutic technique. We do not really believe that the other can or wants to get into where we really hurt, to our uniqueness, to what makes us feel ugly and shameful to ourselves. And we fear the repetition of the hurts we have carried over from childhood.

People often do not like to be criticized because they feel that not only what they *do* but what they *are* is being attacked. They feel that their right to exist is being removed from them by the criticism. That is because they have felt all along that they must justify their existence in order to have the right to exist. People who feel this way will never be confirmed even if they are not criticized. They can never produce enough to make them feel that they have justified their existence, so they anxiously move on to ever-new efforts in the vain effort to fill the inner sense of emptiness. They so identify themselves with their actions and products—their art, cooking, or poetry—that if we say, "I like you but that is not a good poem," they feel that we have attacked them personally.

Every person who works with other persons has faced this problem. I often think of a Vassar student whom I admired both as a person and as a student. After I had read her term paper, I said to her, "I really feel that this paper needs to be rewritten. You did not flunk, but somehow it just does not hold together." She looked at me as if to ask, "Are you merely saying my *paper* is no good or are you really saying that *I* am no good?" My task was not to say, "Oh, yes, you are good and therefore your paper is good," any more than it was to take the opposite position and put her down because her paper needed rewriting. Somehow, as best I could, I had to communicate that I really cared for her, yet I could not confirm what she was doing at that point.

I was often confronted with this problem at Sarah Lawrence College where the "contracts" that the students wrote were not compared with one another but with what each student set out to do. To question the paper and at the same time communicate one's acceptance of the person is a very difficult thing to do, particularly when that person is used only to the conditional confirmation of approval or disapproval of her accomplishments. Yet it is essential. When I first met Martin Buber in person, he said to me, "I am cruel to ideas, but kind to men." What he meant was, "I will not, in order to make a person feel good, tell him that a book that he has written is a good one if it is not."

In our modern culture the mistrust between person and person which makes each person doubt if it is really him or her that is meant and confirmed is much greater than in earlier times. The nature of modern society is such that very few people are really confirmed as persons rather than as well-functioning units in the social system. Yet the problem of the limits of confirmation is not just a modern one. It belongs to the human situation itself.

Confirmation is throughout an undeserved grace. If it were anything other, it would not be true confirmation. It would be so tied to what we have done that it would be simply a reward for an effort rather than that "heavenly bread of self being" that, passed from one person to another, enables each of us to be. We may, of course, hold that our parents owe us an upbringing if they bring us into the world. Yet there is a sense in which the most undeserved grace, certainly the one we shall never be able to repay by anything we do or become, is the love that we have received from our parents. Those who receive this only partially will never be able to make this up in any full way in later life. There are some who receive so little that they remain withdrawn—like some infants brought up in children's homes, without personal care and attention, who never learn how to smile. Such persons never become fully human.

There are some people who are so unconfirmed that they cannot *accept* being confirmed. People really do turn to them with love, really *mean* them and try to give them understanding, but they will not accept it. On the other hand, there are those who desperately need and demand confirmation and never receive it. The more desperately they need it and the more they demand it, the less they get. This is true of "mental patients," but it is also true of those who are not so labelled. There are too those persons who reject as worthless much that is not because they have a fixed notion of the form in which confirmation should come. It may often happen that confirmation is waiting for them on all sides. But having set their hearts on one form of confirmation, they will not recognize anything else.

Real confirmation is often seemingly a quite casual thing. Yet it is often much more important than those obvious forms of public recognition that we crave, high school fantasies which, if they ever were fulfilled, would turn out to be quite empty. People who get hysterically hung up on the notion that "only this will confirm me" have cut the ground from under them. They will probably not get the particular form of confirmation they demand, and, even if they did, it would only satisfy them for a moment and they would then feel compelled to move on to still another form.

In order to confirm oneself or, to use the jargon of transactional analysis, to say, "I'm okay," one must first be confirmed by others. It is a great illusion to imagine that we begin as separate selves or that we can restore our injured existential trust through autosuggestion. On the other hand, no one knows the moments when real confirmation may break in. Even though many things are set when we are children, it is not just as children that we are confirmed. There are other moments of openness that come to us. This is what makes so poignant the hope, as well as the tragic limitations, of confirmation in therapy.

Chapter 7

THE TENSION BETWEEN PERSONAL CALLING AND SOCIAL ROLE

ALL INDIVIDUALS stand not only in person-to-person and person-to-family relations but also, by the very nature of human society from the earliest times, in those technical relations that arise from the specialization of labor in which individuals serve social functions for other individuals. Against this Karl Marx complained when he said that workers are treated as commodities. As a result of this specialization of labor, a large part of the confirmation that is offered by one individual to another is in the nature of how each person functions in his or her social tasks and roles. There is nothing wrong with this. It is an absolute necessity of human existence. Yet from it arises the fact that our interpersonal relations not only include the interhuman confirmation of personal uniqueness but also the tendency to exploit and enjoy one another's individual abilities, usefulness, and charm. This primordial fact of human existence often leads to a standing mistrust, so that even when a person is being offered genuine personal confirmation, he is likely to ask, "Am I being offered this as myself?"

Franz Kafka caught the essence of this human dilemma in his well-known story, *The Metamorphosis*. Gregor Samsa is a traveling salesman. He spends his time during the day traveling to neighboring cities and selling a commodity the nature of which we are

not told. In the evenings when he is free he has two entertain-
ments only. One is to figure out train schedules for the early train
he must take the next morning. The other is to do ornamental
fretwork. Gregor wakes up one morning to discover himself
transformed into a gigantic insect. He shuts himself in his room.
When his employer comes and reproaches him with being a bad
son to his family and a bad worker, Gregor finally consents to
open the door. The employer runs away in horror, and from then
on Gregor lives more and more totally closed off in his room until
finally the family no longer chooses to regard him as their son or
brother. "It can't be my brother," his beloved sister says, "or he
would not bother us," as he did when he came out once to hear
her play the violin. He had been saving his money to send her to
the conservatory and with the rest of it supporting his family
since his father no longer worked. Now the father shows that he
has resilience after all; he gets a job as a doorman with a splendid
uniform replete with fine brass buttons. Gregor voluntarily
starves to death with grateful thoughts of his parents while his
family, rejoicing in his sister's blooming into young womanhood,
goes off on a picnic.

Whatever else we might make of this tale, it is clear that Gregor
had no true human existence even before his transformation. He
was already shrivelled up as a person, for he lived and was
confirmed only in terms of his functions. When he is no longer in
a position to be the breadwinner for his family or to send his sister
to the conservatory, he loses all right to exist. The cleaning lady
throws "the thing" out after Gregor has died, and the family is
greatly relieved. Though the metamorphosis was startling and
sudden, it was no great transition for Gregor to go from being a
cog in the economic machine to being an insect of no economic or
social value. Charlie Chaplin's classic film *Modern Times* pictures a
worker on an assembly line who is fed by a machine as he works,
in order not to hold up production.

It is no accident that both these pieces of art stem from the
twentieth century; for this absence of personal confirmation is
particularly true of "modern times." When the gorgeous blonde
appears on TV and says of the bottle of deodorant that she is
holding, "This is for you," you may want for a moment to believe
she really means you, but you know she does not. "I voted twelve
times for Miss Rheingold," the brother complains in the play *A
Hatful of Rain*, "but what does she care about me?" The nature of

our industrial and electronic society is such that one is hardly likely to get confirmed as a person in one's personal uniqueness. Yet there is something about society as such which makes this threat of nonconfirmation an integral part of the human condition. William Butler Yeats captured this in his beautiful poem, "For Anne Gregory":

> Never shall a young man,
> Thrown into despair
> By those great honey-coloured
> Ramparts at your ear,
> Love you for yourself alone
> And not your yellow hair.
>
> But I can get a hair-dye
> And set such colour there,
> Brown, or black, or carrot,
> That young men in despair
> May love me for myself alone
> And not my yellow hair.
>
> I heard an old religious man
> But yesternight declare
> That he had found a text to prove
> That only God, my dear,
> Could love you for yourself alone
> And not your yellow hair.[1]

This does not mean that she can be loved *only* for her yellow hair, but it does mean that she cannot be loved apart from it or her eyes or her smile or her humor or charm.

Kyo, the hero of André Malraux's novel *Man's Fate*, is told by his European doctor wife May that she has taken advantage of the freedom that they have agreed to give each other to sleep with a fellow doctor in the hospital who keeps pressing her to do so. Kyo's reaction is that she ought not to have used that freedom. To him it is a betrayal and one that is all the more painful coming as it does on the very brink of the Shanghai communist revolution of which he is the leader. Nonetheless, at this very time, he thinks to himself that there are two sorts of people—those like his fellow Communist Party members who judge him by his actions and those like May who love him and who would love him even unto treason, suicide, or baseness of any sort. It is easy to understand why Kyo feels this way. Nonetheless, he is asking for something that no human being can ask for: to be loved as an essence that has nothing to do with his actions as a person. Kyo has a right to ask that those who care about him not judge his actions simply from the outside. That is a different matter. He has a right to hope that those who love him try to understand the relation between himself and his action. He might even wish that they would remember what Kierkegaard said: No person can judge another for no one knows how much of what he does is suffering and how much temptation, that is, in how much of his actions was he compelled to do what he did and in how much of them did he have some real freedom to do otherwise. But he cannot go beyond that and claim that his "I" is some essence that is unconnected with his actions, his situation, and his relations to others.

There is no direct correlation between confirmation and being right or wrong. Some persons are so unconfirmed that they can do the right thing again and again and still not be confirmed. Other persons are so self-confident that they can repeatedly do and say the wrong thing and still come off "smelling like roses." There are, in fact, persons who are wrong even when they are right and others who are right even when they are wrong. It is common enough to find that the more money a person has, the greater is the authority with which he speaks about political and religious matters. But this is exactly what Socrates observed about the Athens of his time: all the poets knew about politics, and all the politicians knew about poetry. The reason that the oracle held Socrates to be the wisest man in Athens was that he was the only one who knew that he did not know! Thus a large part of what appears to be confirmation is inextricably bound up with social status, one's place in the "pecking order," one's role in the family. It has been said that the people who are most subject to heart attacks are not the business executives, as is usually supposed, but the little people who work in lavatories or run elevators—the people at the bottom of the social order on whom everyone else takes out their irritations and grievances.

The paradox of the "contract," of confirmation with strings attached, which originates in the family, becomes intensified and hardened as we move out into the social and economic roles that we must take upon ourselves to exist in human society. We realize our personal uniqueness, as we have seen, only insofar as we answer the call that comes to us from the persons and situations that confront us. Each of us has need of the personal confirmation that can come only when we know our "calling"—our existence in the fullest sense of the term—as an answer to a call. No one is able simply to confirm himself. One may be able to do without the admiration of crowds, but one cannot do without that silent dialogue, often internalized within oneself, through which one places one's effort within the context of a mutual contact with what is not oneself. We need to feel that our work is "true"—both as a genuine expression of the reality that we encounter in our lives and as a genuine response to some situation or need that calls us.

Ronald Laing, who was also influenced by Buber's concept of confirmation, writes:

> Every human being, whether child or adult, seems to require *significance*, that is, *place in another person's world*. Adults and children seek "position" in the eyes of others, a position that offers room to move. . . . Most people at some time in their lives seek the experience, whether or not they have found it in early life, of occupying *first* place, if not the only significant place, in at least one other person's world.[2]

What tortures the paranoid, Laing suggests, "is not so much his delusions of reference, but his harrowing suspicion that he is of no importance to anyone, that no one is referring to him at all." Laing too understands this universal human need for confirmation not only in terms of direct interhuman relations but also in terms of the complexities of group membership and social role:

> Each group requires more or less radical internal transformation of the persons who comprise it. Consider the metamorphoses that one man may go through in one day as he moves from one mode of sociality to another—family man, speck of crowd dust, functionary in the organization, friend. These are not simply different roles: each is a whole past and present and future, offering differing options and constraints, different degrees of change or inertia, different kinds of closeness and distance, different sets of rights and obligations, different pledges and promises.
>
> I know of no theory of the individual that fully recognizes this.[3]

Each one of us must risk himself to establish himself as the person that he or she is and risk failure in so doing.[4] Paradoxically, this means that while the "calling" in its original meaning is an answer to a call, we have to take the first step ourselves and assert that we are called before the call comes. Each of us, no matter how thorough our training, experiences a moment of uneasy tension between our personal and professional self when we first step forward as a "doctor," a "psychotherapist," a "minister," a "teacher," a "lawyer," or even a "husband," a "wife," a "father," or a "mother." At this moment the question, "What am I doing taking on this role?" may well produce an invisible inner panic that has nothing to do with competence or "self-confidence." This is the sense of incongruity that comes when one part of ourselves is consciously "role-playing" while another part looks on and asks whether we can, in all good faith, identify ourselves with this role. If we can make this venture "stick," then we shall be confirmed by others in our "calling" and soon will come to identify ourselves so much with our social role that our self-image will be unthinkable without it. The transition from not having a role in society to having one is soon forgotten, but it is instructive in the problematic of confirmation.

Another deeper problem is that of the tension between personal and social confirmation. The person who makes the assertion that he is a doctor or minister "stick" does not necessarily thereby receive personal confirmation. It may happen, on the contrary, that the more successful he is in his social role, the less he feels confirmed as a person. This is bound to be the case when his social role remains mere "role-playing" and is never integrated in any thoroughgoing fashion with his existence as a person. This is particularly true of those whose social roles elevate them above the populace and make it necessary for them to pretend to attitudes, convictions, and ideals that they do not really hold. But it is also likely to be true of anyone who, in his desperate need for the confirmation of others, prefers to sacrifice his personal integrity rather than run the risk of not being established in a definite, socially approved role.

The person who enters the transition stage stands, therefore, in the tension point between personal and social confirmation. He cannot resolve this tension by renouncing social confirmation, for no one can live without it. Everybody must play a social role, both as a means to economic livelihood and as the simplest prerequisite for any sort of relations with other people in the family and society. On the other hand, he cannot resolve the tension by sacrificing personal confirmation; for this suppression of a basic human need results in an anxiety that may be more and more difficult to handle as the gap between person and role widens. To stand in this tension, however, is to insist that one's confirmation in society also be in some significant sense a confirmation of oneself as a unique person who does not fit into any social category.

Although Carl Rogers points us in this direction in his emphasis upon person-centered psychology, he tends to weaken the tension and oversimplify the situation by positing a simple either/or between social role and personal uniqueness. In a person-centered psychological atmosphere, Rogers claims, *"Roles, and role expectations, tend to drop away and are replaced by the person, choosing her own way of behaving."* Rogers sees the roles and expectations for the man and the woman, the husband and the wife, collapsing in an encounter group or in person-centered therapy or in a women's consciousness-raising group. "The sociological role loses its force in a person-centered experience." Again, in a marriage partnership in which each "becomes truly a free agent, the relationship only has permanence if the partners are committed to each other, are in good communication with each other, accept themselves as separate persons, and live together as persons, not roles."[5] Though basically true as a direction of movement, this is untrue and seriously misleading as an attainable ideal. Rogers himself tells in his book *Becoming Partners: Marriage and Its Alternatives*[6] how two young people who had been living together happily for three years almost ruined their relationship by getting married. Once they were married a host of unconscious expectations entered in that they did not suspect before. No amount of good will and striving for mutuality and equality can entirely remove such expectations or the social roles that they entail; for these are embedded both in the family of origin and in the simple fact of the economics of living together in family, community, and society.

The real thrust behind women's liberation, it seems to me, is the confusion and distortion that prevail in a province that should be that of the highest flowering of the human—the confusion about what it means to be a woman in relationship to a man in this particular historical situation. Somehow it tends to become a mere social role and, what is more, an imposed social role in which women are subject to the tyranny of both men's and women's notions of what it means to be "feminine." "The universal sway of the feminine stereotype is the single most important factor in male and female woman-hatred," writes Germaine Greer in *The Female Eunuch*. The battle for women's liberation is a battle for the wholeness of the human being, a battle for a woman's right to be a person.

Although much has changed in women's situation in the past years, the problematic tension between person and social role remains for them in a more aggravated form than for men. No one ever suggests that a career and fatherhood are incompatible, but, in the past at least, a woman has often been told that she must choose between career and motherhood. Most of the responsibility in the family structure is placed upon the woman, and neither men nor society in general are willing to provide women with the structural means of handling both roles with any ease. For many, a woman's choices are more restricted still: either she must marry and raise a family or face life with no identity at all, an "unwanted spinster." This too is changing with the advent of short-term commitments and "serial monogamy." But it still remains a dominant trend. Kate Millett holds that the rights of women to divorce, protection, citizenship, vote, and property have not affected their continued chattel status in name, residence, sex, domestic service, and economic dependence. Even in the academic world, women must seek survival or advancement from the approval of males who hold power.[7]

Basic to the cultural divisions of roles has been woman's reproductive role. The pill has modified this situation, but it has not fundamentally changed it. Society will not allow woman's reproductive role to be threatened; yet without freedom in this respect, all woman's other freedoms are in danger of being empty. "The real question is not, 'How can we justify abortion?' but 'How can we justify compulsory childbearing?' " At the same time, women are taught not to share love and sex but to use them for profit, for economic ascendancy and status acquisition. And by the same token, women are taught that they are of value when they are young: "Men may mature, but women just obsolesce."[8]

There is another, equally essential, and corollary aspect of this battle, however, and that is the realm of the "between." Equality and dignity cannot be won by women themselves, even by changing the attitude of any number of individual men. It must be won in the dynamic of lived and living relationship—in the concrete situations in which men and women meet and confirm one another as man or woman *and* as person, holding the tension between these two so that, if they can never be simply identified, neither can they ever be separated. If modern man in general knows anxiety, alienation, and exile, it is certain that modern woman knows it in still fuller measure—because she faces the simultaneous breakup of traditional values and of such traditional images of woman as might have satisfied her great-grandmother, grandmother, or even her mother. If the black man is invisible as *man* and *person* through his very visibility as black, woman is invisible as person and human being through her visibility as woman, as D. H. Lawrence has eloquently declared:

> Man is willing to accept woman as an equal, as a man in skirts, as an angel, a devil, a baby-face, a machine, an instrument, a bosom, a womb, a pair of legs, a servant, an encyclopedia, an ideal or an obscenity; the only thing he won't accept her as is as a human being, a real human being of the female sex.[9]

The invisibility of a woman is less obvious than that of a black because of the great respect, veneration, and Mother's Day idolization woman enjoys in our culture, not to mention her unquestionable power to seduce, manipulate, control, and dominate men through her feminine charms and "wiles." But the seduction and manipulation work both ways: Women have been taught to be devious and indirect because it is unladylike or unfeminine to be "too" outspoken, direct, demanding, angry, aggressive, or just plain enraged. Marya Mannes sees the pervasive anxiety in modern woman as the result of the shutting out of the *human* image by the imposed *social* image:

> What I call the destructive anxieties are not the growth of women's minds and powers, but quite the contrary: the pressures of society and the mass media to make women conform to the classic and traditional image in men's eyes. They must be not only the perfect wife, mother, and home-maker, but the ever-young, ever-slim, ever-alluring object of their desires. Every woman is deluged daily with urges to attain this impossible state. . . . The real demon is success—the anxieties engendered by this quest are relentless, degrading, corroding. What is worse, there is no end to this escalation of desire. . . . The

legitimate anxiety—am I being true to myself as a human being?—is submerged in trivia and self-deception.[10]

One cannot legislate the removal of sexual differences arising
from the culture just by recognizing that they are the product of
the culture and not merely of biological inheritance, as Kate Millett seeks to do in *Sexual Politics*. Male and female, she says, are
seen in our society as two distinct cultures, and this division and
cataloguing reduce the human person to half of its potential in its
struggle to fulfill "feminine" or "masculine" role expectations.
This patriarchal system has probably exercised the most pervasive
and insidious control of any other, innocently, wordlessly, install-
ing itself as nature. To agree with this fully, as I do, is not to agree
that one can easily get back to "nature" minus culture or that we
know anything about the human person and society in a state of
nature. The problem is no less real if it is borne by culture rather
than by inheritance, though this may change our attitude toward
it and give us some hope of changing it. One cannot will to see
women as pure person or pure human being minus their
variegated but nonetheless unmistakable feminine appearance
and social role.

All we can do, here as elsewhere, is to hold the tension between the person and the social role, recognizing the necessity of
both and moving in the direction of the freedom of every person
to choose her own social role or roles and not have it imposed on
her by others.

What is true of women in relation to men is also true of men in
relation to women. But for many men in our culture the tension
between personal calling and social role is felt most keenly in the
world of work. Daniel J. Levinson in his perceptive study, *The
Seasons of a Man's Life*, has delineated this tension with especial
clarity in that phase of "Settling Down" which he calls "Becoming
One's Own Man," a period which ordinarily extends from 35 or
36 to 40 or 41 and represents the peaking of early adulthood and
the transition into what lies beyond. Levinson sees the goals of
this phase as including not only advancing on one's ladder but
also speaking more clearly with one's own voice, having a greater
measure of authority, and becoming less dependent, both inter-
nally and externally, on other individuals and institutions. But
Levinson also recognizes a built-in dilemma here, a dilemma

which we have already glimpsed in the problem of the confirmation of otherness:

> On the one hand, a man wants to be more *independent*, more true to himself and less vulnerable to pressures and blandishments from others. On the other hand, he seeks *affirmation* in society. Speaking with his own voice is important, even if no one listens—but he especially wants to be heard and respected and given the rewards that are his due. The wish for independence leads him to do what he alone considers most essential, regardless of consequences; the wish for affirmation makes him sensitive to the response of others and susceptible to their influence.[11]

This dilemma is not just an internal one. As the man advances and comes in contact with senior men who have territories to protect, he receives a double message containing a subtle mixture of support and intimidation: "Be a good boy and you'll go far. Make trouble and you're dead." In the face of these, a man may discover that he is not as autonomous as he thought. "He wants to be his own man, but he also wants desperately to be understood and appreciated" and to have his talents affirmed. As a result, he may find himself in crucial situations too eager to please, too sensitive to criticism, too conforming to speak and act on the basis of his own convictions.

Levinson is also highly perceptive in his description of the "deillusionment" that sets in when at some point in his life a man confronts the omnipotent, fairy-tale quality of his fantasies about advancement and learns the degree to which his experience of success has been based upon illusion. The most poignant part of this illusion is the belief that one is advancing *for* oneself when actually it is often at the cost of one's self:

> Even when a man is doing well in an external sense, he may be gaining rewards that will turn out to have little meaning or value for him. His life may provide genuine satisfactions but at greater inner costs. In order to devote himself to certain goals, he may have to neglect or repress important parts of the self.[12]

The particular value for us of Levinson's periods of adult development is that, in contrast to Erik Erikson's eight stages, they are focused on the "between" and thus cast genuine light on the problem of the confirmation of otherness. Erikson's stages include, among others, Intimacy vs. Aloneness, Generativity vs. Stagnation, and Integrity vs. Despair, the stages of early, middle, and late adulthood. Each of Erikson's stages is governed by a crucial, problematic issue for the self in relation to the external world. "But their primary focus is *within the person*." Levinson's concept of "life structure," in contrast, "is centered more directly on the *boundary between self and world*," giving equal consideration to self and world as aspects of the lived life.[13]

Chapter 8

THE PARADOX OF THE PERSON IN THE MODERN WORLD

EVEN IN the best of conditions, we shall never be free of the tension between our personal uniqueness and our many and varying social roles. This tension is sharpened still further by the social dislocations in the modern world and by the alienation resulting from the loss of a meaningful image of the human—a direction-giving meaning for personal *and* social existence. This is the paradox of our existence as persons in the modern world. Unable to believe any longer in an objective absolute or order through which our personal destiny is determined, or in a biblical God who calls us, we nonetheless know ourselves as persons face to face with reality which transcends us—the other that meets us as we meet it. This reality demands from us response and calls us to account for our failure to respond even while offering no guarantee of confirmation or meaning in return for our response or any sure guidance as to which response is "right" and which "wrong." We need personal meaning for our very existence and continuity as selves; yet we are confronted by an often absurd social and natural reality which seems by its very nature to offer neither confirmation nor personal meaning to the "I."

In our day countless millions of people have been denied their fundamental right of confirmation as human beings, whether through the atomic bombs of Hiroshima and Nagasaki or the dehumanization and extermination of the "racially inferior" in the Nazi death camps or the slave labor camps—the Gulag Peninsula—of the Soviet Union. Even in the most cultured and enlightened of societies, a great many people are left out in the cold because they do not fit what makes the group comfortable, because they, in one way or another, make people uneasy. One of the problems that faces any group of any size—from family to nation—is the extent to which it can confirm someone who is radically other.

Plato's philosopher, following the model of Socrates, cared only for the Good and not for what others thought: "I respect you, Athenians," Socrates said, "but I shall obey the god and not you." Aristotle's man of well-being *(eudaemonia)*, in contrast, not only ought not to do anything shameful, he ought not do anything that other people regard as shameful. If the Athenians said to Socrates, in effect, "Are you not ashamed that at the age of seventy you must die as a common criminal because you tampered with the traditional gods," Socrates replied, "Are *you* not ashamed, Athenians, that you value only money, power, and prestige and take no thought of your soul?" Plato's man was more independent, but Aristotle understood more about compromise and social adjustment.

In Franz Kafka's novel *The Castle*, the stranger-hero K. takes up with the pariah family of the castle messenger Barnabas. Once this family was an integral member of the community, and the father was the head of the volunteer fire brigade. But when Amalia, the oldest daughter, refuses to accede to the insulting summons of a high castle official who demanded that she present herself at the Castle Inn between three and four in the morning to sleep with him, when she indignantly tears up the official's note and flings it in the messenger's face, the family becomes forever outcast. "We did not do anything wrong," Olga explains to K., "and everybody in the Village was just waiting for us to take up our business where we left off. But when we did not, everything we did became utterly shameful and contemptible." As the French gnostic-saint, Simone Weil, remarked from her own observation, the person who suffers and who falls out of the social mold becomes shameful to everyone else. The people regard the suffering servant of the Lord as shameful and rejected by God in Deutero-Isaiah because he was not comely but was smitten with disease. Only much later did they realize that it was *they* who had turned away from God and not he.

The problematic of confirmation has deepened since the advent of what Nietzsche called "the death of God," which can be coupled with the alienation of modern man—not as any sort of theological statement but as a contrast between the relatively greater confirmation that a Roman citizen, the plowman or knight of the medieval world, the courtier of the Renaissance, the Confucian scholar of traditional China, or the Talmudist of Rabbinic Judaism might be able to hope for. Prometheus rebelled on the ground of *moira*, the divine order or cosmos of the Greeks. Job contended on the ground of his created freedom and within a dialogue with God which he sustained even while he protested against God's injustice. In the era of the "death of God," when most people can no longer relate to a cosmic order or to a creating and revealing God, Prometheus and Job live on divorced from their original context and transformed into the Modern Rebel and the Modern Exile.

> The "death of God" does not mean that modern man does not "believe" in God, any more than it means that God himself has actually died. Whether or not one holds with Sartre that God never existed at all or with Buber that God is in "eclipse" and that it is we, the "slayers of God," who dwell in the darkness, the "death of God" means the awareness of a basic crisis in modern history—the crisis that comes when man no longer knows what it means to be human and becomes aware that he does not know this. This is not just a question of the relativization of "values" and the absence of universally accepted mores. It is the absence of an image of meaningful human existence, the absence of the ground that enabled Greek, Biblical and Renaissance man to move with some sureness even in the midst of tragedy.[1]

The crisis of the alienation of modern man is as much as anything a crisis of confirmation. No one illustrates this better than the great Danish theologian Søren Kierkegaard who sought to substitute for the human confirmation of social solidarity the divine confirmation of a lonely dialogue between the "Single One" and the Transcendent. In *Fear and Trembling* Kierkegaard presents two images of the human. One is Agamemnon, the tragic hero or "knight of infinite resignation" who sacrifices his daughter

Iphigenia for the sake of the safety of the Greek ships, thus subordinating his individuality to the universal order. The other is Abraham, the "knight of faith" who is commanded by "an absolute relationship to the Absolute" to "suspend" the ethical principles enjoined by the universal order and sacrifice his son Isaac.

Kierkegaard's "knight of faith" stands, like Job, in a unique relationship to God, not mediated by any order or universal law. In every other respect, however, he differs decisively from Job, as from the biblical Abraham on whom he is modeled. He does not reach the finite directly but through a dialectic in which he first renounces the finite for the infinite and then regains the finite through "faith by virtue of the absurd." Thus he substitutes for Abraham's and Job's direct trust in God a faith of tension and of paradox. What is more, Kierkegaard's "knight of faith" must choose *between* God and creation. There is no longer a possibility of finding God in creation. He rejects society and culture for the lonely relation of the "Single One" to God, thereby losing any check on the reality of the voice that addresses him. In its very affirmation of faith, as a result, Kierkegaard's concept of the "knight of faith" is a consequence and an expression of that "death of God" that undermines the confirmation of modern man: it entails the loss of faith in the universal order and in the society that purports to be founded on it; the "suspension of the ethical" and the relativization of ordinary ethical values that follows from it; the rejection of creation—the world and society—as an obstacle to the relationship with God; and the paradoxical "leap of faith" that is necessary to attain any sort of contact with God.

The "death of God" means the alienation of modern man, as Albert Camus has tirelessly pointed out in his discussion of the "absurd":

> In a universe suddenly divested of illusions and lights, man feels an alien, a stranger. His exile is without remedy since he is deprived of the memory of a lost home or the hope of a promised land. This divorce between man and his life, the actor and his setting, is properly the feeling of absurdity.[2]

The absurd to Camus is born of the confrontation of the human longing for happiness and for reason with the irrational silence of the world. The absurd means life without hope and without illusion: "I want to know whether I can live with what I know and with that alone." "Knowing whether one can live *without appeal* is all that interests me." In conscious contrast to Kierkegaard, Camus asserts that "the absurd . . . does not lead to God . . . the absurd is sin without God."

The modern Rebel-Exile has not the Greek, the biblical, nor the Christian base on which to stand, nor has he the hope of his Renaissance counterpart. He knows himself as being in exile, but he no longer knows anything definite that he can speak of as being in exile *from*. The "infinite spaces" of Pascal and the "heartless voids and immensities" of Melville's Ishmael have taken the place of *moira*, the Garden of Eden, the dialogue with God, and the Christian heaven. Similarly, although he "rebels" against a "Transcendent" that he believes has alienated him from his own creative freedom, modern man knows that this Transcendent is "dead" already, that he is "condemned to be free," that he is a "rebel without a cause." Feuerbach, Marx, and Nietzsche in the nineteenth century and Sartre, Fromm, and even, to some extent, Freud and Jung in the twentieth have all held that if man can liberate himself from the transcendent, he can recover his creative freedom. The contemporary psychologist Erik Erikson, in contrast, has recognized that if last generation's problem was to get rid of the father, this generation's problem is how to become oneself once one has gotten rid of him. When we have recovered our alienated creativity, our problem has just begun. For then we have the problem of how to find a meaningful direction for our potentialities which will enable us to become human in the unique way in which we and we only can become.

I do not mean by this that we consciously set out to become one or another sort of person and still less to realize some particular image of the human. What I do mean is that, by every response that we make in every situation in which we must make a basic choice, we move in one direction or another. To the extent that our response is more whole and more aware, we shall be able to make a more whole response the next time we are called upon for real decision. To the extent that our response is less whole and less aware, we may be less and less able to make a whole response in the future situations that claim us. If we go too far in this direction, we shall reach what I call the problematic of hearing, that to which the prophet Amos points when he says, "There will come a famine not of bread and water but for the words of the living God." From not wanting to hear, we shall reach a place where we *cannot* hear. Kafka pictures many characters like his mole who have encased themselves in an ever-expanding burrow of self-defense. Such persons are so anxious that all they want to do is to defend the burrow from possible attackers. They wish they could be inside and outside at the same time so that they could defend the castle moat while nestling safe inside it. These are people who have built their lives round and round them so that nothing can break in on them. Another such figure is Joseph K., the hero of Kafka's novel *The Trial*.

What is characteristic of all these figures in Kafka's stories and novels is that they try to shut out the world, but the world breaks in on them. They do not want to hear the call that calls to them as the unique persons that they are and can become. As a result, they are called to account. Franz Kafka, more than anyone I know, has grasped the paradox of the person in the modern world. This is the paradox that to exist as a person, one must know oneself as called. Yet one does not know who calls nor, with any clarity, to what one is called. Nonetheless, when one does not respond to the call, one knows oneself as called to account and cannot avoid giving an accounting of oneself.

This is neither optimism nor pessimism. It is, on the contrary, a simple description of our lives as human beings. We would like if possible to rationalize our lives, to make them secure and meaningful according to one or another objective scheme, whether it be that of psychology, sociology, physiology, or astrology. Paul Tillich puts it well when he says that in fact we exist in a great ambiguity of good and evil from which we can escape only at the cost of neurosis and the impoverishment of life. We may try to escape from this "ontological anxiety" through a legalism that tries to make all our actions external to ourselves or an antinomianism which says, "No law binds me"—but either way, we are simply trying to get out of our painful human situation which offers no clear confirmation that what we do is good or evil. There is no one who can answer for us the question of what we ought to do or what we ought to have done in this unique situation.

There are two basic movements in Kafka's works. One is that of the self that tries to protect itself from the world and of the world that breaks in on the self. That is the movement of judgment and of guilt. The other is the one of anxiety in which the self seems to be always seeking for something it cannot find. Like the Hunter Gracchus, it wanders endlessly, never able to find peace. Kafka's "country doctor" can do no good when he answers a "false alarm" because it turns out that the young man whom he has come to see is not sick at all. Then, as he lies beside him in the bed, he discovers that the young man has a terrible wound, a large rose-colored wound in his side out of which worms are crawling and grasping, a wound that he has had since birth. So again the country doctor, the very symbol of help and comfort, can do no good at all. As he returns home, the horses which brought him there so swiftly now walk at the slowest possible pace. Alone in the dark night, he sees his own going astray as a general cataclysm, his own answer to a false call a wrong direction taken by a whole age: "Never shall I reach home at this rate. . . . Naked, exposed to the frost of this most unhappy of ages . . . old man that I am, I wander astray. . . . Betrayed! Betrayed! A false alarm on the night bell once answered—it cannot be made good, not ever."

Again and again in Kafka's writings there is the picture of the person who goes astray. In his great novel *The Castle* this going astray seems to be built into the very system, so that the whole group of people who live in the Village are tied to the Castle by name but can never in fact reach the Castle. If one tries to call on the telephone, one gets a babble of children's voices; if one tries to walk to the Castle, one finds oneself going around in circles. The Castle itself, insofar as one can see it, looks like wretched tenements with ravens crowing in abundance above it. When K. follows Barnabas, the messenger who brings him the first message from the Castle, he discovers that underneath his beautiful messenger's uniform he wears dirty old underwear, that his destination is his home and not the Castle, and that his family are pariahs, exiled from both the Village and the Castle and that the messenger himself doubts that there really was a message. When K. insists he wants to reach the Castle official Klamm in person, he is told that this is impossible because Klamm only exists as a very high official. Even if Klamm calls Frieda, who is his mistress and becomes K.'s, who is to say that it is really Frieda he means?

K. spends his life in endless efforts and exertions and comes near his goal only when he wanders by mistake into the room of a castle official and is told in endless circumlocutions that everything that he wants now lies waiting for him. He knows that something terribly important for him is happening, but he is much too sleepy to be interested in anything important to him, and soon he is out in the hall, his unique opportunity forever lost.

Despite the loneliness of Kafka and of his heroes, there is a sense in which they are representative of the problematic of confirmation that confronts all of us—the paradox of the person in the modern world. Not all persons are artists, and not all need to say, like Kafka's "Hunger Artist," "If I could have found food that I liked, I would have stuffed myself like you or anyone else." Yet each person has need of the personal confirmation that can come only when he knows his "calling"—his existence in the fullest sense of the term—as an answer to a call.

The artist, of course, exists in a specially sharpened paradox of confirmation. He has sacrificed the possibility of a more direct confirmation through his relations with others or of a more certain confirmation through his social role for the loneliness and uncertainty of trying to create something unique that only he can create. His designation as an "artist" offers no confirmation; for unless he succeeds in this unique creation his art is meaningless and his attempt to except himself from the ordinary calling of mankind a presumption. He must make upon his public the impossible demand that only the truly great artist can get away with, namely, that they give him complete freedom to create and at the same time that they confirm his work as meaningful for their lives. No person can *know* himself to be a "great artist," but only that he is called or even compelled to create. No person, consequently, can become an artist without the risk of ending life like the hunger artist—ignored or even scorned by the world while unconfirmed by himself. Kafka's hunger artist is a paradigm of the problematic of the modern person who strives to answer a call of which he is not sure in a way of which he cannot be certain.

K., the hero of *The Castle*, stands squarely in the midst of the tension between personal calling and social role: "Never yet had K. seen vocation and life so interlaced as here, so interlaced that sometimes one might think they had exchanged places." This interlacing can either mean an integral relation between personal and social confirmation or it can mean the opposite—such an insistence on social role that one's personal existence itself seems to derive from that and nothing else. One reason that K. cannot receive confirmation is that he himself must establish his calling as a "land surveyor." The message from the Emperor is for him alone; no one else knows what it says or can help him in answering it. A second reason is that the person who seeks meaning inevitably finds himself in the paradox of losing it as soon as he finds it. Like Maurice Maeterlinck's bluebird which becomes a blackbird as soon as it is caged, "meaning" quickly becomes empty when it is cut off from the living waters that it was meant to channel.

The human being is driven to seek meaning by the very absurdities and contradictions of existence and by the fact that as a self-conscious person one is not simply carried along by the stream of life but stands on the bank and watches it flow. Yet the meaning one seeks is that of the stream. When one brings it up on the bank with one, like a fish that is caught, it gasps and dies for want of the oxygen that it can find only in the stream. The artist is in a better position than the philosopher, for his art remains more closely bound to the concrete. Nonetheless, he too falls within this paradox: all art is an attempt to find the right dialectic between detachment from the concrete and pointing back to it. The artist like Kafka who stakes out a new art and a new realm of meaning must move in "fear and trembling," quite as much as Kierkegaard's "knight of faith."

The artist creates out of his whole existence and cannot circumscribe the part of his existence which belongs to his wrestling with meaning and that which does not. What is more, since he is engaged in creating unique meaning, he cannot have any sure ground on which to stand but must be exposed to the despair that comes when he doubts his own struggle or when existence itself seems to shift beneath him, making all his images and formulations invalid.

In *The Castle* the social is an amorphous realm between the self and the call, a neutral strip, or "no man's land," whose borders on either side are constantly fluctuating. The fluctuation of these borders constitutes the central problematic of *The Castle* in which all its other problematic aspects are included. The problem of the calling, as we have seen, is not merely that a calling is meaningful only as a response to a call and that a call is needed to confirm the calling, but also that the confirmation needs to be personal as well as social, social as well as personal. The impossibility of identifying social and personal confirmation, on the one hand, and of separating them, on the other, is paradigmatic of the whole situation of the self. The self experiences the vertigo of being a free and directing consciousness, on the one hand, and an "eddy in the social current," on the other. This is a contrast of which Kafka himself was all too painfully aware, and his hero K. is a masterful portrayal of the confusion of the anxious and at the same time reflective person who fights for his freedom and independence yet recognizes both the necessity of social binding and the extent to which he himself is not so much an individual as a social unit. If this paradox is heightened in K. and the resulting confusion is consequently greater, it is, nonetheless, an ambiguity that is inseparable from the very existence of the self, one that no human being can escape. The harder a person tries to fight his way through this ambiguity, the deeper his confusion must be if he is both honest and aware.

The other border is between the social and what we might call "ontological reality" in order to distinguish it in some way from the social without erecting it into a separate metaphysical or theological realm. Here too the self experiences great confusion, this time from the side of the call. The call seems to come through the social, yet in such a way that it not only becomes indistinct but often highly dubious. It tempts one to believe, as a result, either that there really is no call or that it comes to one from some metaphysical, religious, or eternal realm quite outside the social. The problematic of the social, as a result, becomes essential to understanding both the self and the call and such confirmation as may arise between them.

The self finds meaning in its existence, not through identifying society and social confirmation with the call nor through turning away from them to some pure call that one hears apart from the world. It finds meaning, rather, through answering with its existence the call that comes to it through the absurd—through the bigoted villagers and the endless, senseless hierarchies of Castle officials—the call that can reach it in no other way. The tension between personal and social confirmation is basic to the relations between Village and Castle in K.'s search to answer his call. K.'s ambivalent attitude to marriage and the community is not to be explained simply by the notion that the Village is his goal and the Castle the means to that goal or by the notion that the Castle is his goal and the Village is the means to the Castle. He never sees any "ultimate reality," he never hears the call except as it is mediated through social reality. He hears the call in such a way, what is more, that he can neither separate social and ontological reality, on the one hand, nor accept social reality as simply reality, on the other.

Kafka's unique contribution to the problematic of confirmation is his probing of the paradox of existence as a person in the modern world. Kafka offers us an image of modern man confronting the reality of an otherness which can neither be dismissed as unreal nor rationalized as anything less than absurd. Kafka's hero is neither able to affirm meaning *despite* what confronts him, as do Nietzsche's Zarathustra, Sartre's Orestes, and Camus' Sisyphus, nor to fix meaning *in* what confronts him, as does Plato's philosopher or Kierkegaard's "knight of faith." Put in the simplest terms, Kafka explores what it means to continue to be "I" in a world that seems to offer neither confirmation nor personal meaning to the "I." He is no individualist; for he sees the person as existing in relation to a world that calls him into existence. Yet he clings too tenaciously to what is given the person in his concrete existence ever to describe who calls or even to assert that anyone does call. He sees the person in the modern world as pure paradox: the self needs a personal meaning for its very existence and continuity as self; yet it is confronted by an absurd reality which seems by its very nature to offer no personal meaning.

Once again what is said here has nothing to do with pessimism or optimism. It is an attempt to face squarely the problematic of confirmation that has always confronted man as man and that confronts the person in the modern world in an especially sharpened way. Only by keeping this problematic in view can we understand with sufficient depth and complexity the possibilities and problems of the confirmation of otherness in family, community, and society.[3]

Part III

CONFIRMATION OF OTHERNESS IN THE FAMILY

Chapter 9

THE ROLE OF THE FATHER IN THE FAMILY

THE FUTURE family will grow out of the culture shock of the present, for the family as we have known it is in an alarming state of disintegration, and it is hard to see what might reverse this trend. In business and industrial centers, urban, suburban, exurban, the extended family is more and more of a rarity, and even the nuclear family is often not intact. This is not, as it might seem, a gain for the confirmation of otherness, but a loss. The greater individuality and seeming autonomy is not complemented by deeper relationship but by alienation, lack of roots, and the coming apart of community in any real sense of the term.

More than 2500 years ago the Chinese family system suffered what was, for them, an even more devastating decay. China's two greatest religious, social, and political philosophers—Laotzu and Confucius—formed their whole philosophies as a response to this event. With the disintegration of the family came the disintegration of the social order. As a result, their discussion of "male roles" was informed by their views of how one might restore the family and the social order. Starting with a common situation and a common tradition, they elaborated almost diametrically opposite teachings. Confucius's overriding concern was with propriety, ritual, and prescriptions of how one ought to act. Laotzu's overriding concern was with spontaneity, flow, feeling, sincerity, and the heart: "The way to do is to be."

The second statement in the *Analects* of Confucius reads:

> Those who in private life behave well towards their parents and elder brothers, in public life seldom show a disposition to resist the authority of their superiors. And as for such men starting a revolution, no instance of it has ever occurred. It is upon the trunk [of the tree] that a gentleman works. When that is firmly set up, the Way grows. And surely proper behaviour toward parents and elder brothers is the trunk of Goodness?[1]

Asked about the treatment of parents Confucius said, "Never disobey!" One virtue Confucius never tired of extolling was filial piety. He saw this as a mutual obligation, to be sure, but one of an essentially unequal nature. Sons owed their parents reverence, respect, and obedience; parents owed their children concern and kindness. "Show piety towards your parents and kindness toward your children, and they will be loyal to you."

Laotzu, in contrast, openly scoffed at Confucius's notions of how to restore the lost social and family order:

> *When people lost sight of the way to live*
> *Came codes of love and honesty,*
> *Learning came, charity came,*
> *Hypocrisy took charge;*
> *When differences weakened family ties*
> *Came benevolent fathers and dutiful sons;*
> *And when lands were disrupted and misgoverned*
> *Came ministers commended as loyal.[2]*

In Poem 38 Laotzu continues this thought:

. . .

> *However a man with a kind heart proceed,*
> *He forgets what it may profit him;*
> *However a man with a just mind proceed,*
> *He remembers what it may profit him;*
> *However a man of conventional conduct proceed, if he be not complied*
> *   with*
> *Out goes his fist to enforce compliance.*

. . .

Conventions are fealty and honesty gone to waste,
They are the entrance of disorder. . . .[3]

To restore the social order and the family, Laotzu taught in Poem 49, we must recover the flow of life, spontaneous reciprocity:

A sound man's heart is not shut within itself
But is open to other people's hearts:
I find good people good,
And I find bad people good
If I am good enough;
I trust men of their word,
And I trust liars
If I am true enough;
I feel the heart-beats of others
Above my own
If I am enough of a father,
Enough of a son.[4]

Laotzu says this in another way in Poem 35:

If the sign of life is in your face
He who responds to it
Will feel secure and fit
As when, in a friendly place,
Sure of hearty care
A traveler gladly waits. . . .[5]

Wisdom has always meant the right alternation between structure and spontaneity, and only wisdom can teach us what that right alternation is. By the same token, only wisdom can tell us the right proportion between social role and spontaneous personal response in the "male role." The "male role" does not mean what men *do* but what people *think* men do or what they *expect* men to do. The most common conception and expectation is that the man of the family be "the breadwinner." In reality, this is often not the case, either because the wife earns money too or because the wife earns it and the husband does not. The tragic fact in many cases is that a family can get more money from welfare if the father is absent than it can from the father's earnings when he is present. A second conception and expectation of the man of the family is that he is or should be "responsible." In actuality, the man of the family is often irresponsible or is responsible according to his own light, which may come to the same thing. Is it a decline in men or the disintegration of the family system or both that makes the man often not want to take equal responsibility for the pregnancy of the woman but instead consider that more her problem than his own?

These sets of contrasts can be multiplied. The man of the family is expected to be decisive; often, in fact, he is indecisive. He is expected to be the authority; often he is lacking in all authority and may even be treated without respect or with downright contempt. He is expected to be the strong patriarch; he may instead be weak, the "eternal boy." Whether he is the biological father or not, the man of the family is expected to be a father to the children. Yet he is not infrequently an absentee father or a father who is "present yet absent." By the same token, the man of the family is expected to be the keeper of values; yet he may not embody any, or any very good ones, himself. He is expected to offer a meaningful image of the human *and* a meaningful image of the male role; yet he may fail to do either. Often these very expectations may lead to his failure, either because he is ashamed not to come up to the expectations that have been built into him by his family of origin, or because he *cannot* come up to his wife's expectations, or because she wants him to reach a standard in conflict with his own value system, and *she* judges him a failure in consequence.

If we take these sets of contrasts seriously, we shall begin to glimpse the fact that we cannot discuss the "male role" without understanding the problems of identity, of confirmation as a person and as one fulfilling a social role, of the relation between the male role and the female role, of the relation of the male role to the image of the human that is exemplified in the family, of the tension between personal uniqueness and social role, of the family system of both the man's and the woman's families of origin, of the present family system, and, most important of all, of the presence or absence of mutual trust in the family. We can touch here only on some of these questions, particularly the relation of the male role to the human image and the problem of personal identity.

The human image, as I use the term, is neither an ideal nor a mere description. It is an integral part of our search for authentic personal and social existence, for a meaningful direction which will enable us to respond from within to what we meet in each new situation, standing our ground and going out to meet the world with the attitude rooted in this ground. The human image does not mean some fully formed, conscious model of what we should become—certainly not anything simply imposed on us by the culture or any mere conformity with society through identification with its goals. It is our becoming in the truest sense of the word—our becoming as persons and as human beings. Our becoming takes place through giving direction to our potentialities, through deciding again and again, with the response of our whole being, what way is ours because it is true for us and we have committed ourselves to be true to it.

The problematic of identity, therefore, cannot be reduced to any simplified issue of individual self-expression versus social conformity. A man needs the confirmation of a woman not only as a sexual being and breadwinner but as a partner capable of giving and receiving tenderness and love. This tension is sharpened still further by the social dislocations of the modern family and of modern culture and by the alienation resulting from the loss of direction-giving meanings for personal and social existence. One of the most serious expressions of this loss of direction is the father-child relationship. The father is the first and often the most lasting image of the human and of the male for the child. It not infrequently happens, however, that the father is not really present for the child, either because he is dead or absent or inattentive, or because he is in no sense a father, or because he is too weak or despicable for a child to be able to emulate him. In such a case the need for the father as an image of the human and a model of the male role remains and often leads to a lifetime search for a substitute father who will supply an image of the human as the actual father has not.

Freud and modern psychoanalysts in general have seen only one aspect of this father-child relationship and have reduced it to fear of castration, introjection of the father's ideals and conscience, or even identification. The aspect which they have missed is the need that the child has for a relationship with the father which will help him or her find direction in the choices he or she must make between one way of life and another. This need is not for identification but dialogue, and it is not a conditioned formation or reaction but a free and even spontaneous response.

The inner division which results when this need is not met is as much a commentary on the absence of a modern image of the human as on the breakdown of the specific father-child relationship. At the heart of this breakdown, in fact, is the inability of the father to give his child a direction-giving image of meaningful and authentic human existence. The inner division in the child that results expresses itself at times in a bifurcation into opposing selves and opposing father images. It may also express itself in a crisis of motives when the child, unable to accept the father, suppresses his or her awareness of that side of him or herself that resembles the father in favor of an ideal self-image. To a large extent, I suspect, child and woman abuse is the product of the absence of adequate male role models and/or the frustration of the man who feels he is failing in his role, including the inability to find employment.

The 1960s and '70s saw the growth of the women's liberation movement and some stirrings of male consciousness in response. In part, this has been an excellent development, even for men. It has made them more aware and responsible, and, in numerous cases, liberated them from those traditional expectations of men that have been enslaving to men and degrading to women. This has led some to contrast unflattering, traditional, "macho" male roles, marked by rigidity, overbearingness, and lack of mutual interaction, with modern male roles, marked by cooperativeness, mutual trust, interaction, flexibility, and openness. These simple contrasts falsify the situation because they treat the male role in abstraction from the all-important questions of the actual resources of the men who are expected to fulfill the role, and of the mutual trust or mistrust experienced by the man in relation to his woman and family. No one can be open and trusting if the partner in an intimate relationship is closed and distrustful. Though we are not simply dependent on the other for our willingness to enter into dialogue, still the other can set the limits to the possibility of dialogue.

One of the traditional conceptions and expectations of the male in our society, which goes with the notion of "breadwinner" and "head of the family," is that he be a successful competitor who thereby provides an image for his children and especially his sons. If he is *not* a successful competitor in the eyes of his family, he is regarded as a failure. But a third possibility may emerge if we can glimpse a wholly different image of true masculine strength—an image of the man who succeeds in cooperating with others, who knows how to meet others and hold his ground when he meets them, who works together with others, giving and taking, and thereby gives his children a meaningful image of the masculine *and* of the human. This is only possible where the family of origin has given this man at least a minimum of confirmation as a person, where a strong father has not seen fit to crush his son or set up impossible expectations, or a strong mother to bind him to her in ties of lasting dependence. It is only possible, too, where there is mutual trust in the family, where the man is not continually put down for embodying *his* kind of strength as opposed to the stereotyped notions of male strength that his wife and in-laws may have.

This image of true masculine strength is close in spirit to Laotzu's image of the sane man, the sound man, the fit man. The "sanest man" "takes everything that happens as it comes, as something to animate, not to appropriate, to earn not to own," as Laotzu shows us in Poems 7, 81, and 54:

· · ·

A sound man by not advancing himself
Stays the further ahead of himself,
By not confining himself to himself
Sustains himself outside himself:
By never being an end in himself
He endlessly becomes himself.

· · ·

The greater his use to others
The greater their use to him,
The more he yields to others
The more they yield to him. . . .

* * * *

. . . Realized in one man, fitness has its rise;
Realized in a family, fitness multiplies;
Realized in a village, fitness gathers weight;
Realized in a country, fitness becomes great;
Realized in the world fitness fills the skies.
And thus the fitness of one man
You find in the family that he began.

· · ·

How do I know this integrity?
Because it could all begin in me.[6]

Chapter 10

SEX AND LOVE IN MARRIAGE AND THE FAMILY

        I HAVE dealt at some length with the subject of "Sex and Love" in two other books, *The Hidden Human Image* and *Aiming at the Self*. What needs to be said here concerns only sex and love within the family itself. As we all know, a large amount of sex and love in our culture does not take place within the family, though some of it, from prostitution and casual affairs all the way to extramarital relations of many years duration, must be understood either as an attempt to escape from the family or as a counterbalance which seems to make it emotionally possible for the person involved not to leave or break up the family.

There is nowhere that the problematic of confirmation is so concentrated as in sex and love. When sex by itself is pursued as a goal, there can be no question of the confirmation of the uniqueness of the other person. At best there is only a mutual exploitation which, usually in the short run, may be satisfying to both partners. At worst there are all types of one-sided exploitation and domination which go far to explain why sex in so many persons' minds is associated with temptation, sin, and evil. When love enters the picture, the situation is different but no less problematic. For if sex is given meaning by love, feelings of love often mask or rationalize what are essentially sexual drives. By "sexual drives" we may mean Freudian instinctual urges and needs. But we may also mean something which is not truly a drive at all, such as Jean-Paul Sartre's understanding of sex as an intersubjective phenomenon which at best is a mutual seduction to become incarnate in one another's flesh but which is even more often the desire of the one partner to make the freedom of the other partner subject to his or her own domination.

To say this is not to imply, as Freud does in *Civilization and Its Discontents*, that civilization in general and the family in particular is founded on the necessary frustration, repression, and/or sublimation of libidinal drives. There is nothing about the sexual per se which makes it impossible to humanize it within genuine dialogue and genuine confirmation of the other, any more than there is about our needs for food, clothing, shelter, and transportation. Sex, Martin Buber suggests, is a sign and a means that the eternal and cosmic power of love may be reborn on earth. "Love needs sex in order to obtain body, and sex needs love in order to attain spirit."[1] Viktor Frankl, similarly, holds that love joins the sexual drive to the spiritual person by personalizing it:

> There is not the least thing to be objected to in the sexual drive as long as it is included in the personal realm: as soon and as long as the sexuality is *personalized*, personalized through us to grasp another person in his being, in his suchness, in his uniqueness and particularity, and not only in his being and his suchness but also in his value, in what he shall become—and that means to affirm him. Love may be defined now as: being able to say Thou to someone—and beyond that to be able to say Yes to him.[2]

Carl Rogers has stressed the revolution in marriage and partnerships that has resulted from effective contraception:

> The availability of effective contraception means that marriage can become more of a partnership, since the wife is no longer fully occupied with pregnancy, nursing, and child-rearing. It also means that physically she is as free as her husband to explore relationships outside of marriage. Premarital sex and sexual relations outside of marriage have increased markedly among women. She also has a chance to choose between family and career, or to balance the two. For the first time in history she is physically a free agent. Effective contraception has made possible the release of woman from her subjugated role. The impact on the politics of the family has been incalculable.[3]

None of this changes the fact that a male must be a man, not just a human being, and a female a woman. But they must also be men and women of our culture, and they must be both of these as human beings. I cannot sidestep the anxiety of being a boy, a lover, a father, through being a "thinking thing," a universal mind, or even an "authentic self." Nor can I sidestep the anxiety of what it means to be an authentic human being by developing myself into a caricature of masculinity. But both of these anxieties focus at the point in history in which our culture finds itself. This is the point at which a father often cannot pass on to his son an image of what it means to be a man and a human being and a mother often cannot pass on to her daughter an image of what it means to be a woman and a human being.

We live in a culture in which men do not feel they are up to their duty as men, and women do not feel they are up to their duty as women. Yet neither men nor women know what it means to be men or women in particular, much less what it means to be human through being a man or a woman. The tendency, as a result, is that each has so much guilt that he or she projects it on the other partner in the love relationship. It may be true, as Kate Millett suggests, that society places the guilt of sexuality overwhelmingly on the female, but within an enduring relationship between a man and a woman, guilt is like a hot potato that each tries to hand over to the other. Some aspects of the Women's Liberation Movement have taken on this Either/Or quality of blaming men for their conscious or unconscious male chauvinism rather than seeing it as a joint problem in which each must help the other to a more human relationship for both. "Those miserable women who blame the men who *let them down* for their misery and isolation," writes Germaine Greer, "enact every day the initial mistake of sacrificing their personal responsibility for themselves."

If men in our society must ask themselves whether they are really capable of loving women or whether their sexuality is not just another expression of their hostility or their need for conquest, men and women together must recognize, as Kate Millett puts it, that "our highly repressive and Puritan tradition has almost hopelessly confused sexuality with sadism, cruelty, and that which is in general inhumane and antisocial." Instead of a genuine image of woman, men and women alike are confronted at every turn by the reigning female fetish—a totally sexless, interminably smiling idol or doll whose lines are those of the castrated female. The passive sexual role assigned to women by our culture is itself a denial of female sexuality in favor of "femininity," or sexlessness. This works both ways, of course. Most men still feel that women *expect* them to be dominant—in bed if nowhere else—and that most women are ready to express a not-too-well-disguised contempt for them if they are not. Women do not have the monopoly on kindness and consideration that some advocates of women's rights imagine when they picture men as educated to harsh competitiveness and women to gentle tenderness.

Women intellectuals are no less "female eunuchs" than their nonintellectual sisters: They are repressed, servile, and disenfranchised of their bodies. Both the feminine and the pseudomasculine roles represent castrations. "Most women who have arrived at positions of power in a men's world have done so by adopting masculine methods which are not incompatible with the masquerade of femininity," writes Germaine Greer. "They still exploit the sadomasochistic hookup of the sexes," in which "we have only the choice of being hammer or anvil."[4] In a phenomenological study of twenty-one women who had entered traditionally male-dominated professions, Pamela Kangas found them overwhelmingly concerned with making it in a man's world rather than with how to remain fully a woman while working in their chosen professions.[5]

Even when men are directly the cause of women's exile, that exile is inseparably tied up with the exile of the men:

> The husband, after all, is trying to protect and bolster his frail ego, not drive his wife insane or force her suicide. He wants in the home to be able to hide from his own inner doubts, his own sense of shame, failure, and meaninglessness. He wants to shed the endless humiliation of endless days parading as a man in the male world, pretending a power, control, and understanding he does not have.
>
> All he asks of his wife, aside from hours of menial work, is that she not see him as he sees himself. That she not challenge him, but admire and desire him, soothe and distract him.[6]

Naturally wives do not exist just to admire and desire, soothe and distract their husbands. But we do not get much farther if we think in terms of fulfilling the "needs" of both partners, as is usually the case. Sex and love in marriage, as outside, is only ultimately meaningful in the realm of the "between," the relationship itself. To establish ourselves as the sexual beings and persons we choose to be, we need to take great and sometimes dreadful risks. Moreover, there is a residual element in sex itself that places a demand on the partners which can only be satisfied if, *in that relationship and in that situation*, the man succeeds in evoking the feminine in the woman and the woman in evoking the masculine in the man, whatever the admixture of masculine and feminine may be in each partner taken separately. The human image only comes to revelation *between* persons and not *in* woman or man in isolation from each other. Hence the unsureness about what it means to be a woman in our culture is complemented by an equal unsureness about what it means to be a man.

Sex, which should be the crown of the interhuman, often in our culture becomes the opposite—the mark of its inauthenticity. A great many persons are inclined to distrust themselves, and they are inclined to mistrust one another. This mistrust arises in part because of the popular Freudian view of the person as a two-layered being whose instincts are likely at any moment to take over control from the rational mind. That ancient dualism in which the body and sex are regarded as evil has been modernized in no less puritanical form by Freud, who tells us that our conscious thoughts *and* feelings are rationalizations for the drive toward fulfillment of libidinal urges which we cannot admit directly to ourselves. If we cannot join Freud in making the conscious mind so much the superstructure determined by and reflecting our unconscious motivations, we can certainly assert that relating to the other as an It and relating to the other as a Thou are nowhere so completely and confusedly intermingled as in sex and love. That would be no problem if the It were transformed by and taken up into the Thou. Often, however, we do not know which is in the service of which. Even if we could rid ourselves of the tenacious notion that sex is something innately evil, we would still have the problem of when it is a "healing through meeting" and when it is a still further wounding through mismeeting.

Although it may no longer be true to say that Freud dominates the psychiatric thought of our time, it is certainly true that he dominates its approach to sex. While many people might quarrel with the central role that Freud ascribes to libidinal sexuality in the human psychic economy, few look at sex itself in basically other terms than those of Freud—namely, as an irrational, instinctual, and largely unconscious drive that must be understood in the first instance in terms of the biological needs of the individual organism and only secondarily and derivatively in terms of interpersonal relations.

If we approach sex instead in terms of the ontology of the between, this means, in the first instance, that it must be seen within the context of interhuman relationships, including love. This does not imply some naive rationalism that ignores the dark swirling forces in the human being that have been uncovered by the romantics and by depth psychology. It means, rather, that human existence can never be reduced to a psychological state, a pure content of feeling, minus the attitude which the person has to that state of feeling and the relation which the person has to other persons. From this point of view, sex is an "urge," or passion, which becomes evil only when we leave it undirected and allow an undirected possibility to turn into an undirected reality without real personal decision. What counts here is not the expression, repression, or sublimation of sexual desire but the response with one's whole being that diverts our powerful desires from the casual to the essential. We are not to turn away from what attracts our hearts but to find mutual contact with it by making our relationship to it real. We are not necessarily torn between a cruel id and a cruel superego. Where some degree of trust and relationship exists, we may bring our passions into unification with a personal wholeness which is itself a by-product of the ever-renewed act of entering into dialogue. Martin Buber calls this shaping of the chaos of matter into the cosmos of personal existence "a cruelly hazardous enterprise." It is, nonetheless, an enterprise that we can and must undertake.

From the standpoint of the philosophy of the interhuman, it is not legitimate to treat sexuality in abstraction from human relationships and, specifically, from the interplay and interaction between the I-Thou and the I-It. By the same token—precisely in the sphere of sexuality—deception, illusion, and bad faith of every kind again and again appear. Here, more than anywhere, monologue loves to mask itself as dialogue—not only because we are all of us "seeming" persons who seek confirmation from the other by trying to appear what we are not, but also because we do not wish to recognize the extent to which we are treating the other as an It and are letting the other do the same to us. If real love is not *in* the person but *between* persons, then we must say that much that passes for love in our age is less than genuine; for it focuses on the precious experience of the I that enjoys the feelings that the other produces in it without giving itself to the other.

True lovers receive the common event from both sides at once and in a bodily way. The lover feels the inclination of the head on the neck of his beloved as an answer to the word of his own silence without losing the feeling of his own self. He does not assimilate the beloved into his own soul nor attempt to possess her freedom. He turns to her in her otherness, her self-reality, with all the power of intention of his own heart. When such love extends into long-term relationship or into marriage, each of the partners must mean the other in his or her real otherness, affirming the other as the particular person he or she is.

To do this, it is necessary to practice what Martin Buber calls "inclusion," or "imagining the real," even in the sexual act itself; for only thus can one imagine quite concretely what the other is feeling, willing, thinking. Once one has really met the beloved in this concrete way, then sex itself becomes an embodiment of the "between" and a mere elaboration of subjectivity is never again possible or tolerable. Each person becomes present to the other for all time. Thus the sexual drive is personalized and brought into the heart of the interhuman. As Viktor Frankl has written, "Only an I that means a Thou can integrate the It."

In *Love and Will* Rollo May shows us sex precisely in the fusion of I-It and I-Thou: "To be human means to exist on the boundary between the anonymous and the personal." The removal of all limits has only increased inner conflict; for "the sexual freedom to which we were devoted fell short of being fully human." The same can be said of the relatively greater education in sexual facts and techniques of our contemporaries compared to the generations that preceded us. The emphasis upon technique in sex has given us a mechanistic attitude toward lovemaking that has left us all the more alienated, lonely, and depersonalized. By a curious inversion people become more wary of the sharing of tenderness than of physical nakedness and sexual intimacy. We call our search for a responding and longing in the other through which to prove our own feelings alive "love," but it has nothing to do with it. Nor is there any real love present in that compulsion to demonstrate one's potency that leads one to treat the most intimate and personal of all acts "as a performance to be judged by exterior requirements." The ironic result of viewing oneself as a machine to be turned on, adjusted, and steered, is the loss of feeling for oneself and one's partner to the point where "the lover who is most efficient will also be the one who is impotent." Another cause of impotence is our compulsively hurried relationship to time. In the age of "short-order sex" sex itself gets shortchanged. Carried far enough this leads to actual impotence—the body's statement that it has been left behind in the compulsive rush to carry out an idea of what we are supposed to want.

We *fly* to sex in order to avoid passion, pushed by an anxiety that cannot know any real presentness even in the moment of intercourse. Sex in our society, writes May, is a technique for a gigantic repression of true passion. Passion is not identical with sex but is a separate force deeper than it. It may be expressed through sex, but it also may be pushed under by it. Only when passion takes over the whole person is there self-assertion and true mutual relationship. Although May says that this relationship "always skates on the edge of the exploitation of the partner," the give-and-take, the experiencing of the other side of the relationship, prevents it from going over the edge while retaining the vitality of the relationship. "The human being has to make the creature with whom he has sexual relations in some way personal, even if only in fantasy, or else suffer depersonalization himself." The need for sex is not so powerful as the need for relationship, intimacy, acceptance, and affirmation. Therefore, exploitation, seduction, and the domination of another's freedom cannot be the last word in sex and love. In attitude as well as in physical fact sex means the ultimate baring of one's self.

Even our feelings are not private but part of the dialogue that takes place in love. They "are ways of communicating and sharing something meaningful from us to the world." "Our feelings not only take into consideration the other person," writes May, "but are in a real sense partially *formed by the feelings of the other persons present*. Every successful lover knows by instinct to pick up the magnetic field of the feelings of the person he is with." Even the wish is not simply individual, as Freud thought, but is a reality *between*: "the wish in interpersonal relationships requires mutuality."

To open oneself to another in love means to be confronted with a vastly widened world including regions of which we never dreamed. This experience produces a vertigo in which we may genuinely wonder whether we are "capable of giving ourselves to our beloved and still preserving what center of autonomy we have." Love may push us toward a new dimension of consciousness in which we transcend our isolation, as May says, but we do not know whether there will be the resources in any particular situation to meet others and hold our ground when we meet them. Still less can we say with confidence of ourselves what May says in a commentary on a traditional people, namely that "the community gives a humanly trustworthy, interpersonal world in which one can struggle against the negative forces." On the contrary, it may be just the absence of this "humanly trustworthy, interpersonal world" that leads to that "crisis of confidence" which, as Buber suggests, sets the stage for the modern split between libidinal passion and superego which Freud took to be the nature of man.

Leslie Farber's "willfulness" that wants to handle both sides of the dialogue is found most often in the contemporary approach to sex. Indeed, Farber goes so far as to assert that "over the last fifty years sex has, for the most part, lost its viability as a human experience." Sexual activity itself has not decreased, but the human possibilities of sex are becoming ever more elusive, and the couplings that take place are "poultices after the fact" which "further extend the degradation of sex that has resulted from its ever-increasing bondage to the modern will." What sex once brought us—the possibility of that mutual knowing and being known within which we regain *our own* body through knowing the body of the loved one—is lost in favor of an empty *knowing about* in which both bodies again escape us. Farber traces this decline in a series of steps: man viewing nature as a variety of energies to be harnessed and utilized, a machine to be kept healthy so it might lead to never-ending progress and prosperity; coming to regard the human body as just such a machine; the decision that the dominant energy of the human machine is sex; the claim of the erotic life as the exclusive province of sexology and psychoanalysis; and the abstraction and isolation of sex into the function of the sexual organs.[7]

Though we cannot return to the unawareness of the past, neither can we remain standing in the pseudoclinical situation of the present, in which frigidity is seen as something *in* the woman, impotence as something *in* the man. Both frigidity and impotence as well as male and female orgasms are essential aspects of an interhuman betweenness in which both man and woman must work together on the sexual, as on the financial and other problems of the relationship. I do not mean that both should deal together with *her* problem of frigidity and/or *his* problem of impotence. I mean that the problems themselves do not belong to and cannot be simply located in one partner in the relationship, for they are a function of the relationship itself.

When and if the mutual trust that upholds the relationship is broken, especially if the separation is traumatic, it is inevitable in most cases that sexual "hang-ups" will be relegated by each partner to the other. Each protects himself from his former closeness by turning the other into a caricature of a person—an object possessing such-and-such characteristics. Actually, he does not know what the other might be in another relationship. I am not denying that some relationships are too difficult to work out. But I am saying that precisely when we know exactly what is wrong with our former partner and wonder why we wasted ten years of our lives with such a person, precisely when we seem to have reached an objective and secure ground, is the point when we have ceased to make him or her present to us as a person and are protecting ourselves from feeling any concern—from living in and with that person.

Only the abstraction of sex into an "experience" somehow supposed to be of value in itself could lead so many to spend so much of their strength and effort trying to prove their "potency" with ever-fresh partners or trying to extend the variety and scope of their experience by the exchange of partners. Many persons in our society are ridden by a deep anxiety concerning their sexual adequacy, that no amount of actual sexual "conquest" or "experience" can ever really allay. People are afraid of fumbling and faltering in sexual relations, for they do not wish to appear un*master*-ly. Few take seriously the extent to which "good sexual functioning" is itself a function of good relationship or the fact that even good relationships, including all the anxieties and worries and fatigues of real life, are not on call to produce good sex at stated periods. It takes courage to falter, to hesitate, to show bewilderment, confusion, and self-doubt. Naturally, we are vulnerable here as in perhaps no other sphere of our lives, and our most personal confirmation is at stake. Yet without the mutual revelation of weakness, of humanness, of hope and doubt, faith and despair, of the very ground in which each of us is rooted, and of the strengths and foibles of our unique personal and human stances, there can be no confirmation of otherness in sexual love.

Often there is little basis for a marriage other than sexual attraction which, even when it lasts, cannot be by itself an adequate basis for marriage and family life. All too often, moreover, this sexual bonding manifests itself in sadomasochism in Erich Fromm's sense of the term, that is, in forms of dominance and submission that function, as a rule, precisely to allow one to escape the anxiety of being oneself or of confirming otherness. Instead of working to build a genuine dialogue in which each accepts and confirms the other in his and her otherness and uniqueness, both partners settle for a symbiotic unity which temporarily staves off the anxiety of loneliness, indecisiveness, and the fear of death. Or there is a Sartrian possession of the other's freedom as subject to one's own—a pseudoconfirmation of oneself and an even more pseudoconfirmation of the other. Or, as Thorstein Veblen has brilliantly illustrated in his *Theory of the Leisure Class*, the marriage mate may be chosen and used as a form of "conspicuous consumption" to show off one's wealth, one's class status, or what an expensive and desirable possession one has.

For Buber marriage is the exemplary bond, as we have seen, precisely because if it is genuine it demands ever again the confrontation and confirmation of otherness. Some people feel that the new attitudes toward sexual freedom imply a corollary disapproval of jealousy as the attempt to possess the other as an object and to impose one's will on the other. There is no question that there is much of real gain for the confirmation of otherness in contemporary attitudes toward jealousy, freedom, and "open marriage." But "open marriage" cannot be understood as merely parallel play in which each is concerned only about her or his growth. At the end of *Open Marriage* by Nena and George O'Neill, there is a section on "synergy" which suggests that whatever enriches each partner in the marriage enriches the marriage. But this is only true if each brings the enrichment of their individual growth back into the mutuality of the relationship. If this is not done, then precisely because of this enrichment, the couple will grow apart.

Carl Rogers tends to fall into the same fallacy as the O'Neills. He concludes a report on a couple who took sexual partners outside their marriage with the statement: "I would suspect that Laura regards her experience with Jay as a growth experience in her life, and hopes that John feels the same way about his closeness to Ruth." Although what Rogers says later represents a modification of this position, there is still the expectation that what enriches the individual will automatically enrich the relationship:

> The politics of a marriage can be one of equality, shared responsibilities, mutual support, and shared decision making, as Trish movingly demonstrates when she says that she and Fred do not so much allow each other the "privilege" of freedom as actually encourage it. This is not the irresponsibility of "I'll do my thing and you do yours." It is in the context of an equal relationship that they go forth to explore and then return to the relationship an enriched person. It has helped to build their independent strengths.[8]

Something of this same approach to relationship as a mere sum of the becoming and self-actualization of two separate persons comes through in a chapter of Rogers' *Becoming Partners* which he entitles "Three Marriages and One Growing Person." He tells the story of a woman who married right out of college the sort of man her mother and her sorority sisters thought she should marry. After ten years this marriage broke up and in another year she married again on the rebound. This marriage was destined to failure and lasted only one year. Finally she met a man with whom she fell in love who was mature enough to resist her demands for a speedy marriage and waited until the relationship had had a chance to grow organically. The story is a meaningful one, not atypical of many in our times. But the title that Rogers gives the story suggests a fatal flaw in his own approach. The third man was mature, but he was not her therapist. To speak of "Three Marriages and One Growing Person" is to suggest that only the woman grew in the third relationship and not the man. Or, more importantly, it suggests that Rogers' only focus is on the becoming of the individual and not on the "betweenness" of the partnership itself.

Although Rogers never states clearly that jealousy can be entirely overcome, he does insist that, to the extent that it is made up of a sense of possessiveness, it can be profoundly altered when the partners give each other real freedom and at the same time maintain a real commitment. His final testimony on this subject is a very moving witness to the betweenness that can develop where there is genuine, lasting commitment:

> One thing that I have relearned from my contacts with this pair is the strong underlying desire on the part of every individual for depth and permanence in any close relationship. They have demonstrated in their own lives a wish which I have come to believe is almost universal—a wish for a lasting relationship in which one can know the other as a whole, complex person, and in which one can *be* known in the same way.[9]

Two aspects of sex and love in marriage and the family which have received increasing attention in the past decades and will receive still more in the decades to come are homosexuality and incest. Both are subjects of utmost complexity about which a whole literature has been written. One thing that homosexuality and incest often have in common is that they represent a fear of otherness, a fear of meeting, recognizing, and confirming a person of the other sex or a person outside the family. This fear results from the absence of a climate of trust in the family of origin that might make venturing forth to meet the other a risk which is not so threatening and anxiety-producing as to kill from the start any chance of a genuine partnership being established. Both also tend to result from possessiveness or domination. (Many homosexual men have overly strong mothers, or fathers who are dominated by their wives or by their own mothers.) In any family where there is not a healthy swing between distancing and relating, autonomy and loyalty, some socio- if not psychopathological result must be expected. Homosexuality and incest, when they derive from the fear of otherness, are examples of such results. Heterosexuality may also express the fear of sameness or even of relationship itself, especially when it takes the form of the male or female Don Juan who moves from one relationship to another in order to avoid closeness and commitment. Without question both homosexuality and incest are overdetermined and are seldom caused by this alone. The results of the absence of a healthy alternation between distancing and relating, conversely, are almost infinitely varied, and we cannot say that they *typically* manifest themselves in the forms of homosexuality and incest.

What is more basic here, as to sex and love in marriage and the family in general, is the tension of opposites that is represented by the male and the female and, within and between every member of the family, by the masculine and the feminine. When fathers forbid their sons to play with little girls or with dolls, it is often an expression of the father's own fear of sexual inadequacy, of not being sufficiently "macho," or even of homosexuality. In this realm too, Freud's Oedipal and Electra complexes take on great social meaning in the complex relationships between mother and son and between father and daughter. "Tea for Two," a popular song of a half-century ago, says, presumably from the man's point of view, "We will build a family / A boy for you, a girl for me." But fathers often want sons as an extension and expression of their own masculinity or even as a fantasied chance to relive their own lives, hopefully without so many mistakes. Mothers often want daughters for the same reason, as the title of Nancy Friday's book *My Mother, My Self* seems to suggest, both from the standpoint of the mother and that of the daughter.

Incest taboos have a long history and are found in every known culture and society. They express both endogamy and exogamy, the desire to keep things within the tribe and yet not have families inbreed. There is undoubtedly a great deal more incest to one degree or another in the contemporary family than is generally admitted or acknowledged. For every one case that reaches the attention of social workers, psychotherapists, and courts, there are probably a hundred that do not. The horror surrounding this "last taboo," as Warren Farrell calls it, makes it all the harder to get a dispassionate understanding of this phenomenon. In part, it results from the natural attractions between members of the opposite and even of the same sex that exist in every family and that proximity and intimacy may promote, especially if the taboo is not openly broken or if it is only gradually transgressed. More often, however, incest is the symptom of some underlying stagnancy or malfunctioning of the family. To take one example of which I know, Nancy's mother drank every evening and undoubtedly shut herself off from the father sexually. Nancy was her daddy's "little girl." He put her and her sister to bed every night while her mother occupied herself with her own woes. It is not surprising, all moral judgments apart, that incest developed out of this situation—between Nancy and her father and to a lesser extent between her father and her little sister.

Blair and Rita Justice's *The Broken Taboo: Sex in the Family*, while confirming the complexity of the interpersonal, familial, and societal causes of incest, also repeatedly confirms our insight into the part that the fear of otherness plays in this whole complex. It also confirms the complementary insight that incest is likely to damage the child's moving toward a healthy alternative of distancing and relating as an adult. To develop, the child needs both to belong and to be a separate person. Incest means a disconfirmation of the otherness and uniqueness of the child because it prevents these needs from being met. Yet the growing stress and change to which the modern family is subject make it ever more likely that certain individuals will turn inward and shut out the world beyond:

> As Erich Fromm has noted, there is a nonsexual "incestuous striving inherent in man's nature" based on deep needs for roots, belonging, warmth, and protection. Frightened and insecure in the world outside, a person turns inside the family to get his or her needs met and closes the door behind. The more stressful a person finds the world, the more likely he or she will turn inside the family. . . . The basic issue in incest is not sex but the need for closeness, nurturing, and stimulation.[10]

It is particularly important to recognize, as the Justices do, that incest and sexual misuse or abuse within a family involve the whole family and not just the person who initiates the activity:

> The nonparticipating spouse is involved in terms of directly or indirectly encouraging the activity. The child is involved in terms of often being an active, not passive, participant or welcoming the activity as a form of special attention. The whole environment of the family is involved in terms of contributing to the conditions under which incest or sexual misuse occurs.[11]

When incest is discovered, this co-involvement often takes on tragic contours. If the guilty adult is sent to prison, the child is left with guilt feelings about having been responsible for sending her father or brother or mother to jail and breaking up the family.

The other aspect that regularly goes with the parent turning to the child for nurturance and support is that the child is parentified, to use the language of Ivan Boszormenyi-Nagy. Not knowing how to get his needs met in a nonsexual and nonphysical way nor how to go outside the family, the father who commits incest turns to sex with his own daughter. The Justices say of the four types of incestuous fathers whom they discuss that "each type shares the inability to reach out to others, to establish closeness, to get attention and affection through daily human contacts." This is particularly true of the introvert:

> The introvert among incestuous fathers feels under attack from the outside world. He sees the family as a shelter that provides him comfort. He turns more and more inward into the family as the pressures outside continue. Much of the outside stress comes from the introvert's cutting himself off from others, asking help from no one, never confiding or blowing off steam. This type father believes he can trust few people, certainly no one outside his family. He sees his family as the place where he should be able to do as he pleases and no one should betray him.[12]

The pathology of such a person has led him to replace the healthy swing between distancing and relating by trying to stick to relating alone. It has also led him to a fixed division between "outer world" and "inner world," so that in the "outer world" he feels totally unsafe whereas in the "inner world" he loses sight of the otherness and uniqueness of the other members of the family and acts as if they were all part of his own self. Undoubtedly there are some people who feel safe only in the "outer world" and never in the family and some, such as certain types of schizophrenics, who swing violently between shutting everyone else out and maintaining a very close bond with the family or with one other person, family or not. The "tyrant," as the Justices describe him, represents a curious combination of "outer" and "inner," with no real relation in either sphere:

> Many tyrants disguise their needs for closeness and intimacy through strong macho attitudes toward sex. Sex is the only way they permit themselves to get close to anyone. They believe that one mark of being a "real man" is to be sexually active and powerful, so to them sex is not for closeness but for expressing manly virility. They have no recognition of how they attempt to satisfy deep needs for warmth through sex. Outside the home their bullying tactics seldom work, so they usually confine themselves to sexual activity with the daughter.[13]

The daughter's acceptance of the father's advances may represent a longing for the closeness of the family on her part and a fear of losing this closeness if she does not comply:

> Even in families where the daughter and mother do not get along, the girl will often protect her from the father's verbal attacks by calming him down with sex. She will go to great lengths to hold a family together that is already deeply split. She often has deep fears of desertion and abandonment and will do any and everything to keep father and mother together.[14]

The mother, on the other hand, may herself want to become the child and may want the daughter to become the mother. In an attempt to get the care and nurturing that she missed in her own childhood, she not only parentifies the daughter but invites her to become her husband's sex partner, perhaps rationalizing her abandonment of the daughter on the basis of helping her husband.[15]

When we follow these lines of thought through we come on an important link between disconfirmation and psychopathology, about which I have written in *Healing Through Meeting: Dialogue and Psychotherapy*. What we have here is not only the existential guilt incurred by the parent who seeks confirmation at the expense of the child, and in so doing either directly disconfirms the child, fails to confirm it, or parentifies it. We also have the tragic aspect of this failure in distancing and relating, namely, that it goes back in turn to the father's not having received the confirmation and nurturance he needed from his mother. This is stated in all explicitness by the Justices:

> Symbiotic personalities, such as those that become involved in incest with their daughters, can be traced back to a mother's keeping her child so dependent that he never learns what it means to grow up and reach out to others or to a mother's never allowing her child to be dependent and receive love and nurturing. In either case, the outcome is the same: the child is expected to meet the needs of the parent. The parent has a need for the child not to grow up, to remain dependent, or the parent has a need for the child to do all the loving and nurturing. In both instances, the child does not feel loved because the parent's needs come first. The child grows up seeking the love and nurturing he never received. Erroneously, he fantasies that mother embodies all-embracing, unlimited love if only he could possess

her and this is the fantasy he pursues with his daughter, whom he believes he can possess.[16]

Only the intergenerational contextual family therapy to which Ivan Nagy points could begin to heal the wounds in a situation like this.[17]

At first glance Warren Farrell's uniquely comprehensive study of incest, *The Family Sex Problem*, seems to contradict much of the above findings. Extending interviews for the first time beyond cases of incest identified by courts, psychologists, and social workers to a sample of the general population, Farrell finds incest neither necessarily pathological nor usually negative in its outcome. Instead of focusing on father-daughter incest, he extends his research to every type (mother-son, brother-sister, brother-brother, aunt-nephew, etc.), and of these he finds 79 percent positive in effects and only 21 percent negative. The only generalization he permits himself is that incest between adult male and preteenage or even teenage female is usually negative and is likely to be so either at once or in later reassessments of the experience on the part of the female involved. Beyond this, he offers some startling tentative conclusions, such as that "the intensity of sex seemed to replace the intensity of rebellion during adolescence," which leads him to question whether adolescent rebellion is a necessity for identity in general or is so "only when the barriers between parents and children are as great as they presently are."

Farrell finds a strong correlation between negative incest experience and negative attitudes toward sex in general, including unhappy family backgrounds and low self-esteem as concomitants. He sees incest as less a question of blood than of social role (relations between *step*fathers and daughters are more likely to be negative than between fathers and daughters). In positive cases, he finds that "the mutual needs served by the sexual contact often created more of a bond than a conflict. The lack of gap [between parent and child] around sex cut down on the secrecy, lying and [the child's] perceptions of [parental] hypocrisy in the positive open relationships. In this context there was almost no need for adolescent rebellion." Because the child did not have to suppress sexuality in the face of parental hypocrisy, when the child reached adolescence it did not have to rebel in order to get in touch with its sexuality. What is more, his findings give no support to Freud's assumption that the acting out of incestuous fantasies between son and mother would leave the son unable to make a break with his mother or to the generally held theory that the taboo is necessary to direct one's energies toward heterosexuality.

> The exceptions, as usual, were preteenage females who had the most traumatic experiences and were "turned off" to men. Most sons who had relationships with mothers had outside heterosexual relationships and brother-brother incest resulted in a higher percentage of continuing heterosexual marriages than any other form of incest.[18]

Even the psychological postulate of some psychologists that incest leads to a split between love and sex is not upheld by Farrell's findings. In the negative cases, to be sure, daughters often said that their fathers expressed little or no affection outside the sexual arena. "But adult women often complain of exactly the same phenomenon among men who are not incest participants—an inability to integrate sex and love."

To get an overall picture of the radical break with past research initiated by Farrell's study, we cannot do better than quote his own concluding summation from his final chapter, "The Psychology of Incest":

> In summary the findings of this study suggest that a number of widely held psychological assumptions about incest must be questioned: It appears doubtful that incest automatically leads to an inability of the child to make a separation from the incestuous parent, that incest is automatically a way of expressing hostility toward the non-incestuous parent, that the Oedipal and Electra Complexes are central to an understanding of incest, that dating is made worse (on the average) by incest (than better), that incest will breed apathetic, aggressive, compulsive, or criminal sexual behavior, that it will discourage heterosexual energy or imagination or cause a split between sex and love. It seems possible it will have implications for our redefinition of what is a necessary part of rebellion, and therefore of the psychosexual maturation process. It seems possible it will add to our understanding of the use of psychology to create self-fulfilling prophecies, the use of mystique, the politics of the unconscious, the uses of traditional and non-traditional psychology, the power relationship between parent and child and

the grey lines between the impact of an event such as incest and the ability of the individual to create a constructive experience out of that event.[19]

Farrell does not, to be sure, examine the effects of incest in the sort of intergenerational family terms that Ivan Nagy would desire or even in terms of a family systems approach in general. He is content to focus on individual sexual good or malfunctioning, on ability to enter into marriage or other outside-the-family-of-origin relationships, and on the subject's own estimate of whether the experience was positive or negative. For these reasons, no conclusion can be drawn, one way or another, from Farrell's study about the intergenerational family effects of incest. Neither does he go into the causes of incest, as the Justices do. His keen awareness of the power coefficient of sexual relations in general and incestuous ones in particular bears out, if anything, the Justices' understanding of the causes of the mostly negative, court and psychologist referred cases that they studied and with it our own analysis of the pathology of distancing and relating that is entailed.

More important still, an internal analysis of Farrell's findings shows that, startling as his conclusions are, they are fully in consonance with our assumption that good relationship within the family and between members of one family and another must bear the outlines of that confirmation of otherness in which each holds his or her ground and meets the other in openness from that ground. Farrell finds, for example, that in a significant number of the positive cases there is a decrease in adolescent insecurity. This might be viewed as healthy, he suggests, if one argues that the insecurities stimulated during adolescence remain with us our entire lives. The counterargument, that these adolescent tensions are a necessary part of growth and learning how to get along with the other sex, he questions on the same grounds that we might: that it "really ends up creating dishonest, gamesplaying and mutually exploitive relationships that hurt both sexes the more they learn how to 'get along by playing games.' " Again, he finds that those who have a ground of their own are better able to establish mutual and open relationships with others: "In my study, *the persons with low self-images were the least likely to have had sex with a wide variety of partners.* People with high self-images and positive relationships had four times as many partners even though they were six years younger." The positive incestuous experiences that he reported were based on mutual consideration in which there was more equality and the maturity of the younger partner was more respected.

The negative effects, quite naturally, were an increase in conflict with the family and within oneself (guilt), increased sexual inhibition, and sexual withdrawal leading to marriage to sexually uninterested men. In the few positive cases of adult male and younger female incest the younger female was assertive, mutual consent was verbalized, the older male expressed attention in nonsexual as well as sexual ways, and the younger partner was never involved sexually for reasons other than sex (e.g., attention, power over the adult). "Consensual" Farrell realistically defines as "cooperatively arrived at with parent or surrogate parent as a guiding force." If almost all negative incest lacks one or more of the conditions mentioned above, so do most negative sexual experiences of any type, Farrell points out.

What Farrell is really doing is pointing out that the family and the home need not automatically mean an undifferentiated ego mass or exploitation of the powerless by the powerful. Even incest may illustrate, *in the right context*, the "family of otherness." The essential dynamics of in-the-home/outside-the-home are still there in his picture and with them the implicit recognition that we *do* live in an age in which many contacts with those not in the family are impersonal, exploitative, stress-creating, and I-It'ish. The son who has sex with his mother who initiates it or even the brother with the close-in-age sister is more likely to find a union of sex and love than in the random and often cruel interactions with casual dates outside the family. This is particularly so because in our culture it is taken for granted that the man must risk himself by taking the sexual initiative.

> The more a man feels he must take the sexual initiative, the more he tends to turn a woman into a sex object. *Men intuitively understand it hurts less to be rejected by an object than to be rejected by a full human being.* That is, the more they become emotionally involved, the more rejection hurts. So many men learn it is *functional* to separate sex from love.[20]

Similarly, if the world outside the family is seen as cold and impersonal, then the warmth and safety of the family might conceivably be the place for children to learn how to love sexually as well as otherwise (assuming, of course, that there *is* genuine warmth and safety in the family, which is all too often not the case):

> A child might also be considered abused who was sent out into the cold world with this raw sexual energy directed "haphazardly" at peers before . . . [he-she] had a chance to learn how to integrate it with love in the safety of the home. Of course, proper socialization can enhance that integration without incest. But we seldom consider parents *abusive* for not explaining how sex and love can be both integrated and separated. Most families still leave most sexual socialization to peer group trial and error.[21]

Chapter 11

PROBLEMS OF CONFIRMATION IN THE FAMILY

I NEVER saw my father with his parents, who lived and died in Poland. But I did see him with his brothers and sisters who were brought over to America one by one by the eldest sister in the early years of this century. Although only two of them lived in the same city, they were so close-knit a group that I often had the impression that in relation to them my father was not so much a unique person as someone playing a prescribed family role. His closeness to his youngest sister, in particular, was a bond that my mother could never make inroads against, even when it meant that she had to come in second. Of course, I also saw my father as a member of our immediate family, and there too he seemed to have a prescribed, though by no means elevated, family role. He became a very successful insurance agent, despite having no education beyond the eighth grade, and he spent most of his evenings seeing prospective clients. I knew him to be a gentle and friendly man, but it was with great surprise that I learned at his funeral how much he was loved and respected in the community at large.

When we add to the roles that individuals visibly play in families the "invisible loyalties" that are passed down from generation to generation, as Ivan Boszormenyi-Nagy has demonstrated, we shall not be surprised that the problematic tension between personal uniqueness and social role is nowhere greater than in the family. A person's whole life is determined in important part by whether s/he is first, second, third, fourth, or fifth child in the family. The eldest child may be the favored one or may be the one who feels quickly supplanted by the others. Or it may be "parentified" and asked to take care of its younger siblings. A person's sense of personal worth, self-confidence, status, and even of social justice is strongly affected by sibling rivalry.

Nor is there any easy or wise solution for the parents in the face of these conflicts. Should every child get an equal share or should they get shares according to their respective ages or should they get shares according to their "needs" as their parents perceive them or their loud and clamorous demands announce them? Neither a strict egalitarianism nor Aristotle's "distributive justice" nor Lenin's dictum, "From each according to his abilities, to each according to his needs," have much to offer us here. Even if the shares of material goods and pleasures were allotted to everyone's satisfaction, which would be a major miracle in itself, how can a beleaguered parent make a wise and just distribution of her or his attention, care, and love? The very uniqueness of relationship that forms in the dialogue between parent and child means that no two parent-child relationships within the family can be the same or even, very meaningfully, comparable. (After dinner, my mother would give my eldest sister the choice of playing the piano or doing the dishes. I had to do the dishes. My turn would come later, my mother said. It never did.) There are, in addition, glaring problems, soluble only through intergenerational family therapy and even then only with the greatest difficulty, of the child who is singled out for a special role in the family—the favorite, the "spoiled child," "mamma's little darling" or "daddy's little girl," the "responsible" child, the bungler, the not-so-bright or not-so-talented child, all the way to the familiar "scapegoat." These roles are so important in the family economy that it is notorious that if an adolescent who is the "identified patient," perhaps a "schizophrenic," gets well, another child must get ill to take its place.

Apart from the particular roles into which children are cast in most, if not all, families, there is also the common phenomenon of the "scarcity economy" in which there is not enough love or confirmation to go around. Shortly after I was married, my wife told me how struck she was by the spectacle of myself and my two sisters all fighting for the piano bench, each wanting to win the "confirmation" of the absent mother by performing on the piano. The effect of such a scarcity economy is that, over and above the handicap of the particular role in which s/he is cast, each child grows up fighting for crumbs from the table. This search for a confirmation that is never really forthcoming ironically leads such individuals to reject the fuller and freer confirmation that they might have from friends, lovers, or mates unlike their parents. Instead they seek out persons who are constitutionally unable or unwilling to give and still try to get "blood out of the turnip." They are still trying to win over their original parents.

We have spoken before of the "contract" through which the child receives conditional confirmation from the parent(s). It would be misleading to picture this simply as the reward given to the good and "submissive" child. The child who can be dominated and is most submissive is often treated the worst. Parents like and often confirm the "rebel" just so the rebellion remains within the confines of the parents' delegations. Often the "rebel" acts out what the parent secretly, usually unconsciously, wants to be. On the other hand, the child that tries to break out of the family system and goes beyond the parents' delegation is going to be expelled from the family in one way or another and not confirmed.

The least favored child is often the one in whom the parents see their own weaknesses, and they therefore reject her. On the other hand, it would be mistaken to imagine that every favored child is really confirmed as a unique person. On the contrary, usually the favored child is the one who is most compliant either to the conscious or unconscious wishes of the parent, and the approval the child receives may have nothing to do with her as a person. I once had a student about whom her father wrote, "Peggy has always been exceedingly beautiful." "Whenever I entered a ballroom, I was immediately the center of attention," she told me. At college Peggy did not receive the attention she was used to receiving in her home town. Neither her family nor her home town had given her real confirmation as a person. The more confirmed she was as a spectacle—"an exceedingly beautiful girl"—the less confirmed she was as a person.

Another whole range of problems of confirmation arises when there is conflict between the parents. When one parent is dissatisfied with the other and (usually unconsciously) fixes on a child for his or her longed-for fulfillment, the child in question gains attention, approval, and support but is not really given a ground of its own on which to stand. The result is that curious mixture of strength and weakness, self-confidence and dependency that is found so often in the child through whom one or another parent lives. Such a child is likely to grow up having a low level of tolerance for frustration and failure and quick excesses of anger and rage when things do not work out for it as the mother has unconsciously programmed it to expect. It may not be the recipient of the "double bind" of contradictory messages from the parent's conscious and unconscious, but it *is* a "bound child" even and most especially when it is delegated.

When there is a serious and continuing conflict between the mother and the father, each child is placed in an impossible, "no-win" situation which denies it the confirmation of both parents that it so badly needs. In the face of this situation, children tend to side with one parent or the other, usually differing from their sisters and brothers as to whom they side with according to such factors as age, sex, temperament, and position within the family. Or one or more children within the family may take on themselves the "mission impossible" of reconciling the two parents and may continue in that role for the rest of their lives and in all their other social relations. Or one or another child may act out the tension and hostility within the family, often in ways that bring down on them the wrath of both parents and of outside authorities. Still another possible response on the part of the child is to take on itself the crucifixion of trying to hold the tension between the two conflicting parents, loving both and hoping to be loved in return, but all too often getting caught in the middle.

Many families are mini-matriarchies in which the mother is dominant. This dominance by the mother again has distinct effects on the problems of the confirmation of the children. It may lead to valuing girls more than boys (as happened in my family) or vice-versa. It may lead to putting down the father, to strength on the part of the girls, and to weakness and even homosexuality on the part of the boys. If the father is put down by the mother and the son replaces the father in the mother's affections, the son will share the mother's contempt for the father. Such a son is likely to become a tyrant in his own marriage or at the very least an overly self-assured and/or self-centered partner. On the other hand, if the father is put down by the mother and the son is also disconfirmed, the son is likely to identify with the father. But such a son will not receive true confirmation through this identification since the father is not really a figure he can look up to and offers him no meaningful role model as a male or as a father.

The rise of women's consciousness during the era of "women's liberation" has focused attention upon the effect of the dominant father on the compliant and dutiful daughter who is brought up to please her father. This is the sort of father that the Jungians call the "senex," a word suggestive of authority as well as age. The Jungian analyst Linda Leonard has performed a great service to the cause of understanding women's roles in the family by focusing on the effects of having a "puer" father instead. The "puer" is the weak father, the "eternal boy," who is charming but not at all dependable and the very opposite of authoritative.

The daughter of the "puer" father Leonard calls the "puella," after the Latin for "girl." Rather than working out her own identity, the puella usually gains her identity from the projections others have upon her, beginning with the father. "Instead of assuming the strength and force of her potential personality and the responsibility that goes with it, the puella dwells in weakness." This is true of such varied types as the femme fatale, the good daughter, the charming wife and hostess, the beautiful princess, the *femme inspiratrice,* and even the tragic heroine. The "darling doll" becomes the image her father and lover expect her to be, adapting herself to their fantasies of the feminine. Another puella existence takes the form of the shy and fragile "girl of glass" who remains apart from life and lives in a world of fantasy. Still another is the "high flyer" who lives by impulse and whim, seeming to be spontaneous and free, forming ethereal relationships and living in the realm of possibilities.

Most significant of all for the problematic of confirmation is what Leonard calls the "misfit," the woman who, because of shame over her father, is rejected by and/or rebels against society. If she identifies positively with her father, she will reject society when it rejects him. If she does not, her "shadow side" unconscious may cause her to live out his pattern anyway. Then the self-righteous mother's criticism of the "bad father" will extend to her daughter, whom she will threaten with the same doom as her father. The daughter, in turn, may rebel against the mother and repeat the father's pattern, acting out his self-destructive side. At bottom of each of these modes of the puella is a lack of self-confidence which drives the woman into a life that is unfulfilled and depending on others for affirmation or condemnation. Puellas avoid responsibility for their own existence, are poor at discrimination and decision making, and have a poor relationship to limit and boundary, whether through refusing to accept limits or "limitlessly" accepting them. They absolutize possibility and ignore necessity.[1]

The contribution of the "puer" father to this lack of confirmation of the puella is shown most clearly by Leonard in her discussion of the "perverted old man" that occupies the shadow side of the puella. This unconscious figure is really a wise old man who is sick and nasty because he has been neglected, and this neglect results from the father's not being there for the daughter in a committed and responsible way.

> In the daughter's view, the father may have been extremely weak and a cause of shame, for example, a man who cannot hold a job, or who drinks or gambles. Or, he may be absent, having left home by choice. . . . Or, he may have been absent not by his own choice, as is the case with the man who dies early, who is sent to war, is sick, or is divorced and separated from his children. . . . [Or he may] indulge his daughter, providing her with no sense of limit, value, or authority. Or he may be prey to his moods and irrational impulses and look down upon and devalue the feminine which is not developed within, often in the name of a "macho" masculine power and authority. Or, he may even be a hard worker, successful in his profession, but passive at home and not really involved in the decisions that go on in his family. Or he may project too much of his own femininity upon his daughter.[2]

The father who is not there for the daughter is often not there for the mother, and the daughter frequently internalizes her mother's embittered, cynical view of her father and other men. The "amazon" responds to the damage of the father image by seeing men as weak, inferior, and powerless. The puella, in contrast, gives up her own power to men with the consequence that her self-confidence and esteem are very low. Unconsciously she may be a princess, but consciously she is a neglected and abused Cinderella.

> In the puella's attitude toward herself, one can often hear a snide and cynical voice telling her she is no good, that she'll never accomplish anything, nor is she worthy of love. When she believes this voice, a vicious circle ensues which perpetuates this negative view of herself as weak and worthless. She does indeed often "fail" in the outer world, but that is because she has given over all her power to this sadistic inner man who tells her she will fail but at the same time also feeds her inflation.[3]

Such a woman gets involved with men not out of mature erotic strivings but out of the need for love and commitment which her father never gave her. She betrays both herself and the usually married or otherwise unavailable men with whom she has affairs since she does not trust them. Or she puts her body on the market. When she goes over from innocence to "sexual freedom," she remains as locked up and closed off from relationship and eros as she had been in her previous naiveté. The woman who has been subjected to sexual abuse or rape by older men when she was a young girl has not only suffered severely damaged self-confidence but has internalized the perverted old man, "a tortuous negative animus continuing that abuse." The prostitute who is brutally rejected by the father reenacts that rejection and the hatred that goes with it by selling herself to men. "But even in the seemingly happy housewife or the young swinger, one frequently finds this pattern operating underneath."[4]

The *son* of a weak father, on the other hand, may well fear that when he marries and raises a family, he will repeat his father's pattern and be ineffective with his own children as his father was before him. Often in families there is a mix-up of masculine and feminine roles because of the emulation of the father by the daughter or of the mother by the son or because the father (or mother) wants the daughter to be a son if there are no boys in the family. In the face of situations like this, it is no wonder that so many modern marriages end in divorce. The misfortune of divorce is not only the conflict between the parents but the inevitable rending and splitting of the children, and the inevitable injury to the confirmation of the children which results. Very often children become mere pawns in the parents' conflict with each other—in the divorce courts or in the protracted "settlements" that they settle down into afterward. "Divorce solves nothing," says Ivan Boszormenyi-Nagy. This may or may not be true for the parents, but it is usually true for the children. On the other hand, coming as I do from an unhappy family which did *not* result in divorce, I have often been grateful to Erich Fromm for his insight that sometimes the hostility that remains embodied in the family may be worse than the divorce which alters if it does not end it:

> Children serve for projective purposes also when the question arises of dissolving an unhappy marriage. The stock argument of parents in such a situation is that they cannot separate in order not to deprive the children of the blessings of a unified home. Any detailed study would show, however, that the atmosphere of tension and unhappiness within the "unified family" is more harmful to the children than an open break would be— which teaches them at least that man is able to end an intolerable situation by a courageous decision.[5]

Extrapolating from what Fromm writes, we may say that one of the most important things a child needs to learn in order *not* to repeat the unhappy pattern of its parents in its own future marriage is that an intolerable situation is not necessarily a permanent one.

The parent who beats his or her children is often someone who was beaten as a child, suggesting a modern application of the biblical insight that the sins of the parents are visited upon the children. Very frequently there is one child in the family that is picked on or beaten more than the others, because of conflict, identification, sexual hang-ups on the part of the parents, or frustration at unsuccessful attempts to assert authority. Recently at a seminar on phenomenological dissertations for clinical psychologists, one participant announced to the group her desire to write a dissertation on the low status of women throughout history. It turned out that her older brother was beaten, and she had concluded that unless she were submissive, she would be beaten too. Yet her two older sisters had managed to hold their ground with their father and were not beaten. What she wished to project onto the screen of history was really the choice that she made as a child in the face of the threat of being hurt by her father.

Each of these topics might well be the subject not only of a whole chapter but of a whole book or a series of books. To deal with them exhaustively here is not our aim. Rather we need speak of them only enough to put them into the perspective of the problems and problematic of confirmation. Two other such topics that are receiving ever greater attention are adoption and the reconstituted family. Both adoption and the reconstituted family intensify the already serious problems of confirmation within the intact biological family. Yet both may also be opportunities for a greater realization in practice of the confirmation of otherness.

Adoption certainly increases otherness by bringing a child or children from one or more biologically different families into the home to be raised as one's own. A whole sheaf of problems of confirmation arises from this act alone. One is whether and when and how to tell the child that it has been adopted and how to answer the child's inevitable (if sometimes unspoken) questions about why its biological parents were willing to give it up for adoption. Another is to deal with the child's feeling of rejection by its original parents *and* its possibly equal feeling that its present parents, who did not give birth to it, must therefore reject it, particularly if there are children in the home who have not been adopted. On the other hand, the child may equally well reject the adoptive parents and use the fact of its adoption as a weapon against one or both of them. In its fantasy, the child is likely to imagine that its biological parents would understand and love it in a way that its adoptive parents cannot. Conversely, I can remember as a child feeling that my mother could not really be my biological mother because of the way she treated me. There are no rules about all this. When there is more than one adoptive child in the same family, one may use the knowledge of its adoption as a weapon and the other may not.

There has been a growing concern about actually finding the biological parents of adopted children, and many stories are told of grown children who have spent years in such a search. Some states have modified their laws to make it possible for the social agency which administered the adoption to disclose the identity of the original parents, and some have not. If the growing or grown child succeeds in finding its original mother and/or father, it will then have to confront a reality which may differ greatly from the previous fantasies about its parents. In André Gide's novel, *The Counterfeiters*, the hero Bernard leaves his father and his home (his mother is dead) when he comes across a packet of old letters that shows that he is, in fact, the product of an amorous liaison the mother had with a lover outside the marriage. At the end of the novel, having matured to the point where he can see his father as a person as well as a role, Bernard returns to his home, knowing that his adoptive father really needs him.

The "reconstituted family" is the name for what was once euphemistically and inaccurately called the "blended family." It is the product of the marriage of two persons, one or both of whom bring into the newly constituted family the children from a previous marriage. From behind a one-way glass, I witnessed recently a family psychiatrist working with such a family. The young wife and mother of two accepted only with the greatest reluctance the presence of the fourteen-year-old son, who was clearly pretty much out of things during his visit to his father, and she refused absolutely to let the college-age daughter even visit, though the daughter lived only a few blocks away. My own experience with a reconstituted family was hardly more encouraging. The competition between the daughter and the new wife for the father, or between the daughter or son and the new husband for the mother, often makes the task of reconstitution an impossibly difficult one.

The result, especially on the part of the children, may be an acting out which will be socially labeled as "crazy behavior" or "mental illness." Actually, as Doris Crisler suggests in her perceptive dissertation on the reconstituted family, such behavior can be seen more constructively as a state of culture shock entered when a new family system threatens personal identity, or, as I would say, leads to disconfirmation.

> As each individual enters the new family constellation, she/he is exposed to unfamiliar customs and relationship responses. Everything from food habits, familiar rituals, expectations, values, verbal and nonverbal communications, myths, to touching, showing approval or disapproval, love or acceptance may change and must be coped with successfully in order to adjust in the new way of life. . . .
>
> It seems logical that breakdown in human trust and relationships, following lack of understanding of this culture shock experience, could lead to eventual breakdown in the individual personality, inability to function socially within the system, and finally to fragmentation of the new family constellation.[6]

Good integration in the family life is often related to good community acceptance, but until relatively recently such acceptance has often been lacking. Suspicion and mistrust and labels of sin and failure have increased the probability of failure in reconstituted families. What the confirmation of otherness might mean in such a situation has been pointed to by Margaret Mead:

> Responsible acceptance by society of the end of marriage is just as important as the acceptance of the beginning of a marriage. Acknowledgment by society that people can change and grow, can succeed in new ventures, may help to alleviate guilt and failure feelings which conceivably could be harmful to new family minicultures.[7]

Communal acceptance and even improvement of communication feedback within the reconstituted family will not in themselves avoid the alienation from self and isolation from others that so often result from the "mismeeting" of the two family segments that were hopefully supposed to "blend" and form a new miniculture. The most obvious fact about the reconstituted family is that it greatly intensifies the problem that is already present in any marriage, namely that at least two family systems are brought into alliance and that no solution is possible by such shortcuts as one family system swallowing up the other or a pretense of harmony when the conflict of value systems is denied and not allowed to be brought out into the open. The reconstituted family makes clear what is already implicit in any family, namely that the realities that must be taken into account are not only the vertical, or intergenerational, ones but also the horizontal and interfamily ones. Only by taking both of these—the vertical and the horizontal—into account can there be any movement in the intact family as in the reconstituted one toward the genuine confirmation of otherness.

Chapter 12

CAN OTHERNESS BE CONFIRMED IN THE FAMILY?

"THE FAMILY," says Ronald Laing, "is a protection racket." To talk of the confirmation of otherness in the family may seem a contradiction in terms in the face of the experience of countless persons the world over for whom the family has become little more than a forced grouping of people who do not like, much less love, one another. For many, perhaps most, people, the family is characterized by dominance and submission, sadism and masochism, and by the practice of every form of overt and covert violence, bullying, manipulation, seduction, collusion, mystification, and chicanery.

Despite all this, Saul L. Brown, M.D., Director of Psychiatry and practitioner of family psychiatry at Cedars Sinai Medical Center, Los Angeles, says that the "sequential evolution of mutual validation occurs in its most intense form in family life." Brown recognizes that once this validation has got off the track, there are lifelong emotional and psychological problems that must be dealt with in family therapy. But with or without therapy, he affirms the mutual escalation of confirmation that can take place in the family. Ivan Boszormenyi-Nagy, similarly, sees the "invisible loyalties"—the fateful commitment and devotion that are important determinants in family relationships—as making for a deeper

binding than the genuine I-Thou dialogue which is possible between those who are not related. My son is "a unique counterpart
of my existential realm" whose meaning for me cannot be embodied by anyone else; for it is part of a multigenerational relationship system that he and I share.

The true meaning of responsibility in the family is the swinging
alternation of distancing and relating, loyalty and autonomy.
Such responsibility is incompatible with parents treating children
as merely an extension of themselves, as with Helm Stierlin's
three modes of "binding," "delegating," and "expelling." What
Kahlil Gibran says in *The Prophet* of marriage applies also, as he
knew, to children and to the family as a whole: "Let there be
spaces in your togetherness." The otherness in families is not just
a problem of in-laws but of husband and wife, parents, children,
and grandparents, and of at least two separate family systems,
each of which goes back through the grandparents, to at least four
family systems, reaching backward and forward in time as well as
horizontally in space. But the problem of otherness must not be
confused with individuality or autonomy. Otherness needs to be
confirmed in its nature and uniqueness, not just set free, expelled, or left to do what it pleases. The ties of relating must be as
strong as the swings of distancing for confirmation of otherness to
take place.

This dialectic of loyalty and autonomy means that there is real
as well as neurotic guilt, interhuman existential guilt as well as
intrapsychic guilt feelings. One may go to the other end of the
earth from one's family and still be paralyzed by amorphous
existential guilt, writes Ivan Nagy, following Buber:

> The therapist who wants to liberate the patient from his concern
> for or guilt-laden loyalty to members of his family may succeed
> in removing certain manifestations of psychological guilt, but
> may at the same time increase the patient's existential guilt.
> Buber distinguished between guilt feelings and existential guilt.
> The latter obviously goes beyond psychology: It has to do with
> objective harm to the order and justice of the human world. If I
> really betrayed a friend or if my mother really feels that I
> damaged her through my existence, the reality of a disturbed
> order of the human world remains, whether I can get rid of
> certain guilt feelings or not. Such guilt becomes part of a sys-
> temic ledger of merits and can only be affected by action and
> existential involvement, if at all.[1]

If autonomy cannot be the sole goal of the family, neither can loyalty. It may be helpful here to distinguish between two types of loyalty. One we might call the loyalty of affinity or like-mindedness. Here the only ethic is loyalty tosole goal of the family, neither can loyalty. It may be helpful here to distinguish between two types of loyalty. One we might call the loyalty of affinity or likemindedness. Here the only ethic is loyalty to the family, with no responsibility to anyone outside the family, as in the novel and film, *The Godfather*. This loyalty may mean a mutual confirmation, but it does not mean a confirmation of the otherness and uniqueness of the family members. Rather each is confirmed only and strictly by how he or she fulfills a role in the family and no room is left for that unfolding of personal uniqueness that might take one in a direction away from what has been defined as the needs and interests of the family. The other type of loyalty is that of the family that recognizes the deep bond that unites them and genuinely cares for one another—cares so deeply that it is ready to confirm the other in his or her uniqueness even when such uniqueness arouses conflict and painful strains in the "family harmony." It is this latter type of loyalty alone that is compatible with and an expression of the confirmation of otherness.

When Martin Buber was in his fourth year of life, he lived in Vienna with his parents in a house under which flowed the Danube Canal. The child used to stand looking at the canal with a sense that nothing could happen to him—nothing could disturb the serene way of life that he enjoyed. Then his mother suddenly disappeared, and for years no one, including his father, knew where she had gone. Young Martin was sent to live with his father's parents, noble people in the exact sense of the term, who probably did not discuss his mother's disappearance with each other more than was absolutely necessary and never with him. He assumed as a matter of course that she was coming back. But one day he was standing on the rectangular balcony of the inner courtyard of his grandfather's estate with a neighbor girl a few years older than himself. "I do not recall asking the question," Buber recounted many years later, "but I can hear to this day her answer: 'No, she will never come back.' "

> I know that I remained silent, but also that *I cherished no doubt of the truth of the spoken words*. It remained fixed in me; from year to

year it cleaved ever more to my heart, but after more than ten years I had begun to perceive it as *something that concerned not only me, but all men.* Later I once made up the word *"Vergeg- nung"*—"mismeeting"—to designate the failure of a real meeting between persons. When after another twenty years I again saw my mother, who had come from a distance to visit me, my wife, and my children, I could not gaze into her still *astonishingly beautiful eyes* without hearing from somewhere the word *"Vergegnung"* as a word spoken to me. I suspect that *all that I have learned about genuine meeting in the course of my life had its first origin in that hour on the balcony.*[2]

Once while in Israel I told this story to a friend who picked up on the phrase "astonishingly beautiful eyes" and pronounced it "pure sentimentality." The next morning I went as usual to do research on Buber at the Hebrew University Library and saw a display of photographs of Buber and his family in memory of his death which had taken place a year earlier. One of them was a picture of his mother with the legend "Moscow, 1897." (She had run away to Russia with an army officer, as Buber learned only after he had grown up and his father had long since remarried.) Not only her eyes but her whole person was astonishingly beauti- ful. What has always caused me wonder about this story is that Buber cherished no doubt of the truth of the girl's statement that his mother would never come back. Why did he not cling to her for a lifetime as Marcel Proust clung to his mother and Franz Kafka to his father? This does not mean that he did not experience a deep inner cleavage as the result of his mother's departure, one that he tried to heal through mystic union and through marriage to an exceptionally mature woman a year older than himself. But it does mean that he accepted the reality and preferred it to living in a fantasy world of wish fulfillment.

It was this acceptance on Buber's part that enabled him to understand ten years later that what had happened concerned not only him but all persons. The acceptance of distance from the original unity with the mother is necessary before it is possible to enter into relation; for relation is never a return to the original unity but only the continual overcoming of the distance that has been established and the continual relinquishment of relation in favor of renewed distancing. It also can help us to understand what at first sight must seem paradoxical, namely Buber's conclu- sion that all that he had learned about genuine meeting in the course of his life had its origin in that hour on the balcony—an hour which gave rise to his inner cleavage and the term "mis-meeting." There had been a genuine meeting with the girl, per-haps, as there was not with his grandparents, at least on the level of his question about his mother's return. But what Buber had in mind in his conclusion, surely, was that genuine meeting begins with the acceptance of distancing and even of the fact of mismeet-ing. Thus in this story the roots of Buber's anthropology of dis-tancing and relating through which we human beings become selves with other selves is already given and with it the recogni-tion that the confirmation of otherness in the family (as in com-munity) rests on this ever-renewed alternation between distancing and relating.

When Richard Stanton interviewed Ivan Boszormenyi-Nagy in connection with his doctoral dissertation, "Dialogue in Psycho-therapy: Martin Buber, Maurice Friedman and Therapists of Dia-logue," Nagy suggested another interesting dimension to this story of Buber's mother: the very fact that people did not talk about what happened with Martin's mother must have been a source of shame to the child. In a traditional family of this sort, the mother's running away must, indeed, have seemed shameful; yet the child must also feel a loyalty to its mother. To Nagy this conflict of loyalties may have been the origin of Buber's philoso-phy of the I-Thou relationship, which Buber, however, applied not just to the family but to all men and to human life in general.

> As I see it now, Buber is a man of *enormous* integrity and pure balancing and facing balances and drawing *hard* conclusions, at great cost. And balancing his survival on a razor's edge many times. That's the way I see him as a human being. . . . Here is this boy [Martin Buber], who is victimized by the tragedy of his mother, the shame of his mother running away. Somehow, I think, to put all of this together, between these extremes of not talking probably about this and absorbing this as a child; on the other hand going back to the orthodoxy of his grandfather and the broken mind of his father . . . and broken heart. Making up for the missing mother, somehow exonerating her—doing the impossible. . . . He's the only child, can't even turn to a sibling with whom to share this. . . .
>
> [He] becomes eventually a self-styled, socialist Zionist, marry-ing a German girl; [he] becomes a great intellectual leader of Germany, leader of Zionist intellectualism, controversial Zion-

istic political figure. Fair to the Arabs, defending what is a heroic legacy of Jews. [He] remains an intellectual figure, turning his energy toward the suffering of [the] psychologically ill. . . . a *tremendous*, tremendous balancing of enormous human realms; at constant cost of misunderstanding and being victimized . . . all of this being done with great talent and tremendous intellectual power.

All of this comes . . . [to] discovery of human relationships as the ultimate resource, provided there is trustworthiness in human relationships. Now, I am rephrasing Buber in what I [say] this is my view. As long as relationships can generate intrinsic trustworthiness, they are the greatest resource.[3]

To what Nagy has said I would add that Buber's I-Thou relationships emphasize equally the distancing and the relating, the autonomy and the loyalty. The greatest loyalty, indeed, is that which can allow autonomy to the individual members of the family.

When the healthy alternation between distancing and relating, autonomy and loyalty becomes unbalanced on one side or the other, then the only road that may be open to confirming otherness within the family may be family therapy. Not all family therapy is of such a nature as to lead to the confirmation of otherness, however. One family therapy that is so to an exemplary degree is Ivan Boszormenyi-Nagy's "contextual therapy." In order to exert a therapeutic influence, the contextual family therapist has to remain a discrete individual, thus impelling the family members to extricate themselves from their wishful symbiotic fantasies. The family therapist has to exemplify and *live* in trust and confidence in the frustrated and often hateful family atmosphere. In order to guide a family to a more meaningful marriage relationship for the parents and separation and meaningful marriages and parenthood for the offspring, he has to remain open to deep, primary process clues in the context of an actual family drama yet not selectively ignore defensive facades that resemble those of his own family. He must not be trapped into wanting to save one family member from another. At the same time, he must be alert to notice the variety of complex ways in which the partners are "grounded" in each other's personality. "As the family's style of interactions moves from symbiosis toward individuation, the capacity of the offspring for genuine encounter increases."[4]

Nagy's goals of family therapy are best understood in terms of Buber's anthropology of distancing and relating as the two ontological movements fundamental to human existence. To Nagy, therapy can never stop with getting out the buried hostility toward the parents; for that would inevitably lead to a violation of the universal legacy of filial loyalty, a rejection of the therapist, or a building up of guilt. "In our clinical experience, no one ends up a winner through a conclusion which predicates a hopelessly incorrigible resentment and contempt towards one's parent."

> While conscious confrontation with one's hateful feelings amounts to progress, it does not represent a therapeutic endpoint. Unless the person can struggle with his negative feelings and resolve them by acts based on positive, helpful attitudes towards his parent, he cannot really free himself of the intrinsic loyalty problem and has to "live" the conflict, even after the parent's death, through pathological defensive patterns.[5]

Frequently the outcome is the rejection and scapegoating of the spouse or the therapist in order to escape from the annihilating effect of victory over one's parents. "The cost of such victory would be guilt, shame, and a paradoxically binding loyalty, disowned, denied, yet paralyzingly adhered to at the same time." The positive goal of therapy is a dialectic between individuation and family loyalty; for the former cannot be achieved at the cost of simply severing family ties. Every step leading toward the child's true emancipation "tends to touch on the emotionally charged issue of every member's denied but wished-for everlasting symbiotic togetherness with the family of origin." The pathological expression of the failure to achieve this coincides with what Murray Bowen calls the "undifferentiated ego mass" or what Nagy calls the "polarized fusion of roles," where instead of a genuinely antithetical dialogue between unique persons, people are symbiotically related to through roles: "The individual can be liberated to engage in full, wholly personal relationships only to the extent that he has become capable of responding to parental devotion with concern." In contextual therapy individual autonomy is not viewed mainly within the confines of ego strength and intrapsychic resourcefulness and effective adaptation, as in individual therapy, but stands in dynamic tension with loyalty to the family of origin.[6]

"In contrast with individual psychotherapy, family or relationship-based therapy proceeds step by step to remove deeper and deeper layers of *inauthentic loyalty definitions.*" The angry and resentful feelings expressed between the generations provide an opportunity to begin to break up what has been projected onto or attributed to the other person. The family therapist can encourage a mutual dialogue so that the aged parent (the grandparent) can reveal his own past, as well as current, longings. When each generation is helped to face the nature of the current relationships, exploring the real nature of the commitments and responsibility that flow from such involvements, an increased reciprocal understanding and mutual compassion between the generations results.

> Our concept of relational autonomy pictures the individual as retaining a modified yet fully responsible and sensitively concerned dialogue with the original family members. In this sense the individual can be liberated to engage in full, wholly personal relationships only to the extent that he has become capable of responding to parental devotion with concern on his part and with the realization that receiving is intrinsically connected with owing in return.[7]

The contextual therapist guides the family members to the multilaterality of fairness in which one person's being heard or being held accountable makes it easier to hear others or let oneself be called to account. Thus the therapist helps them take the first steps toward engagement in a mutuality of trust and trustworthiness. "The lack of trustworthiness in one's relational world is the primary pathogenic condition of human life." The therapist can address this problem of eroding trust by eliciting every family member's own responsible review of his or her side of mutual entitlements and indebtednesses. The balance of relational fairness depends on a relatively equitable investment of trust in caring mutuality; for trustworthiness is the fundamental resource of family therapy. Nagy cautions against a mere prescriptive rearrangement or "restructuring" of family transactions; for this may risk long-range disloyalty and a newly found passive dependence on the therapist. Rather the therapist must become a consultant for the catalysis of a living give-and-take of a more equitable kind. In contrast to traditional psychology and psychodynamic literature which generally underemphasize the self's investment in concern and caring for others, the contextual therapist must have the conviction that caring about the partner's justified merits enables the one who cares to move toward autonomous individuation and growth:

> By investing appropriate new initiatives of trust, he increases his entitlement to acknowledgment of his acts of filial devotion, and to the pursuit of his own autonomous goals, e.g., to forming peer relationships. Consequently, his moves toward autonomy become progressively liberated from encumberment with an immobilizing guilt born of disloyalty.[8]

Through its trust-building strategies, contextual therapy is able to internalize the therapist's concern for fairness and trustworthiness, mobilize the resources of fair reciprocity via an examination of intermember accountability, differentiate between the unchangeable fact of shared rootedness and the vicissitudes of emotional attitudes such as love or hate, realistically rebalance interindividual ledgers, revise and rework invisible loyalties, correct invalid ethical substitutions, deparentify children, and transform passively dependent attitudes into actively accountable initiative and planning.[9] Nagy and his associate Barbara Krasner emphasize that the personal uniqueness of family members is just as much a concern of contextual therapy as their personally exchangeable "systemic roles."[10] This uniqueness includes a person's relatedness to his or her multigenerational roots, with their specific racial, religious, and ethnic facets. Nagy distinguishes the "context" of contextual therapy from "the obvious fit of any individual into transactional systems":

> It is the *ethics* of the personal *sides* of human existence that is the most important aspect of our relational context. This includes each person as a unique center of his universe, rather than regarding him as an item of feedback corrections or escalations.[11]

Liberation from the revolving cycle of destructive action takes place only through discovery of resources of trustworthiness. Contextual therapy helps in such discovery not only through bringing family members into genuine dialogue with one another, but also through teaching them to stand up *against* guilt and *for* their own entitlements. The enhancement of the family's dormant resources for trustworthiness requires mutuality of effort among members through which they become more multilaterally fair and in so doing change and improve the nature of their own entitlement. Here too Buber's meeting others and holding one's ground while one meets them go together: "This is a different and deeper way of standing up for one's self."[12]

Unlike those analytically-based therapists who tend to regard the parents as the cause and the child as the effect, Nagy stresses "the child's reservoir of trust out of which he or she can initiate repayment of trust toward the parents." This reserve of trust has a double source—the legacy of intergenerational relatedness and the human concern for fairness of give and take. Even when the parents act like stones, the child's willingness to come forward with human response can provide the leverage needed to get a "rejunctive" move from the parents, i.e., one that restores relational trust.

The great service of contextual therapy is that it corrects the individualism of intrapsychic and analytical therapy and with it such romantic and illusory notions as that a relationship should be judged only by the degree to which it fulfills the individual "needs" and realizes the individual potentialities of each of its members, or that when two people marry, they marry each other and not their families as well. What Freud did for the field of psychoanalysis, Nagy has done for family therapy: Nagy has uncovered the *invisible* loyalties and the equally hidden multigenerational family ledger of merit that have been overlooked until now. At the same time we must remember that the "invisible loyalties" often represent the pathology of the family as well as its potential health. The emphasis upon the vertical, multigenerational dimension of relationship is necessary in part because the partners in marriage bring their family of origin into their new relationships. Without realizing it they tend to place their mates within the old family system or, what amounts to the same thing, to see them as the magic helpers that will save them from their family system.

The simplest fact about marriage is the one to which Martin Buber points: it means the acknowledgment of vital, many-faceted otherness or it is not a true marriage. Each marriage ideally means the bringing not only of the individual partners but also of their families, their family systems, and their multigenerational ledgers of merit into genuine dialogue, and that means into a community of otherness. When this is *not* done, the new family becomes stagnant and the progress of the children toward their rightful autonomy within the caring community, or the family of otherness, becomes impossible. Thus the healthy ongoingness of the generations not only is not impeded by the dialogue with otherness; it is made possible by it. This dialogue is, in the first instance, on the peer level: one's mate does not come from one's family of origin. But in the second instance, it also extends to the dialogue between the mates and the parents of their spouses, on the one hand, and their own children, on the other. If it is traditionally difficult to relate to one's in-laws as one's family, it is, in fact, no less difficult to relate to one's children as really other and to avoid that trilogy of binding, delegating, and expelling that Helm Stierlin has pointed to as three of the ways in which parents deny children their existence in their own right and seek instead to subordinate them to an imposed family system.[13]

The community of otherness to which I point is not, of course, relationships with peers alone but with any living person—father or son, mother, grandmother, daughter, or granddaughter. It is important to recognize, nonetheless, that, helpful as it is to rebuild trust with the older generations, it is not always possible. The very fact of the merit ledger—the revolving slate that goes down through the generations—means that we must restore relational trust with our children and grandchildren when our grandparents and even our parents are beyond our reach.

Ivan Nagy shares with Martin Buber the belief in the objective reality of the common order of existence and in the equally objective reality of that existential guilt that we take upon ourselves when we injure that order, the foundations of which we recognize at some level as the foundations of our own and of all human existence. The three steps to which Buber points as the way of healing such existential guilt are, first, the illumination of the fact that I, who am now so different, am nonetheless the person who incurred that guilt as a person in a personal situation; second, persevering in that illumination; and third, repairing the injured order of existence by taking up the dialogue again. This reparation can be done with the person whom we have injured if he or she is still living. But if not, it may be accomplished through our taking up the dialogue anew with the other persons to whom life brings us, including our spouses, our children and grandchildren, our friends, and our community. "No one other than he who inflicted the wound can heal it." Yet this person, "in his place and according to his capacity, in the given historical and

biographical situations" is able "to restore the order-of-being injured by him through the relation of an active devotion to the
world—for the wounds of the order-of-being can be healed in
infinitely many other places than those at which they were inflicted."[14] The merit ledger may itself attain balance over the generations, but often the injured individuals remain just that. Even
contextual intergenerational family therapy is unable to heal time
backwards. It too must live in the reality of the present and of the
trustworthiness that may be realized in the present through the
life of dialogue and the community of otherness.

Carl Rogers holds that otherness within the family can be
confirmed through a new politics of the family in which there is
mutual respect which strengthens the relationship between all
members of the family as separate but interdependent persons. In
such a family all members are psychological equals, in contrast to
the traditional family in which the father gives the orders and the
children obey and the modern family in which father and mother
wrangle over control and the children set the parents against each
other. In the meetings of such a family the effort is made to focus
on owned feelings rather than on accusations or judgments of
another. This leads to unexpected self-revelation and deep communication. Because they are continually aware of many of their
own feelings and those of their parents and because these feelings
have been expressed and accepted, the children of such families
develop as highly social creatures, "responsive to other people,
open in expressing their feelings, scornful of being talked down
to, creative and independent in their activities. Thus the politics
of a process relationship between unique persons takes the place
of the politics of control and obedience, with its pleasing static
security."[15]

Part IV

CONFIRMATION OF OTHERNESS IN COMMUNITY

Chapter 13

THE "COMMUNITY OF AFFINITY" VERSUS THE "COMMUNITY OF OTHERNESS"

THE FAMILY itself, like the community and the tribe, is a protection against otherness. Yet it need not mean the smothering of all otherness within the family or of relations between families and among families within community and society. One of the original reasons for the incest taboo was exogamy—the need to bring the family into relation with other families for economic and social and protective reasons. But this is not enough. Families must have to do with families with which they are in no way related by blood or marriage or even kinship ties if true community is to arise. Where there is a climate of trust within the family and within community, there are resources to relate to otherness.

One of those primal demands of the human heart which at any moment, overnight, will break through to actualization and become self-evident, writes Martin Buber, is the longing to have a house. This is not just the *need* for a house but the *desire* to have a house in which to dwell, and that means a home.

> The house is the winning throw of the dice which man has wrested from the uncanniness of the universe; it is his defense against the chaos that threatens to invade him. Therefore his deeper wish is that it be his own house, that he not have to share with anyone other than his own family.

But this house does not just stand in splendid isolation as a place from which he can easily get to his place of work, where for a certain number of hours he shares a space with "strange" men in order afterward to leave them entirely and go home. Rather it must stand between neighboring houses, the houses of his neighbors:

> The unavowed secret of man is that he wants to be confirmed in his being and his existence by his fellow men and that he wishes them to make it possible for him to confirm them, . . . not merely in the family, in the party assembly or in the public house, but also in the course of neighborly encounters, perhaps when he or the other steps out of the door of his house or to the window of his house and the greeting with which they greet each other will be accompanied by a glance of well-wishing, a glance in which curiosity, mistrust, and routine will have been overcome by a mutual sympathy: the one gives the other to understand that he affirms his presence. This is the indispensable minimum of humanity. If the world of man is to become a human world, then immediacy must rule between men, and thus also between human house and human house.

This secret human longing for a life in reciprocal mutual confirmation must be developed through education, Buber points out, but also through creating the external conditions that will make it possible. To this end, the architects must be set the task of building for human contact, of building surroundings that invite meeting and centers that shape meeting.[1]

One of the means through which this longing can be fulfilled is through cooperative housing. Man as man needs to have a ground of his own, and he needs to be confirmed in his existence by his fellow men. One must become what one is called to become in one's uniqueness; yet one must become this through being made present by others and through knowing that one is made present by them. That means that one must work at one's own "self-actualization" and at the same time work together with others. And what is "actualized" is not merely the sum of individual realizations of self or "potentiality" but a reality of the "between," what comes to be in the working together, the cooperation of human beings with one another. For this reason, cooperation is not just a technical means whereby a number of people band together for the fulfillment of individual ends but is itself an indispensable fulfillment of genuine human and interhuman existence. By the same token cooperatives are not merely a pragmatic means to individual ends but a form in which humanity can first find itself as genuine humanity.

What is said of cooperatives and cooperation is true in the same measure of cooperative housing. Each human being needs to have a home, a house, a ground that she can call her own, a life-space in which to show forth the unique life-stance of this particular human being and this particular family. Yet every human being and every family needs to the same degree to have community with others, interaction and dialogue from home to home and from house to house. Cooperative housing is not only an economical means to provide low-cost housing for those who desperately need it. It is also an expression of these basic human needs for cooperation, for living together, for building the reality of the between, for authenticating the interhuman, the life between person and person and family and family.

To understand the authentication of the human in community and society, however, we must make a distinction that is not usually made between two different types of community—the "community of affinity" and the "community of otherness." The community of *affinity*, or *likemindedness*, is based on what people feel they have in common—race, sex, religion, nationality, politics, a common formula, a common creed. The community of otherness, in contrast, does not mean that everyone does the same thing and certainly not that they do it from the same point of view. What makes community real is people finding themselves in a common situation—a situation which they approach in different ways yet which calls each of them out. The very existence in genuine community is already a common concern, a caring for one another. This caring begins with understanding from within the actual people present. Only then does it extend to gather other people in and then to a dialogue with other communities.

A vivid illustration of the problematic of the community of affinity in its relation to otherness is the sociologist Erving Goffman's study of "stigma." While the family and, to a much lesser extent, a local neighborhood can constitute itself a protective capsule for the young, eventually the stigmatized person has to move out of this protection into relation with the "normal" world. While this relation may be eased somewhat by identification with the group of those similarly stigmatized (by blindness, deafness, or any other handicap or abnormality), the stigmatized person in the end is presented with the necessity of making the best of a bad bargain. Those who are "normal" offer this person a token acceptance in return for a "good adjustment" which relieves the normals of ever being presented with the unfairness and pain of having to carry a stigma. They do not have to admit to themselves how limited their tactfulness and tolerance is, and they remain relatively uncontaminated by intimate contact with the stigmatized. The stigmatized person, for his part, must keep himself at such a distance from the normals as to confirm their illusions about themselves. The best he can do is to act so as to imply neither that his burden is heavy nor that bearing it has made him different from the normals. He must not embarrass the normals by testing the limits of their pseudo full acceptance of him. He must accept for himself a self which is, necessarily, "a resident alien, a voice of the group that speaks for and through him."[2]

Community of affinity, or likemindedness, is always ultimately false community. Community of otherness, in contrast, is a way of being faithful and diverse at the same time. This living dialectic of faithfulness and diversity is expressed clearly by Ivan Nagy: "The balance of relational fairness depends on a relatively equitable investment of trust in caring mutuality." It is this that Nagy means by trustworthiness, which he holds to be the fundamental resource of family relationships.

The ultimate issue of the life of dialogue is community—lived togetherness of really unique persons, families, and groups. True community comes into being not through tolerance, adjustment, and compromise but through mutual confirmation. No group is able to confirm all otherness. That is beyond human capacity. But the test of a fellowship is the otherness that it can confirm. If the "spokesman" of the group explains to someone who differs with him or her that that person is really not a member of the group because he or she does not fit the general stamp of the group, then that person will not only have been read out of the group, but out of existence itself as far as this moment and this situation are concerned. The obverse attitude is that of openness and trust. It is our lack of trust, our existential mistrust, that makes us feel that we need to have the security of likeminded groups, groups based on generalized affinity, rather than the concreteness of open meeting with real otherness that is present in every group, down to a pair of friends or a husband and wife.

"Family loyalty" is all too often thought of as a community of affinity rather than a community of otherness, as the film *The Godfather* so vividly illustrates. I do not think that this is the way Ivan Nagy thinks of it, as witnessed by his concern for the uniqueness and autonomy of family members. The dialectic, however, is not just between "loyalty" and "autonomy," as Nagy tends to put it, but between distancing and relating within the loyalty of the family of otherness, the "caring community." Nagy's concern that children not be parentified or everlastingly burdened by loyalties to their family of origin and that they be allowed to establish new families of their own suggests that he does, indeed, mean by family loyalty the dialogical interrelationship of the community of otherness.

If a father and mother must decide whether to abort an unborn child which an amniocentesis has shown to have a spina bifida condition or some other serious birth defect, the issue is not adequately grasped through an ethics of individualism or an ethics of utilitarianism any more than it is through pitting family against society. In general, the question is not one of the rights of the individual versus the rights of the community or the family versus society, but of the person's or family's being open to growth *and* accepting the conditions and limitations of growth as an organic member of the community. Such a member of the community must stand on the ground of its personal uniqueness and demand what freedom for growth the situation at any time allows while at the same time recognizing that its growth does not take place through relationship to itself. The person or the family must confirm other persons and families in their uniqueness and in their need. It must confirm the common ground of communal existence as a meaning larger than that of the person and the family but inclusive of it. The communal existence here does not equal harmony or obedience to authority, but building together— each person or family from where it is and from what it is—the "community of otherness." Communal responsibility must begin with the individual and the individual family. But it is only possible through overcoming false individualism, through recognizing the interhuman and social corollaries of its own growth, and through its stake and trust in the community.

But the communal responsibility is also that of the community. It has to encourage the maximum growth of the individuals, families, and small groups within it. The community must set limits where necessary, but, if it is a real community, if it has real communal concern, it can never just cut off the person and cease to be responsible for her. It cannot offer only a conditional confirmation. Venture and risk are a part of all life. Risk is implied in the very notion both of communal growth and communal authenticity. Today, however, the venturing on all fronts in order to break out of the unlived life that has confined us greatly multiplies the risk. There is no simple formula that helps us, no Either/Or of risk or no risk which is of any value. Our problem is to draw the demarcation line responsibly and ever anew: This much risk this family, this group, this community can take and no more in this hour, this situation. This is not at all the same as that self-protection engaged in by the community in casting out the person who raises anxieties or threatens its happy harmony.

We live in a time in which we find ourselves painfully trying to rebuild real communities within the larger social bodies. One of the dangers of this effort, as the commune movement has shown, is the temptation to betray the community of otherness by designating one's own commune or cell "the blessed community" and consigning everything else to total meaninglessness, if not to the profane. The "encounter group" which flourished in the '60s and '70s and which still exists in many places and many forms also provides us with an opportunity for grasping concretely the significance of this distinction between the community of affinity and the community of otherness.

It makes no sense to talk of pure spontaneity; for structures are necessary and without them we would not have that margin within which spontaneity can arise. But there is an all-important difference between the structure which makes possible spontaneity and that which takes its place. There is nothing wrong with planning as long as we do not try to plan the spontaneity itself, or, what amounts to the same thing, bring such strong expectations of specific results that one type of event is reinforced whereas another is played down or ignored. It seems to be our human fate that again and again the structure alters from something that is life-promoting to something that gets in the way of life. Carl Rogers sees the encounter movement as "a growing counterforce to the dehumanization of our culture." Yet, as he himself recognizes, it may, in fact, promote that dehumanization because of the tendency to turn structures that arise organically out of a unique group in a unique situation into omnicompetent techniques that may be carried over to any occasion.

Sensitivity training is no substitute for sensitivity, openness, and responsiveness, and that always means to the unique, concrete situation in all its fullness—not just to what one is looking for. True sensitivity is wedded to the moment. William Coulson, in this spirit, chides a fellow facilitator for suggesting a risk to two people rather than allowing it to be produced between them and quotes Buber's statement that "every living situation has, like a newborn child, a new face, that has never been before and will never come again. It demands of you a reaction which cannot be prepared beforehand. It demands nothing of what is past. It demands presence, responsibility; it demands you."[3]

One of the most important distinctions to be made among encounter groups is between those that lead to the real openness of the "community of otherness," that is, a group in which each cares about the others for what they are, and those that lead to a cult, a community of the like-minded. Cults give their members the false security that they are in the know and everyone else is really outside. Cults destroy the person by destroying his or her responsibility before the other who does not fit the model of the group. They also destroy the reality of the group because people do not meet each other in the freedom of fellowship.

To what extent does the human potential movement represent what Martin Buber has called "the lust for overrunning reality," in which the person "becomes at once completely agitated and crippled in his motive power," a crisis of temptation and dishonesty in which "the realms are overturned, everything encroaches on everything else, and possibility is more powerful than reality"? To what extent is the encounter movement a lust for instant life, instant joy, instant intimacy, instant relationship? It is salutary, in the midst of our heightened mobility, to realize that there is an organic tempo to life, that not all human realities can be poured into an atomic crucible and transmuted with the speed of light, that some suffering and sorrow and pain must be lived through for their duration and not at the "souped-up" speed which we willfully will. The "Evil Urge," says a Hasidic master, "goes around the world with his fist closed. Everybody thinks that just what he wants most in the world is in that fist, and so he follows him. But then the Evil Urge opens his hand, and it is empty!"

In order to counteract the danger of "inappropriate self-disclosure, scapegoating, tyrannizing by the group, inappropriate reassurance, provocative behavior, tyrannizing by the leader, favoritism by the leader, and forced confession ('psychological rape')," Louis Paul sets forth a set of ethical principles for facilitators, the first of which is an encouragement to informed self-determination which will lead him or her at times to "endorse, protect, and value a member's choice to remain silent; to decline another's urging toward action; to deviate from the position of the majority; to remain an observer." The facilitator may wish to help the other enlarge his or her perceptions, options, and independence, but even this the leader does not force. "The facilitator does not browbeat, intimidate, mystify, dazzle with his brilliance, or intellectually seduce." Neither does he or she take advantage of the awe in which the member may hold him or her to seduce or touch the other sexually, though he or she may touch the other as "a companion along the way." This touching is not exploitative but a genuine contact with reality. "To touch is human, humane. An alerting, a solace, a seeker connecting with the Other, flinging a bridge across the separateness."[4]

For a facilitator to steer groups into being like ones he has known in the past, says Thomas Greening, is a "cop-out" "from the frightening existential challenge and responsibility to create one unique new being from the many potential beings." The unpredictable venture of creating relationships means a movement from marketing orientation to Buber's I-Thou meetings, and this means, says Greening, "to gamble on the emerging humanness of the participants without taking over and trying to shape them in one's own image." Recounting the way in which a group led by Gerald Haigh worked through the problem caused by the presence of a disturbed member, Greening points to precisely what I have called the "dialogue of touchstones" and to the possibilities of healing through meeting that are present in such dialogue:

> This capacity to trust and risk enabled him to offer her and the group the choice of valuing and exploring her emotion, rather than narrowing down her choices to either alienating herself from her feelings so as to "adjust" to the group or erupting with emotion while alienated from the group.[5]

Only an experienced facilitator and a group of people coming in touch with what is deeply genuine and meaningful in themselves and each other can break through the facade of "group games," "I-Thou jargon," and "peak experiences" to the real person inside, says Greening. Although the pressure to experience awareness undoubtedly exists, an effective group "will encourage deep and sustained confirmation of the authenticity of the awareness rather than hastily praise its semblance." It is "from one man to another that the heavenly bread of self being is passed," Greening quotes Buber. The challenge of the future, says Greening, will be "to create a world in which encounter will no longer have to be an encapsulated, specially arranged event." He sees this challenge as being met in part by those colleges and universities now offering intensive group experiences in order to tap the vast potential for authenticity, relatedness, and creativity in their students.

It is no accident that it is out of the very institution which Greening sees as particularly rich in "the shared search for meaning"—Johnston College, a new experimental division of the University of Redlands—that there has emerged a reply to Fritz Perls' famous credo. "I do my thing and you do your thing," says Perls, one of the gods of the human potential movement, in a poster to be found in innumerable growth centers and "turned-on" homes. "I am not in this world to live up to your expectations, and you are not in this world to live up to mine. You are you and I am I; if by chance we find each other, it's beautiful. If not, it can't be helped." Building on Buber's understanding of dialogue and the mutual need for confirmation, Walter Tubbs, a fellow in psychology and philosophy at Johnston College, rejoins:

> If I just do my thing and you do yours, we stand in danger of losing each other and ourselves. I am not in this world to live up to your expectations; but I am in this world to confirm you as a unique human being, and to be confirmed by you. We are fully ourselves only in relation to each other; the I detached from a Thou disintegrates. I do not find you by chance; I find you by an active life of reaching out. Rather than passively letting things happen to me, I can act intentionally to make them happen. I must begin with myself, true; but I must not end with myself: the truth begins with two.[6]

Greening also points to the existential trust which I have

characterized in *Touchstones of Reality* as "the courage to address and the courage to respond." Such courage is frightening, he points out, for it entails vulnerability to disconfirmation. Too often in everyday life the gestures of self-disclosure and humanness go unnoticed or are rejected, as a result of which people develop a self-fulfilling prophecy which says that existential risk-taking is useless. Greening recognizes that there is no guarantee that mutual confirmation will happen in encounter groups, to which I may add that the courage to address and respond also includes the courage *not* to address or respond when you are not really addressed as a unique person but only triggered off. The encounter group can be, as Greening himself concludes, a way toward the realization of the community of otherness: "Few social inventions can equal encounter groups as a method for enabling people to learn from their differences and discover or create their unity."

Coulson also points to the community of otherness in his recognition that what matters is not so much whether words hit or miss the mark but whether the members of the group really care for one another. He also recognizes the all-important difference between providing an occasion for encounter groups and structuring the encounter itself. An encounter group goes better when the leader yields to the process and shares in its suffering, vulnerability, and surprise. What is primary and healing, according to Coulson, is not professional training but the relationship itself. Coulson makes an important distinction between the irresponsible release of possibilities which characterizes some groups and the proving of one's humanity through the responsible return to the people given in one's life situation. If the facilitator becomes involved in the suffering of the group activity, he or she is less likely to stimulate the group into being overwhelmed by new possibility and more willing to wait attentively and discover what he or she wants in gentle interaction with others. The facilitator helps others meet, not by arranging a cautious experience as opposed to an experimental one, but by providing an occasion for meeting, and arranging nothing at all. The foremost learning of an encounter group, states Coulson, is that one can call on people. Encounter is not useful. "It is at most a celebration of the mystery that lies between us."

The La Jolla Program does not encourage participants to establish themselves as "encounter gurus" but "to apply their learnings to the settings in which they already find themselves." The value of the special encounter group is "getting people relating again person-to-person rather than function-to-function." The humanizing need within institutional life is for occasions for genuine meeting; for it is out of such meeting that real community will arise. Community means mutual teaching and learning, influencing and being influenced, letting others have a say and asking them to let you in, taking the time necessary to build up close human, trusting relationships, helping each other to speak personally. It is significant that Coulson ends his book not on the note of "encounter," the word with which Walter Kaufmann renders Buber's *Begegnung* in his translation of *I and Thou*, but with "meeting," the word Buber himself preferred. Unfortunately, it is less the rule than the exception that the spirit of encounter groups has been that of genuine meeting.

If the death of dialogue is the split which leads one group to be entirely "objective" and content-oriented and another to be centered on looking at feelings, the life of dialogue might be a "basic encounter-discussion group" in which the members are called forth in such a way that they respond from the depths without making that response their conscious goal. This is a structure which makes spontaneity possible without taking its place. One of the purposes of the "basic encounter-discussion group" structure is to encourage a return to wholeness beyond the tragic split between thought and feeling that marks our culture. But even this holistic structure cannot be imposed. In an interdisciplinary seminar on religion and psychotherapy, I found the group evenly split between those who wanted academic content and those who wanted pure exchange of feelings; no one was ready for my third structure in which the two might be joined in a single response to the problems and issues shared by the group. But it is a goal that one can move toward, refusing to accept the split as a permanent one or as a description of how things are. I was gratified to learn that Carl Rogers shares this identical goal and the identical experience:

> In any group to some degree, but especially in a so-called academic course I am conducting in encounter group fashion, I want very much to have the *whole* person present, in both his affective and cognitive modes. I have not found this easy to achieve since most of us seem to choose one mode rather than

the other at any given instant. Yet this still remains a way of being which has much value for me. I try to make progress in myself, and in groups I facilitate, in permitting the whole person, with his ideas as well as his feelings—with feelings permeated with ideas and ideas permeated with feelings—to be fully present.[7]

Another aspect of the "basic encounter-discussion group," and potentially of any encounter group, is that it is a structure that will help to avoid the danger of looking at the interactions of the members of the group only in terms of the feelings that they produce within one and not as real events in themselves. The artificial time and space of the weekend or week group adds greatly to the danger that even the most profound interactions among the members are likely to have an unreal, set-apart quality radically different from a genuine commitment to and concern for other persons. On the other hand, the idea of being in an "encounter group" may tend to obscure the unique and unrepeatable character of this group. It may tempt one to carry over what one has learned in one group as a technique to be applied to other similar groups rather than as a "touchstone of reality" that can be made present again in a unique way in each new meeting. The very notion of coming together in order that each might realize his or her "potential"—as if this were a fixed substance within that only needs to be liberated by some catalytic agent—promotes this turning away from real response to events and persons toward a focus on the impact of the group happenings on the individual psyche. When this takes place, the true meaning of "here and now"—the sphere of the between that transcends all individual feelings and psychic aftereffects—is screened out of awareness and often irreparably injured.

It is not only psychologizing individualism that is at work here but a relation to time that robs us of true presentness. If our goal is to get rid of our hang-ups, to be turned on, to become free, then, like it or not, we are using ourselves and the other members of the group as functions of a process. But the reality of the group is not made up of the sum of the feelings of the people in it. It is this particular togetherness and interaction with its specific possibilities and limitations. There will be as much true openness as the resources of this particular group make possible and no more. True openness is not attained through the manifest or concealed pressure to "let go" and express emotions. Just as in individual therapy the patient often has dreams that fit the school of the therapist, so in encounter groups people often express the emotions that they feel are expected of them without ever sharing a moment of true presentness with the group. There has to be that reality, fully itself, of this group experience; there has to be intrinsic meaning, of the group's value in itself as well as in its future effects, or the very stuff of life is being destroyed.

Even the term "group process" obscures the concrete reality of what has come to be in this group that will never again exist in any other. If we take our potential seriously, we shall discover that it is not in us as something that we possess nor is it waiting to be pried out of us by one technique or another. It is what comes to be in the two-sided event, the grace that comes from both sides of the happening, from within and from without. Often it is true that all that is present in an encounter interchange is mutual projection which entirely obscures the unique person one is confronting in favor of some person or persons in our past. But we must not rule out a priori the possibility that many other things can take place. Perhaps two persons will break through to each other and then really oppose each other because each stands on a fundamentally different ground. This, too, is meaningful encounter and confrontation. But I have also observed that when an interchange which began in hostility and anger began to change into one in which one of the parties in a generation battle was beginning to sense the sorrow of the other from within, the group leader cut it off in favor of expressions of anger and hostility on the part of others in the group. On one occasion a surgeon of about fifty-eight and a young woman of about twenty-two were having a bad time with each other because he was "establishment" and she, with her long skirts and motorcycle, was a "hippie." Yet they were deeply involved with each other, and they came to the point where she seemed finally to begin to sense the painful meeting from his side of the relationship. At this point the leader deliberately cut it off; for he was looking for individual revelations and had ruled out in principle the "between."

We can and do experience the other side of the relationship—looking in each other's eyes, touching each other's face, involving ourselves deeply with another's suffering, pain, or anger. Even when two people cannot stand each other, they can glimpse for a moment what it is like to be the other person. This glimpse is fully as real a part of the feeling aspect of encounters as those self-referring feelings that we entertain within ourselves and tend to make our goal. I would claim, in fact, that the deepest feelings arise, not when we are focusing on our own feelings, but when we are really responding to someone else. Is it really worth our while to discover that we can feel and touch if we do not use our feeling and our touching for real contact at this moment? The very notion of touching means touching what is not yourself. If instead we focus on having experiences of touching, or on having feelings, we cut off our contact with real otherness and isolate ourselves still more. Coulson has expressed this paradox of touching turned in on itself with incomparable clarity:

> Sad it is that touch, which in our culture could imply the existence of an affection between people that is real and risky, which might take account of the individual uniqueness of both toucher and touched, . . . sad it is that this possibility for confirmation between persons has been appropriated as a gamer's self-display rather than as the knowing implication of a betweenness.
>
> This indiscriminateness of touch is sad for the recipient, for it implies the denial of his hope that what it is to be himself will not turn out to be interchangeable with what it is to be anyone else. . . . The game-based touching is saddest, I think, for the toucher, for he misses the thrill of presence, which is only to be found between persons, never to be placed there. . . . Cued by a voice from an electronic box, a man and a girl, strangers, embraced. Science had synthesized I-Thou.[8]

Without time spent in working out mutuality and "gradually gaining knowledge of each other, there can only be blind guesswork, a mechanical forcing of one person on the other, in which both will be diminished."

In a community of otherness, even a marriage or friendship, as close as it may be, is not a simple unity. Rather each goes out from his or her ground to meet the other in his or her otherness. This is not a matter of comparison and contrast but of seeking someone from where he or she really is. In many groups in which I have been involved, whether they called themselves encounter or not, something has happened which has gone beyond anything we can understand in terms of individual psychology, something which cannot be parcelled out to the individual members of the group as the mere sum of their feelings.

We can grow in the strength to be there for another, really there, in such a fashion that we are not at all concerned at that moment about whether we are realizing ourselves or our potentiality. All great self-realization is a by-product of really being present in the situation in which we are involved. If we come to an encounter group with the concern, "How may I grow through this?" or "What can I get out of it?" we will not grow at all. The concern will stand in the way of our really being spontaneously and unselfconsciously present for the other members of the group. Carried far enough, we will miss the trip entirely; for the present will be seen only as a means to the end of the future, and the group event will never seem real enough to call us out in our wholeness.

What is really called for is a faithful response to the situation, including the otherness of the people in it. Then in really meeting these people, in really being present for one another, our "shadow" also comes into play and we begin to understand the reality of the interhuman more deeply than before. Such understanding includes a caring about the others for themselves, a caring that is sometimes strong enough to bridge the gap between one lonely person and another. If, in contrast, we look at the others merely as sources of feedback, then we regard each person's words, gestures, and actions as useful bits of information about ourselves without any genuine response to them seeming necessary. Thus the emphasis upon realizing our possibilities may profane the situation by turning it into a function of a self-becoming which is not true self-becoming since it does not grow out of faithful listening and response to the call that comes at every moment. Our resources for responding come into being as we are called out by the depth of our caring about someone or something not ourselves. "By never being an end in himself, he endlessly becomes himself" (Laotzu).

Only when the encounter group is seen as a concrete happening, unique and unrepeatable, not subject to manipulation or techniques which will produce given results, can there be a really deep and lasting effect on all those who share in the group's life-reality.

The therapeutic communities which Ronald Laing and the

Philadelphia [brotherhood] Association established at Kingsley Hall and at other places in and outside London give us some insight into the concrete ways in which Laing's dialogical approach to healing schizophrenia may lead to the community of otherness. "Ronnie" is pictured by his coworker Leon Redler as sitting at the head of the long rectangular table at mealtime, "speaking in a moving, searching and penetrating way," and allowing "himself and others a lot of freedom of movement and action." He was "very much there," " a strong and vibrant presence." Similarly Redler saw how he himself was with people at the Archway community "in terms of being present as openly and honestly as I can." It was less a matter of using techniques of doing anything special than of being attentively and caringly present. In this setting, where no distinction was made between "doctor" and "patient," Redler found that it took him quite a while to begin to realize how much he had maintained barriers between himself and suffering—his own and that of others; for much of his doctor/psychiatrist training and institutional practice supported his defensive barriers and evasions. "Even in an ambiance which allowed for and encouraged a more naked and honest meeting," he found that he continued to maintain them, and he found this maintenance of masks even while struggling to let go of them very exhausting. Eventually he learned to let go of his medical and psychiatric learning and training and to just let himself be there. "It was a scene where assumptions were put in question, illusions shaken, preconceptions cut thru—and where if you depended on others for cues as to how to behave you would soon be bewildered."[9]

Redler shared Laing's faith that *a breakdown can be seen as a potential breakthrough*:

> The *breakdown* is the breakdown of a way of being that is characterized by contradiction, deception, cutting off of experience, engaging in defensive and calculating maneuvers with one's self and with others. The *breakthrough* can be through to a freer, more authentic, integrated, centered, harmonious, more open way of being. The movement may be like out of a prison—often with the first realization that one's been in a prison.[10]

The founders of the Philadelphia Association discovered that the conventional medical model impeded both in theory and practice working through the experience of the "breakdown." "To explore the contradictions in communication that at times may lead any of us to act, or to be seen, as mad, we needed a community with a flexible structure, where people did not have to be forced into such roles as doctor, social worker or patient." The therapeutic communities of the Philadelphia Association came very close to what I have called a "community of otherness.":

> All groups of free people struggle with issues of tolerable and acceptable limits of behavior within the group. In these house-holds these limits change as people grow and develop, come and go. With few set rules or defined limits, the struggle is a fresh one with each new situation. . . . I've been trying to con-tribute to the development of a place of asylum or refuge, a relatively safe place to be; a place where one can fall apart, be untogether, recognize and realize how untogether one actually is—as well as a place to come together; falling apart and coming together; death, rebirth. There needs to be much more atten-tiveness, clarity and love in the system than we've had. Atten-tive care rather than intrusive control.[11]

Carl Rogers' person-centered approach to community is so close to the community of otherness that it is instructive to con-sider where these two understandings of community converge and diverge. The attitudes that make for improved relationships, says Rogers in his book on "personal power," are the willingness to "indwell" in the perceived reality of the other and the valuing and respecting and caring for the other person. These attitudes lead to communication, a responsible and responsive stance to-ward others, and an absence of facade that draws out realness in the other and makes possible "genuine meeting" (to use Buber's term).

In *A Way of Being*, Rogers recounts that he has been involved for fifteen years with colleagues at the Center for the Study of the Person and elsewhere in the United States and abroad in building temporary communities most of the members of which "feel both a keen sense of their own power and a sense of close and respect-ful union with all of the other members." Mostly these com-munities arise in workshops of one kind or another, workshops in which persons are free to be creative, diverse, contradictory, pres-ent, open, and sharing. These workshops are characterized above all by openness, acceptance of difference, and a desire to *hear*, all of which make them remarkably close in spirit to the "community of otherness."

> We listen especially to the contrary voices, the soft voices, those that are expressing unpopular or unacceptable views. We make a point of responding to a person if he or she spoke openly, but no one responded. We thus tend to validate each person.

Rogers feels that the most dramatic and far-reaching future significance of their work is their way of being and acting as a staff—open, with no leader and no hierarchical organization, leadership and responsibility equally shared. The revolutionary implications of such an approach can be easily seen by comparing it with the dominant attitude toward power in administration:

> Our schools, our government, our businesses and corporations are permeated with the view that neither the individual nor the group is trustworthy. There must be power *over*, power to control. The hierarchical system is inherent in our whole culture.[13]

Rogers sees these temporary communities as pilot models for future permanent community when the society will proves ready to use them on a larger scale. There are several senses, nonetheless, in which they fall short of the "community of otherness." There is insufficient recognition, first of all, that the success of even these temporary communities depends upon the facilitators and, despite the lack of structured hierarchy, on the guiding presence of Rogers himself for that climate of trust and resources that makes community possible. Equally serious is the tendency on Rogers' part to see what is happening in these communities in terms of an Either/Or—the individual versus the society or the organic whole, the inner versus the outer. Either "the welfare of the total organism, the state or nation, is paramount . . . and each person is helped to become conscious of being but one cell in a great organic structure" or there is "a stress on the importance of the individual." Rogers fails to see the third alternative that lies at the heart of the "community of otherness," namely the reality of the between that links the individual and the community. For this reason, he claims that "the locus of evaluation is in the person, not outside" and that "the good life is within, not dependent on outside sources." The young woman who goes from a Rogers

workshop to face 800 people at a public county school board
meeting around the issue of racial integration reports her experience in typical Rogerian terminology of the organism: "I felt,
more fully than ever before, my strength and confidence in my
organism." The organic analogy which Rogers uses to explain
community, sap rising in a tree, the bud opening, the cactus
shrinking and swelling, the seeds of plants that lie dormant and
later bloom, is inadequate to capture the reality of the community
of otherness for the precise reason that the organic excludes true
otherness.[14]

Even more serious is the fact that Rogers' temporary communities tend to take place in abstraction from the concrete situation. Rogers claims that the dynamics of the process stand out in
his workshops "because there are relatively few factors extrane-
ous to the experiment." "They are free from any conditions except
those that they establish themselves." But this very fact makes
them less and other than a true community of otherness, which
must exist in the concrete situation and in relationship with other
communities. Rogers himself recognizes that their experience is
limited almost entirely to the formation of temporary communities and that where they have had to deal with existing
structures, such as groups in which political positions are already
laid down, they have had only partial success. The Camp David
meeting of Egyptian President Sadat and Israeli Prime Minister
Begin is heartening, as Rogers suggests, as is the experience of
the Center for Studies Belfast Group in promoting discussion between antagonistic Protestant and Catholic groups in one block of
Belfast.[15] But neither experience serves as a pilot model of community for the larger society, as Rogers claims, because neither
has been realized in larger structures than the meeting of individuals. The true community of otherness must have endurance
in time, the concrete situations of everyday lived existence, and
meaningful interaction with other communities of otherness
within the society.

Chapter 14

THE LEARNING COMMUNITY

THE LEARNING community is, quite simply, the "community of otherness." It is the community that confirms otherness within climates of trust to the extent that these are made possible by the educational structures and the persons working within those structures.

Looking recently at the manuscript of my three-volume "dialography," *Martin Buber's Life and Work,* I was astonished to discover how explicitly Buber himself stated this thesis in a 1935 essay on "Education and World-View" that I myself translated ten years before the metaphor of the "community of otherness" came to me in a context far removed from education. The background of this essay was the adult education and the training of teachers that Buber led in Nazi Germany during the time when all Jewish students had been excluded from public education. Buber was the leader of this demanding and difficult undertaking, which he and Ernst Simon who assisted him saw as effective spiritual resistance to Nazism and its full-scale attack on the Jewish community.

In bringing together formerly conflicting Jewish youth groups, Buber rejected the language of "tolerance" and "neutrality" in favor of that of "making present the roots of community and its branches" and of "solidarity, living mutual support and living mutual action." In these designations he saw the "model of the great community," the "community of communities." "For the formation of the person and, accordingly, for the formation of the great community growing out of persons and their relations," Buber wrote in the bulletin of his central educational office that he entitled "Education and World-View," "everything depends upon how much one actually has to do with the world that one is interpreting." Therefore, the decisive question about a world-view is whether it furthers one's vital relationship to the world or obstructs it. The world-view does not need to get between the person and the world. On the contrary, it can help one strive to grasp the facts faithfully if it keeps one's love for this "world" so alert and strong that one does not grow tired of "perceiving what is to be perceived." One can in one's own spirit put a stop to the politicization of truth, to the identification of truth with what is useful.

In his work as director of the Central Office for Jewish Education, Buber set as the goal of its educational program bringing groups with different world views into contact with one another in the experience of community. "Only in lived togetherness, indeed, do they really come to sense the power of the whole." Those teaching periods in which the leader united some youth groups according to a single *Weltanschauung* remained in the minority. As a rule several groups of varied orientations came together. Buber himself characterized these two types of groups as homogeneous and heterogeneous.

> The former was an idyll, bright and warm, uninhibited, in the first hour it grew to its full shape. The latter was a drama, hard and eventful. We enjoyed the otherness of the other person. We had something to develop to the full; we did so. We were at loggerheads and then we fell into each other's arms. On the third day, matters had reached a critical point. We had known all along that things couldn't go on like that. . . . On the fourth morning sport and singing revealed a new impulse in our togetherness. The first of these two types of class belonged fully to the "Mittelstelle." I would not like to miss it. But only the second does the real work.

Here Buber pointed the way to the "community of otherness." The great community "is no union of the like-minded," Buber wrote, "but a genuine living together of persons of similar or of complementary natures but of differing minds. Community is the overcoming of *otherness* in living unity." This is not a question of some formal and minimal understanding but of an awareness from the other side of the other's real relation to the truth—"inclusion." "What is called for is . . . a living answering for one another . . . not effacing the boundaries between the groups, circles, and parties, but communal recognition of the common reality and communal testing of the common responsibility."

Vital dissociation—the sickness of the peoples of our age—is only seemingly healed through crowding persons together. "Here, nothing can help other than persons from different circles of opinion honestly having to do with one another in a common opening out of a common ground." This is the "andragogy" (the adult pedagogy) of our educational work. "We live—one must say it again—in a time in which the great dreams, the great hopes of mankind, have one after another been fulfilled—in caricature!" This massive experience Buber saw as caused by the power of fictitious conviction, the uneducated quality of the person of this age. "Opposed to it stands the education that is true to its age and adjusts to it, the education that leads one to a vital connection with one's world and enables one to ascend from there to faithfulness, to standing the test, to authenticity, to responsibility, to decision, to realization."[1]

Community is the overcoming of otherness in living unity. This is the essence of all true community, but it is the very heart of the learning community. We shall understand learning better if we go back to the root meaning of the term educating—the Latin "educe." Education is educing. The scientific method is made up of a combination of deduction, in which one applies a general thesis to particulars, and induction, in which one goes from particulars to a general thesis. But Socrates used neither deduction nor induction; he used eduction, he educed, he led out. He started in the middle of the situation and mostly, if you follow Plato's Dialogues carefully, that is also where he ended, or at least it is where his hearers ended. This has very serious consequences. If educing means leading out of, it means starting with the situation where you are—not just pulling out something that is already in there, but evoking, calling forth.

Martin Buber characterizes the "old" way of looking at education by the metaphor of the funnel. The student's head is empty, you bore a hole in it, and you pour into it whatever you want to. The "new" metaphor for education, Buber suggests, is the pump.

Progressive education, which was all the rage in the 1920s in Germany and became the rage in America some years later, was like the pump. Everything was already in the child. All one needed was to pump it out, or, to change the metaphor, the teacher watered the plant, pruned the leaves, kept off insects, i.e., facilitated the unfolding of the powers of the child. The funnel approach is the educational philosophy of Robert Hutchins and the "Great Books." There are certain great books which the teacher teaches the student to analyze and through that they become educated persons. The pump approach was the philosophy of John Dewey that had such a powerful influence on educational thinking in America. Dewey talked about the potentialities of students and what they needed to develop them.

I taught for fourteen years at Sarah Lawrence College, which was developed in the late 1920s under the impact of the John Dewey type of progressive approach to education. We used to say, "We don't teach material. We teach the student." There is something to that, of course, but it led at times to a "student-centered" approach to education that emphasized the one side of the dialogue at the expense of the other. I was still more troubled by the assumption of Harold Taylor, the president of Sarah Lawrence College, that there would be an ideal harmony between the teacher and the students. The teacher would want to teach in the most progressive style, and the student would want to learn in the same way. Therefore, the integrity of both would ideally be preserved. But Sarah Lawrence women who dated men from Columbia, Yale, and Princeton sometimes felt that their boyfriends' courses were better, even though they were more traditional ones. In the years since I left Sarah Lawrence, the traditional system of evaluating the student by a paragraph has been replaced by grades, *at the request of the students*. The ideal harmony between what the teacher wanted and what the student wanted did not hold.

A fatal inner-outer, subjective-objective split accompanies these contrasting approaches to education. The funnel side assumes that the student is there as a mere receiver of knowledge while the pump side assumes that the teacher is merely the facilitator to bring out what is already there and needs only be unfolded. Speaking to a group of progressive world educators in Heidelberg in 1925, Buber suggested that there is a third approach. This third approach has to do with learning as dialogue, and by dialogue

Buber did not mean simply Socratic dialogue. He meant people really being present one to the other. The true opposite of compulsion is not freedom but communion. Buber even went so far as to say that the basis of education is trust: "Because this human being exists, in the darkness the light lies hidden, in fear salvation, and in the callousness of one's fellow men the great Love." This is "the inmost achievement of the relation in education."

In an article on the encounter movement, Viktor Frankl, the distinguished logotherapist, points out that there has to be an objective content of the encounter, or meeting *(Begegnung)*, as well as people talking with each other. There does have to be an objective content, but the objectivity of that content, Frankl to the contrary, is a *social* one. The meaning of what you take up between you is right there in the meeting itself. That does not mean that it is merely subjective. For years, I have asked my students to keep a "personal-academic journal" in place of an examination. This journal has four steps. The first is for the student to select from the reading or the class discussion something that strikes her and to write it down in the journal. Step Two is to try then to put it into one's own words. Step Three is coming back to one's own side and responding—both intellectually and emotionally—from where one is. Step Four is to relate what one is commenting on to ongoing issues of the course. Step Two does not mean translating into familiar categories or constructs. It means trying to go imaginatively over to where the other person is and to sense where that person is speaking from, be it author, lecturer, or fellow classmate. I have said that most education is miseducation because it teaches us to abstract from where people are and think only in terms of abstract ideas which we then are taught to put in categories. We call that education, and the student becomes very expert at it.

Learning, when it takes place, is an event. We are being bombarded all the time with information, but that does not mean that real learning takes place. Real learning is deliberate. It is, as Buber suggests, effective selection by the teacher of what the student needs. Most true learning in our day is not a matter of taking in more but of taking in less, of focusing, of letting something come to us. We might well ask, "How do we know what of the effective world to select?" The teacher educates herself, Buber suggests, through discovering what the student needs. How do we then discover what the student needs? Through dialogue—not *asking* the student what he or she needs but experiencing the other side, imagining the real. The pupil has something that no one else in the world, including the teacher, has—a unique experience. To discover that, the teacher must ask *real* questions and not just Socratic ones.

I have since learned that real dialogue and real learning is possible in many settings. What is more, I have learned that it is not necessarily the students who are the most verbal who are most in dialogue. Once I gave a lecture to 1500 people on Existentialism at Cooper Union in New York City. After the lecture and the long question period, I was warned by the moderator to get away through the back before anyone came up to me. One person came up to the stage, and I knelt down to ask what her question was. Suddenly there were about thirty people there, every one of whom was trying to talk at once or at least raising their hands to show me they wanted to say something. In the back of a group stood one woman who was not trying to talk and who did not raise her hand. Yet there was something in her face that made me want to call out to her, "What are you saying to me?" She was really in dialogue.

There is no structure that guarantees the presence and reality of the learning community. There are many structures that tend to get in the way of it. By community I mean people who are in some way there for one another, not doing the same thing but also not simply each going his or her own way. This means caring enough to have an interchange, verbal or nonverbal, caring enough to share. Much in our society is so polarized that people cannot hear one another; yet hearing and responding to one another is the simplest prerequisite of the learning community. In almost any professional meeting what seems to be most rare is real hearing as opposed to people putting what other people say into their own categories and then cutting them down on that basis.

This is academic polarization, but in recent years we have also seen political polarization operating even more strongly. Once after a speech at the University of Massachusetts in Boston on "A Dialogue with Today's Youth," I was immensely struck because it seemed that all my listeners were programmed to hear in a certain way. The editor of a student newspaper, who had just announced that morning in headlines that there was a great rebellion going on in what was in fact one of the most quiescent campuses in the United States, said, "You mentioned Job in the Bible, and Job is obviously a cop-out." A young woman said, "There cannot be a dialogue between a teacher and a student because a teacher has power over the student." Another young woman, despite the fact that I had not said one word about religion or God, asked "What *do* you mean when you speak about God?" "I cannot answer a question put in that way," I replied. "That's the trouble with the establishment," she retorted. "They always want to have the dialogue on their own terms!" Finally, the Chancellor of the university, who happened to be there, remarked, "As I hear it, you are saying that the administration should be as rigid as possible so that the students can have a healthy rebellion." "Is there one person who even heard what I said?" I asked myself.

This sort of programmed response easily goes over into almost willful mishearing. The prophet Amos said, "There will come a famine not of bread or water but of thirst for the words of the living God." We go over from not listening to the place where we can no longer really hear what someone else is saying. No real learning can take place when that is the case.

One of the obvious problems of structure is size—classes of two thousand, universities of 30-, 40-, and 50,000. Yet size alone does not prevent learning from taking place. There are possibilities for learning even in the largest university if one can create within those structures a "climate of trust." Sometimes that has indeed happened. Clearly, there are *limits* to creating climates of trust in situations where the larger climate is one of mistrust. Once I was part of a group of faculty and graduate students at a professional school who created a qualitative, or nonstatistical, dissertation track which flourished for a time and attracted many students. But this climate of trust was directly threatening to the larger climate of mistrust that dominated the school. Every graduate school that I have been associated with has seemed to me to produce an unnecessary amount of anxiety for its students, who are already anxious enough by virtue of their pressured and demanding situation. This additional anxiety is created by bureaucracy and by professors of the department who are concerned with *their* reputation, *their* discipline, *their* methodology. But this professional school went far beyond that. It actively mistrusted the students and created an overall "paranoia" such as I have never experienced before or since. In this atmosphere it was self-evident that any faculty member who was an "advocate" of the students was an enemy of the administration. This experience taught me that if you want to change a structure you may, at times, have to create a whole new structure—if you can. We *have* to live in structures, and we have to decide when we can fight to change them, when we shall leave them, and when we must try to create new ones. In the process we discover what strengths and resources we have.

The learning community is the community of otherness, and the community of otherness means the recognition that wherever there is more than one person there is more than one point of view. By "point of view" I do not mean opinion or idea but what Buber says about true marriage—that the other person has another touch from the regions of existence, another soil, another faith. Each person brings something quite concrete and unique into the relationship. If that is not recognized, it is usually the fault of *all* the persons involved. There tends to be an implicit contract through which one or more persons allows his or her self to be dominated.

One of the reasons that we have communities of affinity or likemindedness is that we are so afraid of difference, of conflict, of otherness that we imagine if we admit any, we shall kill each other down to the last person. Some time ago *The Herald Tribune* used to bring high school students every year from many countries to spend a year in America. These students would come to Sarah Lawrence College for a week's workshop before separating to attend high school in cities throughout the United States. I was teaching a course in Comparative Religion at the time and was invited to conduct a workshop with these students. I accepted eagerly since I had never had contact with so many students of so many different religions all in one group. I asked each of them to write a short statement for me to use as a basis for discussion. The Catholic student from Africa and the Catholic student from South America wrote the identical catechism, but once we got into discussion we found that their religions were by no means identical. The atheist from Indo-China was a Buddhist; the atheist from Paris was a Sartrian existentialist. These young students loved these interchanges, and I did too. The woman who ran the week's workshop called me up afterward and said, "I am going to take four of these students on television and try to do what you did about religion. But, of course, I am not going to allow any issues to arise"!

The American novelist Kurt Vonnegut distinguishes in his

novel *Cat's Cradle* between a "granfaloon," which is something like an alumni reunion where everyone has something superficial in common, and a "karass," in which the persons involved may have nothing in common but a common concern which brings them together. That is very similar to the distinction between a community of affinity, or likemindedness, and a community of otherness. The key to the community of otherness is its readiness to confirm the otherness in its members and in those outside the community, insofar as the resources of that community make it possible. No community can confirm all otherness; that is beyond its possibility. However, there is a great difference between discovering what we can confirm in practice and the hysteria that says, "We can't allow anyone in who does not have *our* words, *our* mottos, *our* creed, *our* way of speaking."

What gets in the way of the learning community being a true community of otherness? Size, structure, program boxes, mistrust, lack of real communication, concern with public relations, *and* the specialization through which professors know more and more about less and less. There is no learning community, no community of otherness, if we use our language games in such a way that they shut out people who do not use our language. This is extremely pervasive. Disciplines and departments are good, but they are not ends in themselves. The problem with specialization arises when it is no longer content to be a useful tool and claims instead to be the only real province of knowledge. As soon as one says that there is only one right language, then the community of otherness is endangered—not by specialization per se but by allowing it to become a dogma, a shibboleth. David Hume said that if a book has anything in it but reasoning and matters of numbers it should be cast into the fire. We see the same attitude in the modern logical positivist who says that literature, religion, and most philosophy do not mean anything. Or the linguistic analyst who reduces every statement of values to personal preference—"This is what I like. I wish you would like the same."—so that there is no referent beyond oneself. This adds to the mutual mistrust. Instead of trying to understand why a person says what she or he says, one is already seeing through and unmasking that person in advance.

The community of otherness is not an ideal. It is a direction in which we are trying to move, a reality that we are trying to build in every situation in which we find ourselves. I would question in the most serious fashion whether anything worthy of the name of learning is going on if there is not this dialogue that is open to otherness—not just in the sense that you may say your piece and I will say my piece, but in the sense that we grow together even in opposing each other, even in conflict, because we really are coming up against each other.

Heraclitus of Ephesus spoke of his fellow Ephesians as being "present yet absent." What teacher has not had that experience with his or her students? Presentness is not a thing. It is a presence with and toward others. The French Catholic existentialist philosopher Gabriel Marcel speaks of being with someone else who robs you of your own sense of presence through the way they are removed and detached. Presentness is a reality that happens between persons. What threatens this presence in learning is the tendency to divide thought from feeling so that we may imagine we are present if our thought is there even though our feelings are quite repressed. Not so long ago people turned that upside down and said that the only important thing is to have feeling—gut level hostility—and the rest is "mind-fucking." Presentness means being present with our whole being as we are at that moment. It means not withholding ourselves, but it does not mean saying everything that comes to mind. One way of not withholding ourselves is to have "the courage to address and the courage to respond." But not withholding ourselves also means *not* to address and respond if we are merely triggered off, if it is not really we who are being addressed and called to respond with our wholeness.

A curious form of nonpresentness that I have often seen is where people ask questions, putting the question forward but hiding themselves in the background. Once at a Pendle Hill lecture, a man whose face was deeply etched by the encounter with life asked a question about evil. After I had answered it, I said to him, "Perhaps you would like to say something from your experience." "Oh, I've never had any experience of evil," he replied. He was withholding himself, probably without being consciously aware that he was doing so.

The corollary of presentness and not withholding oneself is the recognition of truth as a manifestation and expression of the "between." For Martin Heidegger, truth is *aletheia*, the "unconcealment of Being," and *Logos* for Heidegger is the meaning of Being. For Buber, in contrast, *Logos* is the speech-with-meaning that arises in common in the process of building together a common cosmos. The truth that comes into being *between* us is far more and other than the sum or expression of our individual truths. It is a reality that would not have existed without real address and real response and the courage and risk that both of these entail.

Our truth, then, is a human truth. We do not *have* it, but we relate to it and witness for it. It only remains ours, moreover, if we are willing to bring our touchstones of reality into a dialogue of touchstones. The "dialogue of touchstones" is the way in which we share the unique events that become touchstones of reality for us. Sometimes we do this without speaking, just by the way we are—the way we bring ourselves to a situation, as I point out in *Touchstones of Reality*.

> We cannot say with what we make contact minus the touching, but the touching itself *is* a contact. It is not just that we have the *experience* of touching. On the contrary, to touch is to go through *and beyond* subjective experiencing: if I touch, if we touch, then there is a communication which is neither merely objective nor merely subjective, nor both together. The very act of touching is already a transcending of the self in openness to the impact of something other than the self. When two people really touch each other as persons—whether physically or not—the touching is not merely a one-sided impact: it is *a mutual revelation of life-stances*.[2]

Once I was addressing a large group of graduate students at the Humanistic Psychology Institute at Sonoma State College in northern California when a young man said to me, "Why can't you speak in such a way that a little child could understand you?" "I am speaking to graduate students," I thought to myself. "Why should I?" Later one of the professors present suggested that we have a "fishbowl." A group of twenty students sat in a circle with me and the rest stood around us and watched. We had a warm, lively conversation. Then a young woman in the circle said, "I had a feeling that you were annoyed with that young man." "Yes, you are right," I responded, assuming for some reason that he had left. "But when I looked in his face, I realized that he *was* that little child." No sooner had I said that than I realized that he was still there. "You can't tear the covers off the Bible," he exclaimed. (I was applying "touchstones of reality" to psychotherapy and had not mentioned the Bible or even religion.) "You have to start where the Bible starts, with Jesus Christ!" The beautiful, warm feeling in the fishbowl circle suddenly vanished. "What if I say, 'That is your bag, man, and this is ours'?" a student in the circle asked him. "Your bag is false," he retorted, "for *I* speak with the truth of God and *you* speak with the pride of men." Feeling called upon to make some response, I shared how I had known fundamentalists of many kinds when I was in Civilian Public Service camps for conscientious objectors during the Second World War and was often deeply impressed by their witness. But I could not confirm him in his notion that only *he* had the truth, nor his desire to impose his touchstone of reality on others without being willing to enter into a dialogue with their touchstones.

We discover the limits of the learning community in the concrete situation. In classes that most students take only because they fulfill a requirement, it is hard for true learning to take place, no matter how good the teacher may be. But even where the students are genuinely interested, they are often inhibited from taking part in class discussion by the fact that students are rewarded for articulateness. The students who are more facile with words than others get the best grades. Schools ought to be places where students could experiment and make mistakes. Instead they are all too often places where students are afraid to speak up for fear that what they say will not sound smooth and finished to the teacher or even to their fellow classmates. For years I wondered why it was that students would put their hands up and then invariably begin their comment or question by saying, "No." I finally concluded that that "No" was a disclaimer, a denial, something that made it safe to go ahead.

Even in very small colleges there is often very little chance for real learning and dialogue to take place because of lack of real communication. During the more than thirty years that I have taught I have again and again been struck by the fact that small colleges and even very small departments often have wretched communication. If you add to this the complexity of hierarchies, ranks, competitive grades, power and mistrust, the situation becomes more and more difficult. Once I thought it would be insulting to characterize as "Janus-faced" a dean's statement that as chair of a department of philosophy I would represent the administration to the faculty and the faculty to the administration, a term which she herself promptly proceeded to use. Yet this situation is far from the worst. In many departments, even small ones, the chair represents only the dean and the administration and does not really fight for the needs and legitimate interests of the faculty. There are scholars, moreover, whose thinking becomes altogether different when they ascend from professor to dean. Once such a person shocked me by saying to a woman professor in a grievance case, "I wish you good luck, but not in this case." She felt, and rightly so, that he was acting as a lawyer, an advocate of the administration.

At the heart of the learning community, as we have seen, stands genuine hearing. Yet hearing is not something we can aim at; it is a spontaneous matter. It cannot be done by an effort of the will. Still if we let it happen, we shall, sooner or later, find ourselves hearing on more levels than we could have imagined. Real hearing is not something that we *do* but something that takes place *between* us and the other. On the other hand, we must have made our lives such that presentness, openness, trust, and hearing are integral parts of them. If real hearing has no place in our actual life as persons, we shall not be able to practice it as teachers.

In the learning community too we cannot know our resources except by using them.

Chapter 15

Dialogue in Mentoring and Research

DANIEL J. LEVINSON sees initiating, modifying, and terminating relationships with mentors as "an important yet difficult task of early adulthood," and he defines a good mentor as an admixture of good father and good friend. Like the hierophant who initiated the devotee into the sacred mysteries, the mentor is guide, teacher, and sponsor in one—"a transitional figure who invites and welcomes a young man into the adult world." Levinson's study dealt only with the development of men, but what we say here applies equally to men and women. The good mentor not only helps the young to find their way and gain new skills. S/he enables them to identify with a person who exemplifies many of the qualities they seek and through this identification to internalize a figure who offers love, admiration, and encouragement in their struggles. The mentor not only represents the skill, knowledge, virtue, and accomplishment that the young hope someday to acquire. S/he also gives her blessing to the novice and the novice's Dream while conveying the promise that in time they will be peers. Levinson is fully aware of the possible negative aspects of a mentor-protégé relationship which may result in the suppression rather than the confirmation of otherness:

> There is plenty of room for exploitation, undercutting, envy, smothering and oppressive control on the part of the mentor, and for greedy demanding, clinging admiration, self-denying gratitude and arrogant ingratitude on the part of the recipient.[1]

Levinson defines mentoring as "a serious, mutual, non-sexual loving relationship with a somewhat older man or woman." Like all love relationships, its course is rarely smooth and its ending is often painful. In the course of termination, "both parties are susceptible to the most intense feelings of admiration and contempt, appreciation and resentment, grief, rage, bitterness and relief—just as in the way of any significant love relationship." But mentoring relationships are far less common than other types of love relationships. Despite emphasis on loyalty and teamwork, they are more the exception than the rule for both workers and managers. The system of higher education has inherited the institution of mentoring from classical Greece and the medieval universities, and it professes to continue it. Yet the reality in most institutions of higher learning falls far short of this profession: "Our system of higher education, though officially committed to fostering the intellectual and personal development of students, provides mentoring that is generally limited in quantity and poor in quality."[2]

One exception is the small progressive college, such as Sarah Lawrence, that has a built-in system of individual conferences and advising that is structured to bring the mentor and the protégé into close and regular contact. Another is the various "universities without walls" that have sprung up, such as the Union Graduate School, the Saybrook Institute, and Fielding Institute, all of which have cluster leaders and/or mentors of individuals and groups. One of these, International College, with headquarters in Los Angeles and a Guild of Tutors spread out over America, Europe, and parts of Asia and Africa, prides itself on reviving the medieval tradition of the tutor-student relationship. International College centers its education on the mentor-protégé relationship more than any other educational institution of which I am aware, particularly at the graduate levels leading to the M.A. and Ph.D. The 1981 Catalogue of International College sets forth its basic idea as that of bringing "mature and able students into close association with gifted and established leaders in a wide variety of disciplines."

While this may appear innovative today, the concept of an intensive tutor-student relationship is not new. Centuries ago students sought knowledge through close association with a sage or philosopher: Confucius in Lu, Socrates in Athens, Abelard in Paris. . . . The student enters the Tutor's world, physically as well as intellectually, residing near the Tutor and using . . . resources available there. Work and study are free from bureaucratic restraints and requirements. The Tutor's personal guidance, the Plan of Study, and the student's self-discipline determine the content and tempo of the educational process.[3]

Levinson holds that not only a change in institutions but also a change in the understanding and cultivation of middle adulthood is necessary for the mentoring relationship to flourish:

> Until middle adulthood is a better time of life, most of those who are in it will be unable to contribute the mentoring urgently needed by younger generations. Many middle-aged men never experience the satisfactions and tribulations of mentorhood. This is a waste of talent, a loss to the individuals involved, and an impediment to constructive social change.[4]

According to Levinson, not only mentoring relationships but mutual friendships are largely noticeable by their absence. Both friendship between one man and another and friendship between a man and a woman are rare in adult life in America. "Most men do not have an intimate male friend of the kind that they recall fondly from boyhood or youth," nor do they have an intimate, nonsexual friendship with a woman. This is surely a poignant commentary on the absence of "communities of otherness" and climates of trust in our society.

The doctoral dissertation, which should be the very flower of the mentor-protégé relationship, is, in fact, a prime example of Levinson's claim that our system of higher education provides mentoring that is limited in quantity and poor in quality. The original idea of a dissertation is that it should be a new contribution to knowledge. Yet in most places dissertations mean the opposite: learning the methodology of one's chief adviser and feeding that back in such a way that one's adviser and a couple of others are satisfied, without venturing beyond.

When we began to create the nonstatistical track at the California School of Professional Psychology-San Diego, we formed a science and psychology workshop which met over many months and then a support group that used to meet every week where students could share anxieties, problems, and methodologies. While it lasted, this support group was enormously important for the students who belonged to it. Most persons have threads of meaning—life concerns that are important to them. Yet they often lose touch with those threads because of professional pressures. Therefore, the task may be one of going back and getting hold of these threads. One may have to go through a disintegration of what I have come to call "premature professional crystallization" in order to integrate these threads into one's life. This can be greatly helped by such a weekly support group and by an hour to an hour-and-a-half per week of dialogue with the mentor. These threads are important because they are the way of organically moving forward—searching together for lost threads, finding what genuinely interests the student and what at the same time represents a significant and limitable problem. Starting with these threads, one identifies a field of interest; then one identifies certain problems within that field; gradually one delimits those problems to something that is doable. One does not start by delimiting; for that would shut off the real interest. This whole process can only be accomplished through genuine dialogue between mentor and student.

The mentor's effort to help in finding the lost threads of the person with whom he is working can even be a type of psychotherapy in the sense that one lets the other flounder and does not demand that the other always be conscious and articulate or clear about where he or she is going. At such times the student may fundamentally change what s/he is doing and feel her way along. It is then that it is particularly important for the mentor to understand where the student is coming from. This organic dialogue grows from week to week, sometimes taking place above and sometimes below the surface of consciousness. What is essential to it is the tact that is needed on the part of the mentor in sometimes allowing the protégé to be unclear and inarticulate and to go through trial and error. In this sense the task of the mentor stands at the borderline between the teacher and the therapist. The mentor is neither interested in the protégé just as a mind nor in the learning of a method by itself without concern for the person who is learning it. At the same time, the mentor *is* concerned about facts and about faithfulness to what is being done, because it is part of the human way that this person is taking. If the mentor insists on the protégé being too structured at every point in the process, it will prevent essential intellectual and personal growth and will frustrate what might have been accomplished.

After the mentor has helped the protégé to get back in touch with lost threads, he then helps him to identify an area of interest and then within that area to find a focus. Only after this is accomplished over whatever time it takes is it possible to find the central problem on which the dissertation will center and after that the methodology that fits this problem. The mentor is not just a nondirective person who listens and does not respond. The mentor at times places demands—demands that grow out of the dialogue itself. This cannot be done according to any prearranged schedule or as a technique. It must grow out of a relationship of trust and out of a tact that respects the tempo with which the protégé develops. The more there is a fixed time line and the more anxious and pressured the protégé is, the less this organic process can take place.

I once talked with a young man who wanted to do a clinical psychology dissertation on the modern Hindu sage Krishnamurti. I responded with some enthusiasm, yet he dropped out of the nonstatistical track for a year and a half and only returned when enough security had been built up in the program to change the overall atmosphere of the school and to allay his anxiety. I also discovered when he returned that the very creativity of my response to him, in which I suggested a combination of Eastern and Western psychology and philosophy, had made him feel that now it had become *my* dissertation instead of his. In my very effort to respond I had failed to be attuned to a delicate process that was going on and had unwittingly taken over. The task of the mentor is to help this person become his or her self in response to the world this person stands in relation to. This person needs help. Yet the mentor cannot take over for her.

To help a person grow toward independence and to find a ground of his or her own is a very subtle thing, one that depends not upon the mentor alone, moreover, but on the dialogue itself. In this sense the mentoring relationship depends upon existential trust *and* upon existential grace. When the protégé really responds to the mentor in the dialogue, the mentor is not the cause and the protégé is not the effect. Rather it is, in the most exact sense of the term, a matter of betweenness. The mentor cannot expect to receive from the protégé the confirmation that comes in mutual friendship or love, but if the protégé is willing to let the mentor help, that is the greatest gift that person can give. In this dialogue, both mentor and protégé come to life in the fullness of their beings.

The demands that the mentor places upon the protégé arise from the relationship itself. One time it may be telling a student who is inclined to pick what appears to be an easy topic without its having any special meaning for him or her that s/he ought to accept the challenge of a more difficult topic that is personally and intellectually meaningful. Another time it may be dissuading the student from dropping out. Always it is getting a sense of what that person's threads are and holding the person to that while being open at the same time to a number of changes of topic so long as these seem to be genuine attempts to stay with these threads. If the mentor at times allows the protégé to be conscious and at times inchoate, the mentor too is intuitive and at times acts without consciously knowing why. There is a sense of leading, but this is not leading according to any prearranged end. Rather it is getting a sense of the protégé's thread of meaning and moving with it. That is why it is so important that there be regular dialogue between mentor and protégé. The mentor brings his or her own context to that of the protégé, but s/he also gets a sense of the protégé's context as other than his or her own.

If we were to try to describe this in stages, we might speak, first, of a mutual attraction in which mentor and protégé get to know each other, a stage of excitement and unfolding. Then there is a stage of building mutual trust in the relationship. The third stage is that of working together. This stage includes the subtle listening and tact of which we have spoken, the musical, floating response of the mentor to the protégé. We might speak also of a fourth stage that comes with the occasional crisis that arises—the inner turmoil which goes beyond the task of finding a topic to the person in the whole sense, including, of course, his or her intellectually struggling forward. This stage calls for patience and for love. Finally there is a stage of completion, one in which the protégé accomplishes his or her task and moves from being a protégé to a peer, even though in the best relationships an informal mentor relationship may persist throughout the lifetimes of both.

Being a good mentor is really a matter of walking the "narrow ridge"—being involved but not too attached or too personally invested. Because the mentoring relationship is a personal one, it includes not only the possibilities of conflict but also of tragedy, where there are not enough resources on either side to bridge the gap and convert painful contradiction into creative growth. One of the built-in aspects of this conflict is that the person the mentor is working with has to make a living, to get a job. The mentor must be respectful of this need and of the structures that go with it. Yet the mentor must at the same time resist becoming a tool of the protégé's professionalism which wishes to exploit the relationship exclusively in terms of making it in the profession. The mentor needs to encourage the protégé to take risks yet recognize that the protégé may not have the personal resources that the mentor herself had or that the situation which faces the protégé may be worse than the one which the mentor herself originally faced. The mentor holds this tension between professionalism and personal growth not just for the personal satisfaction that the mentor may attain but also for the sake of the protégé himself who must learn to hold creatively the tension between personal calling and social role.[5]

What we have said of the mentoring relationship has already given us some intimations of the way in which the protégé may carry on research which can in itself be a genuine dialogue with and confirmation of otherness. This is particularly true of "non-statistical" research—theoretical, philosophical, historical, phenomenological, existentialist, humanistic, or case study. Of central significance to such qualitative research is that in every case the proper methodology is developed only *after* the tasks of discovering the larger area of interest, delimiting the parameters of this area, and focussing on issues and problems within this delimited area is completed. The researcher begins with some general methodological approach, but the specific methodology that the researcher uses should develop in dialectic with the research itself, particularly as it moves into depth studies of individual cases. Scientism is the adulation of certain methodologies that have worked well in physics, chemistry, or biology and the uncritical application of them to psychology or the social sciences. There is no one right methodology for all cases but only the methodology that best helps one investigate the problem that one has chosen.

The basic tool of qualitative research is an open-ended dialogue with the persons one interviews. No interviewee will be fool enough to pour out her heart and soul if one presents oneself as a sort of machine. The researcher must take part in the dialogue, and the way in which one takes part is going to have an enormous impact on the results one obtains. The more one presents oneself as the detached observer, the less response one will get. Human beings, as Buber points out in "Elements of the Interhuman" (*The Knowledge of Man*), know how to shut others out; they know how *not* to reveal themselves to the other. This is especially true when they are confronted with someone who wants to see what makes them "tick." Only as a person, only as a partner in dialogue, will one be able to get any understanding of the other person's wholeness and uniqueness, for it cannot be understood as an object.

Everything that you present in an interview is setting a tone, a stage. The more structured you are, the less you will have a chance to discover the unique that this person can give you and the depths from which this person can speak. The scenes in court-rooms offer a real anti-model; for there people are told to stick to the question and are not allowed to bring themselves in in their own way. One has to give the people one investigates a chance to talk in depth. Only in that way will one also begin to discover the highlights—what is important to someone and what is not. Otherwise, everything is at a dead level. If one focuses the inter-view in such a way that one gets the interviewee to answer ten questions, then one does not know how to rank those questions in terms of their importance to this person.

Of course, a lot depends on the interviewer. If interviewees see that one is only in it as a business, that one's only interest in them is to get data for one's research, they are not likely to talk very much. An open-ended dialogue is not one where one brings so much that one prevents the other from answering but where one brings oneself. There are people who will disclose themselves to one person because they trust that person and not to another because they do not trust him or her. That may not have anything to do with what the person says.

People imagine the I-Thou to be subjective and the I-It objec-tive. Actually it is the other way around. The I-It is *subjective* because it brings with it its categories and looks only at what fits them. The I-Thou is *objective* in the sense that it does not bring categories. It tries to perceive the unique. For example, Kurt Wolff, a distinguished American sociologist and anthropologist, lived among the Loma Indians for three years after which he wrote a book called *Surrender and Catch*. Instead of coming with his questions and categories already formed, he lived with the Loma Indians long enough to understand from *their* side what was unique to them. The "surrender" was the surrender to them—to their uniqueness. The "catch" was his response.

The contrasting and much more usual approach is illustrated by Abraham Kardiner, a distinguished psychoanalyst and direct disciple of Freud. In the 1950s Kardiner gave a talk about a society where children were raised differently from those of any other society, pointing out all the nefarious effects of such child rearing. Since he was unmistakably talking about the kibbutzim in Israel, I asked him after the lecture about his stay in Israel. "I've never been to Israel," he replied. "I am a Park Avenue anthropologist. I send my students to Israel, and they bring back to me the results of the TAT tests they administer."

It is not possible to remove all one's biases and assumptions, but it is possible to be more aware of them and more aware of what one is bringing to the dialogue and what one's part is in it. One should show the process one goes through so people can understand where one is coming from. The investigator should be present, including his or her passion. It is possible to have passion and still allow the other person to be free. It is bad only when one lets one's passion override the situation so that the other feels s/he has to fit in with one or fight against one. While one does not want to impose the answer on the person one is interviewing or to straitjacket them, one should give the other person a feeling of one's lived concern.

What we are talking about is not easily attained. No degree or license guarantees that one has reached that level of personal wholeness through which one can be truly present. Yet that is a direction worth working toward; for only such presentness makes possible the open-ended dialogue of meaningful qualitative research that has its part to play in building the community of otherness.

Chapter 16

REFLECTIONS ON INTENTIONAL COMMUNITY

WHEN THE nineteenth-century German sociologist Ferdinand Tönnies made his famous distinction between *Gemeinschaft* and *Gesellschaft*—organic community and that loose association that we find in most institutions—he used as his model for *Gemeinschaft* the hereditary family, class, and guild systems of the Middle Ages. When Martin Buber took over that same distinction, he extended the meaning of *Gemeinschaft* to intentional communities, communities that are neither hereditary nor familial in basis but seek to make up for the lack of organic community in our time by living together in larger or smaller groups.

In *Paths in Utopia*, his classic study of utopian socialism, Buber devotes a chapter to "Experiments"—the utopian communities of nineteenth-century England and America, the producers, consumers, and full cooperatives of Europe and America, and the religious communities such as the Hutterite Brothers and the Dukhobors of Canada.[1] What Buber concludes from the history of these experiments is of significance for the confirmation of otherness in community: 1) the smallness of the communes was not in itself a drawback; 2) the full cooperatives had more meaning than the producers' or consumers' cooperatives; 3) the religious communities proved more enduring than those founded upon the basis of utopian socialist theories because they had a center beyond the mutual benefit of cooperation; and 4) communication and even federation among communities is necessary for their fruitful interaction. In addition, the young will not tolerate being isolated and cut off. In the last chapter of *Paths in Utopia* Buber points to the kibbutzim in Israel as an example of an experiment that did not fail. They combine the production and consumption of the full cooperatives and the village commune with the devotion of the religious communities.

In our own day the famous behaviorist psychologist B. F. Skinner has offered a somewhat mechanistic formula for the confirmation of otherness in community in his utopian novel *Walden Two*.[2] Reasoning, quite correctly, that no one likes to do all the dirty work, he suggests greater credit for less pleasant work, a method of calculation which his followers at Twin Oaks, a commune in Virginia, have tried to put into practice.

The story of the communes of the 1960s and early '70s has yet to be written. Some of these communes were centered on drugs, some on radical politics, some on religion, some on sexual freedom or nudity; some were city communes and some were agricultural. One particularly short-lived commune in Germantown, Philadelphia, had as its motto, "The family that lays together stays together." All of them represented interesting experiments in intentional community; few of them demonstrated an ability to last beyond the cultural milieu which created them and endure in the later, more conservative era that followed.

Linda Savage, who has lived for a decade in city communes in Miami, Chicago, and San Diego, has made an impressive witness to the community of otherness in her writings on communes and intentional community. Beginning with the distinction between "enclaves of cultures, geographic locations, or blood groups and physiology which set men apart from each other" and "the new consciousness" which "sees every individual difference as an addition to the richness and fulfillment of all," she rejects the tendency of people of the "old culture" to see a "commune of the new consciousness . . . as creating like minded and like behaving 'homogenized' people":

> Fulfillment *is* difference and, at the same time, the appreciation and sharing of others' differences is fulfilling to one's own being as much as his ability to be unique. The mistake of communes of the past has been the emphasis upon sameness, whether it be beliefs, life styles or needs.[3]

At the same time she recognizes that "communal living . . . has to be based on some goals or values held in common or the assertion of 'community' would be meaningless." These things that are held in common, however, do not need to be at the expense of the uniqueness of the individual members or the realization of the community of otherness:

> The trick, of course, is to negotiate a minimum of commonly agreed upon norms which will make living together possible. These shared norms must never be locked into rigid rules since needs will change with the growth of the individuals within the community. Because living is an ever-moving trip, we cannot apply previous rules to future circumstances. If individual uniqueness is to be encouraged and appreciated, nothing must be locked in, final or absolute. The amount of trust, of giving, of going with the flow must be enormous. *Trust is the foundation principle upon which all else is built.*[4]

Savage's recognition of the fundamental importance of trust means, of course, that there can be no techniques which will ensure that the commune will, in fact, be or remain a community of otherness. Some of the most successful of communes, such as Findhorn, have begun, in fact, on highly autocratic, centralized lines and only later allowed delegation of responsibility and trust in the community to enter in. Nonetheless, Savage has some practical suggestions for communes which themselves are based on a distinction between what I would call a climate of mistrust (Theory X, which assumes that people are basically lazy and must be watched, prodded and clocked) and a climate of trust (Theory Y, which assumes that work is as natural to people as play and celebration and that the right kind of structure coupled with the involvement of the work force in decision making would lead to work being done in an efficient yet noncoercive manner):

> Members should be given areas of responsibility and they will be responsible for completing a task with a minimum amount of supervision. Goals and timetables should be mutually agreed upon both for the completing of the task and the growth of the individual. Some spiritual communities, particularly the more traditional ones, have fallen into the trap of Theory X organizational structures. The leadership is not shared and inflexible

rules stifle the individual's creativity. However, the majority of the emerging new communities are leaning toward Theory Y.[5]

Particularly significant in Savage's pointers for intentional communities of otherness is her emphasis upon the need for flexible interaction between structure and spontaneity:

> There needs to be a stable balance between the Gestalt, free flowing, spontaneous way of life and the development of linear structures which enable the flow to go on without being diverted by unwarranted disorganization. A certain amount of linear planning and organization can guide a well-intentioned group through all of the early crises in developing a community. However, there should always be built into these linear structures a way to continue changing them as the needs of the community change. Nothing should remain fixed or absolute. Our basic organization goal is transformation, which does not thrive on rigid linear structures. Transformation transforms and does not stop, it is the ongoing process of ever-changing change itself.[6]

This also means, as Savage points out, that the community should be sufficiently flexible to be able to carry on without its founders and central leaders since these too change and leave.

Linda Savage and her co-author Jerry Spiegel make an interesting tie-in between the problem of confirming otherness in the family and the problem of confirming otherness in community. They point out that the nuclear family is itself an experiment, only fifty years old, motivated by the desire of young couples to break away from stifling traditional norms. Before that, marriage existed as a part of an extended family, tribe, or clan. The price of this newfound freedom for the nuclear family was the loss of the crucial emotional support and work sharing of the larger family. In the face of the failure of this experiment, with a divorce rate of 50 percent and rising, Savage and Spiegel propose the commune as a form that can combine emotional support, work sharing, and the integrity and freedom of the marriage couple:

> The Intentional Community can provide for both the individual expression and the support of a larger social grouping. People express fears that living in a commune will break the bonds of a strong couple relationship, but this is not necessarily the case. In

fact, the Intentional Community can enhance rather than detract from this relationship.[7]

My own reflections on intentional community are based upon my direct and indirect contacts with these communes and with other attempts at organic community in our time. The houses at Harvard were established to promote fellowship among the students. At Eliot House, where I lived, the richer students lived on the ground floor in expensive suites while the scholarship students, like myself, lived on the fifth floor. In the dining room no student would sit with another whom he did not know, or even talk with those who had not been to prep schools at least as good as his own. It was with some surprise that I discovered, when some of my fellow Eliot House men got drunk after one of Harvard's rare wins at the football field, that some of them actually knew my name. If a black student sat down at a table with them, they would get up and move away. When I sprained my ankle and had to be on crutches for six weeks, I continued to hurtle down five flights. It was not until I was almost well that the Eliot House Secretary said that she should have thought of putting me up in some first-floor suite during this time.

My own friends hardly made me feel more at home. They made up for what they lacked in social status by engaging, whenever possible, in intellectual putdowns. When I went to an International Student Service work camp between my sophomore and junior years, I was so rubbed raw from Harvard that I resolved not to speak to the first work campers I met there unless they spoke to me first. By the end of the summer, I was so impressed by the social democracy at the work camp that I thought of transferring to Swarthmore College, where one of the work campers went and which I imagined to be a small informal college somewhat after the pattern of the work camp itself.

The following year at Harvard I established weekend work camps, or "work-ends," as we later called them, with Harvard and seven other colleges in the Boston area. In the cities we worked at settlement houses and slums. In the country we picked apples. In both places we sang songs and danced and lived and felt the spirit of community. None of this prepared me for what it would be like to spend three and a half years in Civilian Public Service camps for conscientious objectors, as I did during World

War Two. The curious mixture of compulsion (behind these camps lay the threat of prison) and the attempt at continuing the spirit of voluntary community we captured in our songs:

> *The other night at dinner*
> *They fed us chicken soup,*
> *And right there in the middle of it*
> *We found the "will of the group."*
> *I don't want to stay in C.P.S.*
> *Ma, I wanna go home.*
>
> .   .   .
>
> *Working at forty below,*
> *Working at forty below,*
> *Working at forty below, Lord, Lord,*
> *And I ain't gonna be treated this away.*
>
> *Working for eight cents a day,*
> *Working for eight cents a day,*
> *Working for eight cents a day, Lord, Lord,*
> *And I ain't gonna be treated this away.*

(The German prisoners of war were paid a salary by the government while we were literally slave labor. The eight cents a day referred to the $2.50 per month which the American Friends Service Committee gave us as an "allowance.")

In a side or "spike" camp in California where we were on standby for fighting forest fires, we discovered that we were something less than the blessed community we aspired to be. The Harvard men in one tent could not get on with the four fellows from Rochester in the next tent who wore cowboy hats and pretended to be shooting each other all the time. This conflict gave rise to a variation on the *Titanic:*

> *It was sad,*
> *It was sad,*
> *It was sad when Dog Valley Camp was found,*
> *Yellow C.O.'s*
> *Very nearly came to blows.*
> *It was sad when Dog Valley Camp was found.*

After the war I concluded that I would not voluntarily again go into a system that so destroyed the personality with its meaningless "make work," digging ditches in the winter that any tractor could have done in one thousandth the time, throwing rocks off the road. It was conscription and punishment (we were not allowed to be within 600 miles of our draft boards since they did not want us returning home on our rare furloughs) in the disguise of "work of national importance." The enthusiasm of my work camp days quickly vanished in the face of the reality of that strange anomaly—a compulsory system of meaningless work run voluntarily by the Mennonite, Brethren, and Friends Service Committees in the name of religion, pacifism, and high ideals. Recently I was invited to a reunion of Civilian Public Service men who had been at Coleville camp in California. Though the reunion was nearby, I found I had nothing to celebrate from those years, and I did not want to relive one of the most painful periods of my life.

I spent three and a half years in Civilian Public Service camps and units (I worked for a year and a half in "detached service" as an attendant at what would today be regarded as a fairly medieval institute for the "feebleminded"). During the last year of my service, I came in contact with the "Creative House" about which I have written in *Touchstones of Reality*, a group of young people living together in what would have been called twenty years later a commune. I have already described the Creative House as a "modern gnostic" venture in "overrunning reality." In terms of the confirmation of otherness, what was striking about it was the appearance of an organic group in which each member was going through deep transformation that concerned not only his or herself but every other person in the group. The deeper reality was the domination by "Caroline," the twenty-six-year-old leader of this totally nonprofessional "psychodrama."

My next experience with intentional community was as a house parent for a "Students-in-Industry" summer in Columbus, Ohio, in the summer of 1947. My chief memory of this is the difficulty of getting the boys (including the director!) out of the girls' house at curfew. The students came from various parts of the country and got jobs in industry as best they could. Perhaps the most important influence on the young people was the black cook who acted and spoke with an authority that none of us leaders could command.

It might seem strange to include my years at Sarah Lawrence College in my experiences of intentional community. Yet we did try to build something and for a while we seemed to succeed. One of the ways we did this was through the "Teaching Faculty" which operated as a committee of the whole until, as an expression of mistrust in the faculty, the Board of Trustees abolished it. After this came secret meetings of "Young" or "Middle-Aged Turks" and the Sarah Lawrence chapter of the American Association of University Professors, an informal and certainly unauthorized replacement for the Teaching Faculty.

During the 1950s, I came to know Staughton Lynd. Staughton carried the political liberalism of his parents, Helen and Robert Lynd, into the social by joining Macedonia, an intentional community in Georgia. Macedonia, like Celo Community in North Carolina (founded by Arthur Morgan of the TVA) was one of the few successful agricultural communes in the South that lasted over several decades. It was an organic community, but it was also a democracy. It was with some dismay, therefore, that I learned that Macedonia had been taken over by the Bruderhof. The Bruderhof was a religious community, or rather group of related communities, originally founded by Eberhard Arnold in Germany after the First World War. Originally a product of the German youth movement, later it identified itself with the Anabaptists of the seventeenth century. When Hitler came to power, it took refuge in South America and then moved to the United States. The Bruderhof is an excellent illustration of what Buber has said about the need for federation, but its methods leave something to be desired as far as the community of otherness is concerned. It is, in fact, a not too well concealed theocracy in which the decisions are made by a small group of leaders at the center. This applies not only to the taking over of Macedonia and the running of their communities at Reston, New York, and elsewhere, but also to the private lives of their members. While he was there, Staughton Lynd was instructed to divorce his wife who was then made to move out of the community leaving the children behind.

Pendle Hill, during the twenty years when Dan Wilson was director, offered a notable contrast to the Bruderhof. Pendle Hill was not a pure democracy. There was structure and order, yet there was individual freedom in the deepest sense and there were attempts to build real community through common work, common study, and common prayer. Although not all or even most of the resident community were Quakers, much of the spirit of Pendle Hill was Quaker—from its subtitle, "A Quaker Study Center," to the daily silent meeting for worship in the barn, to the business meetings which were carried out, insofar as possible, in the spirit of the Friends Business Meeting according to the "sense of the meeting" rather than majority vote and parliamentary rules. This spirit also carried over to the volleyball court, where poor players and children were accorded equal rights with good players and adults.

This spirit was not quite sufficient to sustain Pendle Hill during the turbulent years of the late '60s. Once we organized a Pendle Hill Seminar. Our attempts to have meetings of the whole were disrupted by students pounding the benches and shouting at the speaker (a fellow Pendle Hiller like themselves, though in this case a professor who really knew something), "Who do you think you are? God?" In the groups of about twelve each, we met with no better fate. Two Pendle Hillers undertook to lead a session on some of the problems they had encountered as psychiatric social workers. Though the leader of the group, I said nothing for forty-five minutes. The session was taken over by three young men: one a Nietzschean romantic, one a self-styled Zen Buddhist, and one a self-styled Tibetan Buddhist. When I finally did try to say something, one of these three clapped his hands above his head the whole time, claiming that I was interrupting him, which the Tibetan Buddhist, who was also my advisee, kindly explained to me later was because I was "irrelevant." It was not only I who was irrelevant but the scheduled speakers and everyone else, old or young, who was not as "in" as they were.

There were some real gains in those years in the realization of a community of otherness at Pendle Hill, from the nature of the classes to interest groups started and conducted by various students, to participation of the faculty and students in decision making. Many of these gains have been "corrected" in subsequent years in the name of restoring Pendle Hill to what it was before Dan Wilson and of making it a more truly "Quaker" institution. Even at the height of Pendle Hill as a community of otherness, there was always a certain measure of fear and mistrust of uncomfortable voices, a mistrust which expressed itself by the Board going into "executive session" at regular intervals, at which point they excluded the faculty members of the Board.

It was during the '60s that a remarkable offshoot of Quakerism and Pendle Hill came into being which was also, in its way, a true community of otherness. This was the Working Party for the Future of the Quaker Movement, which I have described in

Touchstones of Reality. Some of what I have written there is of sufficient importance for our understanding of the confirmation of otherness in community that it merits being repeated here:

> Despite its grandiose title, our Working Party for the future of the Quaker Movement really consisted of a small group of eight or nine intellectuals who met three weekends a year for intensive sharing of where we had come from, where we were, and where we felt we were going. Sometimes we thought of our sessions as autobiographical excursions, sometimes as confirming each other in our *daimons,* or callings, sometimes as a dialogue of metaphors, or the interchange of the myths that "spoke to our condition."
>
> In an important way these four years advanced my own understanding of touchstones of reality; for we met across all differences in an intense mutual sharing and caring that went beyond the search for common formulae. My very presence in the group, as a Jew and not a Quaker, already implied that loyalty to the Society of Friends did not preclude fellowship with committed seekers outside of it. At times we had to make a distinction between the Society of Friends and the "Quaker movement." If the Society of Friends creates an environment in which its members feel at home, that raised for us the question of whether a feeling of belonging and being a vanguard movement, or thrust into the future, go together. There is a persistent danger of confusing affinity and community. . . . Is there not a community of otherness that would make Quakerism really a movement and not an institution?
>
> What the Friends call the "gathered meeting"—the silent meeting in which the presence is at once personal and communal—tells us something important about the nature of religious truth. We do not need to use the same words as others or even to affirm that beneath our different words and images we really mean the same thing. . . . Our Working Party could never reach the place where it could agree on Christ-centeredness as a central term for everyone, nor could it reach the place where everyone would agree to dispense with that term. The greatness of the gathered meeting lies in the fact that it does not start with an *a priori* unity but with a genuine trust. We receive from each other without ever being identical with each other; we are able to affirm and respond to what we receive, and grow through it. The genius of Quaker worship, at its finest, lies in the fact that it does not seek any sort of abstract or conceptual unity or criterion

of faith. Nor can one speak of an experienced unity attained during the meeting—only community and communion, which enables us to be really different and yet together. To some members of the Working Party, Christ remained an ultimate beyond which they could not go to any sort of higher abstraction that would be more satisfactory to them. Yet in contrast to those who turn their Christology into an exclusive way to God, they were not imprisoned in it and had no trouble talking to non-Christians as well as to Christians for whom Christ was not central. . . .

One of the ways in which the members of the Working Party shared their witnesses with each other was bringing into the group from one time to the next some of the important life-issues they had had to wrestle with in the interim—operations for cancer, changing one's vocation, moving to a different community, facing death. But an equally important form of witnessing for us was our dialogue of metaphors, our expounding and mutual testing of the myths that best embodied our own touchstones of reality. We were soon forced to recognize that we would never find a common myth that would unite us. We shared our myths with each other and grew in the strength to live without a single or an all-encompassing myth. . . .

In the course of our discussion of myth I glimpsed . . . a "metamyth" which included both the individual daimons of the members of the group and that spirit which joined us together as a group. . . . In contrast to the myths of process, evolution, and the unconscious which we had, *it* possessed *us*. We could not objectify or articulate it. It removed the very desire for a common myth; for it held us together, borne in a common stream. . . . Wherever persons of no matter what religion or none at all meet in a spirit of common concern, ready to encounter each other beyond their terminologies, this "myth" can come into being and with it the lived reality of community. . . .

What emerged for me from our four years of the Working Party as the uniqueness of the Quaker movement is . . . a way of being faithful and diverse at the same time. . . . The distinctiveness of the Quaker movement might be precisely a quality of gathered presence which would give us the trust that would enable us to affirm religious pluralism. . . . One of the geniuses of the Friends has been the recognition that the spirit moves in the group, and that no one *has* it. The spirit that speaks through us is a response to the spirit that we meet in others, the spirit that meets us in the "between." . . .

Without ever reaching an overarching word, our Working Party glimpsed the meeting of one *logos* and another, felt our "ultimate concerns" touch one another through and beyond all words. This going *through* the word to a meeting *beyond* the word can be a more powerful witness to the imageless God than any dogma, creed, theology, or metaphysic.[8]

Another high point of Pendle Hill as a community of otherness was the national conference on communes and underground churches held in the summer of 1969. At that moment we were able to touch the pulse of a great striving for community of otherness that manifested itself in many different places and forms during those years—and as quickly disappeared during the years after 1974. At the same time I must record some aspects of this conference on underground churches and communes that showed the limits to the community of otherness. Aside from problems with people who wanted to camp their campers on Pendle Hill grounds and the surprising defection of one of the members of the planning committee to some sort of unscheduled alternative conference that suddenly arose out of nowhere, there was the realism of the wife of the black leader, Mohammed X, who pointed out that, although communes had a lot to offer the black population of Philadelphia and other great cities, the blacks in general did not have the leisure that would make the imagining and planning of such communes possible.

The enemies of the community of otherness are rigidity, mistrust, fear, hysteria, insensitivity, and unconcern. The confirmation of otherness in community is only possible through a respect for the spirit of the community so deep, realistic, and concrete that the diversity and otherness of the members and the smaller groups and relationships are included in that respect. This means in turn a flexible interaction between structure and spontaneity, genuine listening and genuine response, and mutual openness and trust. But by the same token it means an openness to other communities that can lead to the confirmation of otherness in society and even toward a genuine community of communities.

What is most important to remember is that the community of otherness is neither an ideal nor a specific goal. It is a direction of movement within particular, ever-changing situations. The support group of students doing "nonstatistical" (qualitative or phenomenological) dissertations at CSPP was in its own way a community of otherness as has been a Hasidic tales discussion group that has met once a month for more than four years now. This group meets at some home in the greater San Diego area for a potluck supper. Before supper we begin by focussing on one or another section of Buber's *Tales of the Hasidim* or, at times, my own selection of tales that I call "Hasidic Healing and Helping." The members of the group are psychologists, social workers, professors of philosophy, graduate students, and other kinds of persons, many of whom are neither Jewish nor religious.

Each time, two or three persons share with the group a tale from the agreed-on section that has spoken to his or her condition, reading the tale aloud and explaining its impact on his or her life or thinking. The other members respond from where each of them is not only to the tale but also to the person who is sharing the tale. At the end of the discussion of that tale, the person who read it originally asks another member of the group to read it aloud again. This reading aloud adds another voice, another interpretation, another life-stance and meaning to those that have already arisen in the original reading and the discussion of the tale.

At the beginning of each such meeting the members introduce themselves (there are never the same people twice though there is always some core of those who continue). The participants report what has happened to them in the month since the group met or what is important to them at this moment in their lives. Over the years it has become a sort of floating community that others hear about and join. It is never very large, not more than twenty or so, and there is no formal structure. Yet every time the group elects to meet again the following month, even through the summer.

One more form of "intentional community" to which I can witness out of firsthand knowledge is the International Center for Integrative Studies (ICIS) of New York City, and its offshoot, "The Door." When I first became acquainted with ICIS in the early 1960s, I thought of it as an exceptionally high-powered organization of intellectuals who were rapidly building a worldwide system of communication among scholars and thinkers of all disciplines and were promoting communication among them through their organ, *The Forum*. Some years later, however, I took part in an intensive weekend that ICIS sponsored among a handful of *Forum* members, and I discovered that the intellectual organization rested on the foundation of a genuine community inspired by ICIS Director, Erling Thunberg. Over the years, I have remained close to this community which showed its genuineness and staying power in the mutual presence and caring which nourished Erling in his months of final illness and carried the group forward in the years after his untimely death.

A new stage of ICIS began in 1972 with the establishment of a community-based multiservice center for youth appropriately named "The Door—A Center of Alternatives." In the course of repeated visits to The Door, which has become in the last ten years a flourishing institution which serves as a national and international model, I discovered that the spirit of genuine community which informed ICIS had been carried over to the management of its offspring—so much so, indeed, that I became convinced that here, as nowhere else, was a true exemplar of the "community of otherness." This has continued to be the case even amidst administrative crises which have led to the departure of some of the original administrators of The Door.

I know of no better way to convey the importance and scope of the "community of otherness" which The Door has become than to quote extensively from the brochure *Inside the Door*, which celebrates The Door's coming of age on the occasion of its tenth anniversary.

The Initial Development

In the late '60s and '70s, drug abuse, violent crime, delinquency, alienation from families and other problems were having an unprecedented impact on the lives of urban youth. Problems ranged from teenage pregnancy, prostitution and venereal diseases to mental illness, low academic achievement, dropping out of school and high unemployment. It was clear that many needs of urban youth were not being met. . . .

Accepting this challenge—and seeing it as an opportunity—the original team of young professionals in the fields of medicine, psychiatry, law, education, social work and the arts set out to develop a model program to offer young people relevant services, programs and meaningful life alternatives. . . . At the start, there was no money, no space, no equipment and no staff—only a group of deeply concerned volunteers who recognized the crisis of inner-city youth and were determined to do something about it. . . .

In January, 1972, The Door opened and, with an entirely volunteer staff and no funding, began to provide free services to youth from throughout the city. . . .

Since its inception, The Door has emphasized the value of a holistic and human approach within the context of an intensive working relationship between young people and staff.

The Door Family—Young People and Staff

The clients range in age from 12 to 20, with the majority between the ages of 15 and 18. Fifty-one percent are male, and forty-nine percent female. Drawn from all ethnic backgrounds, they include 43% Black, 23% Hispanic, 22% white, 2% Oriental, 10% other.

The vast majority live in decaying areas of the city, under conditions of poverty, in unstable family circumstances and with substandard educational and vocational opportunities.

Forty-eight percent are no longer in school—most of these are dropouts; twenty-eight percent have no regular means of support; nearly fifty percent are not living at home.

Despite their many and often deep-seated problems, the young people who come to The Door are often wise in practical knowledge and possess vitality, team spirit and untapped creative potential. . . .

Many youth need a nonthreatening environment where they can find help. In a real sense, The Door—with its supportive milieu, holistic philosophy, caring and concerned staff—is a direct response to such needs.

Staff members are selected on the basis of their human qualities, their professional skills, their concern for young people and their ability to work sensitively with youth.

The staff consists of full-time and part-time professionals and paraprofessionals, as well as volunteers who contribute their services on a regular basis. The disciplines include: internists, gynecologists and pediatricians, family planning and sex counselors; nutritionists, nurses, health educators; psychiatrists and psychologists, social workers, caseworkers and mental health workers; lawyers, teachers, and educational, job, drug and alcohol counselors; theatre, dance and music instructors; artists, craftsmen, and youth workers. . . .

A climate of mutual concern and trust encourages young people to share experiences, express themselves creatively and change for the better.

Treating the Whole Person

The Door is a client-centered, supportive and socially constructive environment where young people are free to explore new patterns of interaction and behavior with peers and adults, as well as values and life directions. Within this reality-oriented setting, youth are motivated to deepen their insight into their own life situations and to cope more effectively with their various life problems.

Toward Basic Change

The Youth Leadership and Youth Worker Program provides paraprofessional training for young people who wish to be of service to others and are ready to assume leadership among their peers at The Door and in their schools and communities.

Links with the Community

Since its inception, The Door has made it a priority to develop close working relationships with existing youth-related agencies and institutions throughout New York City. Links with the neighborhood, the community at large, and a broad sector of youth service institutions have been steadily expanded and The Door currently has an extensive network of interagency liaison, referral and back-up arrangements with more than 350 agencies and institutions throughout New York City. These include schools, hospitals, health and mental health facilities, social service agencies, churches, courts, legal aid agencies, residences for adolescents, residential drug and alcohol treatment programs, public health and other youth care agencies.

Managing the Door

Making The Door work well takes a combination of tough-minded practicality, flexibility and a visionary sense of future potential. The Door's management systems and practices have evolved through an open-ended process over several years and have included strong emphasis on team management, with an interdisciplinary professional team sharing overall responsibility for the program.

The Door's organizational structure centers around a three-tiered management system with each group responsible for a realm of decision making and functioning.

The Administrative Staff consists of seven senior professionals who have worked closely together since founding The Door and are responsible for overall programmatic and financial management. . . .

Each service area is headed by a Coordinator. The Coordinating Staff supervise service functions and program areas, and direct and supervise service staff on a day-to-day operational level. The Coordinators work closely together as a group and, together, are responsible for the daily management and integration of the overall program.

The third tier consists of the general staff, both professional and paraprofessional, from all service and program areas. All staff have substantial freedom and responsibility within their service and program areas. Creativity and initiative-taking are encouraged. . . .

The Door Looks Ahead

An expanded programmatic commitment will be made toward the many "more together" young people who are searching for greater meaning in their lives. To deal with this need, the Adolescent Identity Program will be expanded to help larger numbers of young people cope better with normal "growing-up pains," sexual identity, personal and social relationships and development of their human and social potential.[9]

With our discussion of The Door, we have already anticipated Part Five—"Confirmation of Otherness in Society" and particularly John Friedmann's call for "task-oriented working groups" which I second in Chapter 21—"The Community of Otherness and the Covenant of Peace."

At the end of his essay, "The Psychologizing of the World," Martin Buber makes a profound statement about the community of otherness, one that sees the instability and even breakdown of community as a part of the way of community in our time:

The community does not have its meaning in itself. It is the abode where the divine has not yet consumed itself, the abode of the coming theophany. If one knows this, then one also knows that community in our time must ever again miscarry. . . . But the disappointments belong to the way. There is no other way than that of this miscarrying. That is the way of faithful faith.[10]

Part V

CONFIRMATION OF OTHERNESS IN SOCIETY

Chapter 17

WOMEN'S LIBERATION

ALTHOUGH WOMEN have won the franchise in most Western countries, equal pay for equal work and equal opportunity for getting work are nevertheless anything but a reality for them in most so-called democracies, and their supposed equality in the Soviet Union is more a matter of social role and function in the collective than of their equal dignity and worth *as women*. Churches, governments, law firms, businesses still perpetuate in greater or smaller measure the myth of male dominance, and the jokes and laughter of men at women's movements betray not only anxiety but a desire not to face the issue squarely for fear of losing cherished prerogatives. If the Orthodox Jew prays consciously, "Thank God, I was not born a woman," most men pray it unconsciously. What John Stuart Mill wrote about the damage to boys that arises from reinforcing them from earliest days in their notion of superiority over the other sex is just as applicable today, Kate Millett points out. "When the feeling of being raised above the whole of the other sex is combined with personal authority over one individual among them," writes Mill, this becomes to men whose strongest points of character are not conscience and affection, "a regularly constituted Academy or Gymnasium for training them in arrogance and overbearingness."[1] The images of woman as tender, receptive, healing, and helping; as wife, mother, homemaker, and housecleaner; as witch, bitch, shrew, and nag; as the eternal temptress, the courtesan, and the bunny girl—all do their part in making each woman invisible to many men and even to many women as the unique person she is.

For all this, I do not believe that men really do feel superior to women in our culture. They *need* to feel superior and to dominate, but that very need is a great dependence on the confirmation of women, which often gives the woman the whip hand or at the very least a far stronger role than is generally imagined.

The unique qualities of women's minds must be brought to flower in situations of mutual confirmation and appreciation which our present competitive business society hardly leaves room for and cannot envisage. The same applies to all of women's other talents and abilities. How many women secretaries today can afford to come on as thoroughgoing independents without losing their jobs? How many women teachers can talk back to men superintendents as "man to man" without losing their jobs? How many young women in middle-class society can dispense with all the flirtation and subtle flattery that men expect without losing dates and eventually even mates?

The sexual is only one of myriad manifestations of women's exile. The society's image of woman has been so internalized by women themselves that they have tended to justify it, taking on the passive role that is expected of them, being afraid to speak out, feeling that if they are not married they will not have an identity, feeling the obligation to remain young if they are to retain their hold as women, buying a career at the price of feeling "less of a woman." By the time most women are in high school, they begin to do worse in intellectual tasks and in productivity and accomplishment in general, thus giving justification after the fact to the characterization that they are inconsistent, emotionally unstable, lacking in a strong conscience, weaker, intuitive rather than intelligent.[2] In her focus on the male as source of security, she cannot build mutuality with her fellow women.

Ironically, woman's greatest and most universal exile occurs precisely where she is supposed to be most at home, namely, in marriage and family life. In his study of *The Origin of the Family, Private Property, and the State,* Friedrich Engels already identified the family as the basic unit of capitalist society and of female oppression. The family is founded upon the open or concealed domestic slavery of the wife, and society is founded on a multiple of families. In the family the husband is the bourgeois, the wife, the proletariat. There is no free marriage contract unless both are free in every respect, including the economic. The same situation prevails today. A great many American men are not accustomed to doing monotonous, repetitive work and are loath to realize that in their daily lives they have been accepting and implementing the very oppression and exploitation that they deplore in public life. "All men everywhere are slightly schizoid—divorced from the reality of maintaining life," says Pat Mainardi in "The Politics of Housework" *(Sisterhood Is Powerful)*. By foisting the housework onto his wife, he gains seven hours a week to play with his mind and not his human needs, hence "the horrifying abstractions of modern life." The family is supposed to be the place where everyone can find relief from the commodity relations that dominate the rest of society, but it is not so; for family functions and woman's functions are almost synonymous. The nuclear family unit forces woman "into a totally dependent position, paying for her keep with an enormous amount of emotional and physical labor which is not even considered work." Women have to purchase from men what should be theirs by right—equal opportunity for making money, for doing work they like. "Sex and love have been so contaminated for women by economic dependence that the package deal of love and marriage looks like a con and a shill."[3]

In her remarkable book *The Dialectic of Sex*, Shulamith Firestone, one of the young leaders in the Women's Liberation Movement, gives us further insight into the exile of modern woman. In order to be acceptable in the eyes of men, women must force and mutilate their bodies. Love and status are so intertwined for woman that she is never free to choose love for its own sake. But male culture, too, is parasitical. It takes from woman without giving and flourishes on the confirmation and support that women give to men. What is worse, woman cannot see herself directly but only through the eyes of male culture and values herself accordingly. Yet through the blindness of "sex privatization," women imagine themselves to be related to as individual persons and do not perceive that men treat them in terms of their class generality.[4]

Outside marriage as well as in, woman, while not being allowed to have control over her body, is held responsible for its products, for her pregnancy. There are numerous women who have been granted hospital abortions only on the condition that they agree to be sterilized, i.e., to be permanently punished for sexuality or for daring to do something active about not wanting a child. Firestone says that among Puerto Rican women in New York City, *La Operacion* has been so encouraged that between a fifth and a third of them have been sterilized. Not unconnected with this surely is the fact that in a recent three-year period 79 percent of New York City's abortion deaths occurred among black and Puerto Rican women. The abortion death rate was forty-seven times as high for Puerto Rican women and eight times as high for black women, as for their white sisters. "It is obvious," concludes Lucinda Cisler, "that poor women have almost no access to information about legal or safe illegal abortion sources, to friendly doctors who do abortions, or to the money to pay the exorbitant charges involved."[5] Sadly the repeal of the New York State antiabortion law has not made much difference in this situation.

The situation of black women and Puerto Ricans and Chicanos, while testifying to the common oppression of women, is sufficiently specific to discourage claims that the Women's Liberation Movement is or can be one unified movement of all women. Black women, for example, have very special problems arising from their situation than other women do not. Doubly oppressed and doubly burdened, they have for the most part chosen to fight beside their black brothers, fighting racism as a priority oppression. "Most black women have to work to help house, feed, and clothe their families." "Black women make up a substantial part of the black working force." Black woman in America is justly called "a slave of a slave," says Frances Beal, since she has so often been used "as the scapegoat for the evils that this horrendous System has perpetrated on black men." For these reasons black women cannot identify in their struggle with any white women's group that does not have an anti-imperialist and antiracist ideology but lays oppression simply to male chauvinism.[6] Mattie Humphrey sees the black woman's situation as even more exposed: Caught between the black-consciousness struggle and the struggle for women's equality, the black woman must recognize that she can benefit only indirectly from either movement and that she may be accused of betraying the other movement in the process.[7]

The exile of women in the professions and in other labor is perhaps too well known to need many indications here. Although thirty-five million women work and many, if not most, do so out of sheer economic necessity, women everywhere represent only a small percentage of the professions—law, medicine, chemistry, editing, journalism, university teaching—and their jobs are usually less responsible and interesting and their pay notoriously lower than that of men. Though more women proportionately are in secretarial, clerical, service, and factory occupations, their treatment and their pay are no better, indeed far worse. Quite regularly, women do not relate directly to their work as their accomplishment and many of the petty jobs women do seem to have no purpose other than emphasizing, as one secretary puts it, that "women are shit and men are king." In any case, the much heralded entry of woman into man's world has not meant either the end of "shitwork" for the woman or in most cases that she is really accepted as a man's equal. Women with Ph.D.'s make less money than men with B.A.'s. There are also countless women who cannot get steady employment but who occupy the position of a reserve labor force that can be used, in almost classical Marxian fashion, to hold down the wages of others.

> Considered as a whole, female employment in Britain and the United States displays the same basic character, that of an inert, unvalued though essential force, considered as temporary labor, docile, ignorant and unreliable. Because more than half the working women are married, the assumption arises that the family is their principal concern, that work outside the home brings in a little extra spending money, that they have no ambition. Not only are women paid less than men in most of the instances where they do work identical with men, but most women work at a lower level than men in the same industry, so that the question of parity can never arise.[8]

Even in the radical movement, as Marge Piercy testifies, the relationship of men to women is still predominantly a sexual one. Women are used to prop up men, used up and cast aside, and they are "not able to keep tenderness and sensual joy from being converted into cooperation" in their own manipulation. The women the radical movements want to reach—the working-class women and those on welfare—need to have a movement for liberation which will take a whole new form, attacking exploitation on the job and in the home together in a way that neither tradi-tional male unionism nor middle-class feminism can do.[9]

The sexual, however, is only one aspect of the battle for Women's Liberation. This battle cannot be won through relegat-ing the blame to men or women but through seeing the task as a common one—a task of the "between" to be shared by men and women in their relationship to each other in the concrete situa-tions of their lives. Women stand in need of dialogue with and confirmation by men if they are to become what they are called to become as persons: "Women be-ing or bring-ing the New Woman into being," says Miriam Carroll of the Philadelphia Task Force for Women in Religion, "depend on a response—a dialectic with men for the process to continue or go to completion without damaging or wasteful detours." Rebellion, says Rosemary Ruether following Camus, is an affirmation of a common human-ity—a breaking of the silence between oppressed and oppressor that is the beginning of humanization. The chief act of rebellion for a woman, according to Ruether, is an internal grasping of faith in full personhood and a rejecting of the limiting self-images that women have taken over and internalized.[10]

"The women's liberation movement must seek the liberation of all people, men as well as women," writes Florence Bryant. "This putting down of men must stop. . . . One can only be as free as one allows others to be." This freedom for both men and women is not just laissez-faire: It is interdependence, cooperation, dia-logue. Starting with the indubitable fact that "men and women as they are, are the products of complex social relations in an ongo-ing historical process," Mary Daly stresses that personal liberty and growth are not opposed to, but are essential to, love and commitment. The way forward, for her, is the way of the "be-tween," rejecting "the old obsession with sex roles, in order to focus upon the problems of persons in relation to others."

> We should strive, therefore, toward a level of confrontation, dialogue, and cooperation between the sexes undreamed of in the past. . . . The directing principle . . . should be commitment to providing the possibility of ever more profound, complete, dynamic and humanizing relationships.[11]

In her *Dialectic of Sex*, Shulamith Firestone sees the feminist movement as the first to combine effectively the "personal" with the "political." It is developing a new way of relating, a new political style "that will eventually reconcile the personal—always the feminine prerogative—with the public, with the 'world outside,' to restore that world to its emotions, and literally to its senses." To reintegrate the emotional with the rational is to reintegrate the female principle with the male. What is more, she insists on including the oppression of children in any program for feminist revolution. Otherwise, women will be open to the accusation of missing an important substratum of oppression merely because it did not directly concern *them*. Only the elimination of the very conditions of femininity and childhood themselves will clear the way for a fully "human" condition, she says. The most important characteristic of revolution, according to her, is flexibility—an emphasis rare among revolutionaries.[12]

Against men's probable desire that if they are not free, women should not be free either, Germaine Greer replies that by securing their own manumission, women "may show men the way that they could follow when they jumped off their own treadmill." In the end the task is not that of women alone, of course, it is a task of the "between." To achieve a stable relationship between the forces of creation and destruction, we have to abandon the polarity of male sadism and female masochism and translate a universe of aggressors and victims into a cooperative endeavor. "The great renewal of the world will perhaps consist in this," Greer quotes Rilke, "that man and maid, freed from all false feeling and aversion, will seek each other not as opposites, but as brother and sister, as neighbours, and will come together as human beings."[13]

For Kate Millett too, in *Sexual Politics*, the sexual revolution means a liberation of men as well as women, of the slavery of the master to his domination over the slave. When male supremacy is overthrown, it will be possible to replace the present constriction of roles by a reevaluation of "masculine" and "feminine" traits which might reject violence and excessive passivity in either sex and encourage intelligence, tenderness, and consideration as appropriate to both sexes. This is surely the attitude of the confirmation of otherness, as is Mary Daly's statement that "individual men and women find themselves not in static conformance to roles but only in dynamic relationship to each other." But Mary Daly also calls for a striving for authenticity that recognizes "the ambiguity of concrete reality, which cannot be contained in abstraction."[14] Precisely because of this ambiguity, we cannot altogether dispense with the idea of the "social role," though we can guard ourselves against taking it as the reality itself and see it instead within the dialectic between more or less static conceptions of roles and the actual dynamic of our relationship to them. We cannot deny the specialization of labor and the continual rationalization of that specialization in terms of job descriptions, problems of the exercise or sharing of decision making and authority, and the obvious need to call for people not as the unique persons they are but as abstractions, such as professor, secretary, machinist, crane operator, doctor, or bank clerk. What we need not accept is that the convenient label and the social role either adequately describe what in fact goes on or exhaust the reality of the person for the hours during which he works. On the contrary, his own unique relationship to his work is of crucial importance not only for the success and meaning of the work but for the human reality that is here becoming event. What is more, we can recognize the necessity for a continual critique of abstractions to make them more and more flexible and more and more in line with the actual situation at any one time. In terms of this critique, it is a part of the task of man and woman alike to reject the unfair "burden of always responding to a situation in a catalogued way." But this means to reject a life in which the human has been all but smothered under the weight of technical, social, and bureaucratic abstractions, and this is a cultural and spiritual revolution that must concern us all. Indeed, this, if I may be so bold, is the deepest level underlying all the rebellions of our day—those of the blacks, of women, of youth, and of the Third World.

In each of these spheres we come upon the plain signs of the fragility of our life together, of the life between man and woman and between man and man. Our hope for the "greening" of America or the world can only be meaningful if we begin with the realism that shows us caught in an immense corporate state or network of military and industrial complexes in which the pervasive alienation removes our being with one another in community, not to mention our realization of our personal uniqueness in that being together, and leaves us only pseudofreedoms that we imagine we enjoy. But if there is a fragility in our life as human beings there is also strength. The deeper the human image is hidden, the greater the possibility that resources may arise from the depths through which we can rediscover in each situation the human being, man and woman.

To stress that the problem is one of the between and that the task is one that men and women must work on together is not to suggest that socially men and women are in an equal position of authority and power. Despite the gains that have been made in recent decades, women are still far down on the social scale. In some respects the situation is analogous to that between parents and their teen-aged children. The greater power and the greater responsibility lie on the side of the parents though the teen-agers already have considerable ground of their own and are surely, if not steadily, moving to greater power and equality.

Whether the coming changes will mean moving toward androgyny, as some think, or even a return to the matrilineal, it will certainly be a different picture than the one we have now. The greatest problem in the fight for women's liberation is the steps and stages that must be gone through to reach this different and better relationship between the sexes. In order for women to learn to hold their ground in relationship to men, they may have to pull away at various points and strengthen their sisterhood with one another. But this will only be meaningful if that distancing leads later to a stronger and more equal relating than before. When this takes place, the dialogue will evoke the human in men as well as affirm the human in women, and it will manifest the human image that lies hidden between the two.[15]

Chapter 18

AGING AND THE COMMUNITY OF OTHERNESS

Grow old along with me,
The best is yet to be,
The last of life
For which the first was made.

Robert Browning, "Rabbi Ben Ezra"

OUR MOST typical association with aging, in our culture, is not wisdom, serenity, fullness of life, or bringing in the harvest, but a long, terrible period of increasingly failing powers. This image is not based on observation so much as it is on dread, on anticipation of one's helplessness at the onset of aging. This anticipation was already clearly present in T. S. Eliot's earliest published poem, "The Love Song of J. Alfred Prufrock," written when he was still a very young man.

I grow old . . . I grow old . . .
I shall wear the bottoms of my trousers rolled.

Shall I part my hair behind? Do I dare to eat a peach?
I shall wear white flannel trousers, and walk upon the beach.
I have heard the mermaids singing, each to each.

I do not think that they will sing to me.

Eliot was, of course, trying to portray a general alienation and futility, but the symbol he chose for this was the failing powers of age.

This was still more explicit in the first of Eliot's 1920 poems, "Gerontion," the fictitious central character of which is an old man awaiting death who realizes that he has not really lived:

> *I an old man,*
> *A dull head among windy spaces.*
>   . . .
> *I have no ghosts,*
> *An old man in a draughty house*
> *Under a windy knob.*

We have liked to imagine that death confers some dignity and meaning in the manner of the Greek tragedies. But when this old man's life protracts itself into death, no closure or meaning is to be found:

> *Think at last*
> *We have not reached conclusion, when I*
> *Stiffen in a rented house.*

All that he can say is that perhaps the failing powers of age are less poignant than the presumed rising powers of youth because age, at any rate, offers no illusion of meeting, no hope of contact with real life:

> *I have lost my passion: why should I need to keep it*
> *Since what is kept must be adulterated?*
> *I have lost my sight, smell, hearing, taste and touch:*
> *How should I use them for your closer contact?*

At the age of forty T. S. Eliot incurred Edmund Wilson's ire by writing "Ash Wednesday" as if from the standpoint of an old man resigning the powers of youth:

> *Because I do not hope to turn again*
> *Because I do not hope*
> *Because I do not hope to turn*
> *Desiring this man's gift and that man's scope*
> *I no longer strive to strive towards such things*
> *(Why should the aged eagle stretch its wings?)*
> *Why should I mourn*
> *The vanished power of the usual reign?*

"Ash Wednesday" is, to be sure, a religious poem of purgation, in contrast to the Waste Land world depicted in the earlier poems; yet the theme of age as associated with failing powers is as central here as there.

We might hope for something more positive from the *Four Quartets*, Eliot's greatest and most mature summation of human existence. If we are not entirely disappointed in this hope, nonetheless the burden of Eliot's plaint about aging remains the same. We are told in "East Coker" that old age was not "what one had expected." Yet as portrayed here it seems to be almost exactly what Eliot had expected all along:

> *What was to be the value of the long looked forward to,*
> *Long hoped for calm, the autumnal serenity*
> *And the wisdom of age? Had they deceived us*
> *Or deceived themselves, the quiet-voiced elders,*
> *Bequeathing us merely a receipt for deceit?*
> *The serenity only a deliberate hebetude,*
> *The wisdom only the knowledge of dead secrets*
> *Useless in the darkness into which they peered*
> *Or from which they turned their eyes.*
> 　　　　　. . .
> 　　　*Do not let me hear*
> *Of the wisdom of old men, but rather of their folly,*
> *Their fear of fear and frenzy, their fear of possession,*
> *Of belonging to another, or to others, or to God.*

These negative thoughts on aging have, of course, a positive context, the limited value of the knowledge derived from experience, the recognition that "The only wisdom we can hope to acquire / Is the wisdom of humility," the purgation and descent into the dark night of the senses and of the soul. Yet the final stanza of "East Coker" is only a little more promising than the earlier lament, as far as age is concerned:

> 　　　*As we grow older*
> *The world becomes stranger, the pattern more complicated*
> *Of dead and living. . . .*
> *Old men ought to be explorers*
> *Here and there does not matter*
> *We must be still and still moving*
> *Into another intensity*
> *For a further union, a deeper communion*
> *Through the dark cold and the empty desolation,*
> *The wave cry, the wind cry, the vast waters*
> *Of the petrel and the porpoise. In my end is my beginning.*

In "Little Gidding," the crown and recapitulation of the other three poems in *Four Quartets*, the mystic serenity is punctuated by an Ecclesiastes-type irony at the fruits of old age:

> Let me disclose the gifts reserved for age
> > To set a crown upon your lifetime's effort.
> > First, the cold friction of expiring sense
> Without enchantment, offering no promise
> > But bitter tastelessness of shadow fruit
> > As body and soul begin to fall asunder.
> Second, the conscious impotence of rage
> > At human folly, and the laceration
> > Of laughter at what ceases to amuse.
> And last, the rending pain of re-enactment
> > Of all that you have done, and been; the shame
> > Of motives late revealed, and the awareness
> Of things ill done and done to others' harm
> > Which once you took for exercise of virtue.
> > Then fools' approval stings, and honour stains.

Once again, the context of this bitter refrain is the need for purgation—to be "restored by that refining fire / Where you must move in measure, like a dancer"—and the deeper meaning that may open itself to our exploration so that we can "arrive where we started / And know the place for the first time." Age, then, is not a bad preparation for mystic realization precisely because it is the inevitable preparation for death, as Eliot makes clear in "The Dry Salvages":

> There is the final addition, the failing
> Pride or resentment at failing powers,
> The unattached devotion which might pass for devotionless,
> In a drifting boat with a slow leakage,
> The silent listening to the undeniable
> Clamour of the bell of the last annunciation.

The "last annunciation," whose clamor we cannot deny, is, of course, death. Many dread age because it represents the threshold of death with an inevitability that does not attach to any other time of life, unless one is struck by a fatal disease. This is an unassailable insight if for no other reason than because our life is future oriented and our movement toward the future, in one sense or another, must take place in hope. Yet for the aging there is no future, no hope except for death—if we stick to the moving finger of time on the surface of the sphere and do not descend, as Eliot bids us, into "the still point of the turning world." We cannot deny "the undeniable clamour of the bell of the last annunciation" even if we hold immortality or reincarnation as a trump card in reserve. Yet a deeper examination of our attitude toward death lays bare that it is not the event itself but our relation to it that terrifies us. Our dread of *both*—aging and death—is rooted in our lack of organic community, our alienation from nature and time, as I have pointed out at length in my book *The Hidden Human Image:*

> Man's attitude toward death has always been bound up in the closest way with his posture vis-a-vis nature, time, and community. Although he is aware of the seasons, modern man hardly lives in the time of nature. His time is abstract, calendrical, and conventional, and his relations to nature are more and more detached—whether nature be the object to be exploited, the scene to rhapsodize over, the terrain for a holiday from the city, or the great Earth Goddess that was only recently celebrated every year to ward off the threat of pollution and ecological imbalance. As a result, it is hardly possible for modern man to see his own death as a part of the natural rhythms and cycles of nature, to be accepted with the wisdom of nature itself. . . .
>
> Like K. in Kafka's novel *The Castle,* modern man's attempt to find a foothold in present reality cannot succeed because he is always using the present as a means to some future end. This functional relation to time is caused in turn—and reinforced—by that sense of isolation, rootlessness, and exile which makes modern man feel, in moments of awareness, that he knows no real life. He is cut off from the nourishing stream of community; the prospect of his own death takes on an overwhelming importance that robs life itself of meaning. . . .
>
> Certainly, even in the best of communities, death is an individual affair. Even in traditional religions, the journey of the soul to some Hades or Sheol must be facilitated by the community through *rites de passage*. Death *is* that uttermost solitude of which every other abandonment is only a foretaste, as Martin Buber suggests, and time *is* a torrent carrying us irreversibly and inexorably toward "the starkest of all human perspectives"—one's own death. But our obsession with our own deaths, our focus upon them, is in no small part caused by our exile and isolation in the present. This same obsession leads us to use our

cults of youth, of having "experiences," of realizing our poten-
tials, as ways of not looking at the facts of old age and death.
Our culture gives us no support in hearing Hopkins' "leaden
echo" of old age in which we give up all the "girl-graces" of
youth in favor of that vision in which every future is cut off
except death. Yet this fear of time, old age, and death is woven
into every moment of our existence, so that we have no real
present and no real mutual presence for one another.[1]

Old age and death are not the same; yet in our imagination and
in our anticipations they are inexorably woven together. Our fear
of aging is not to be explained by our fear of death. Both have
deeper roots in our relation to existence itself, particularly in our
culture in which an organic flowing with the Tao often seems an
impossibility. Our experiences of abandonment in old age are a
foretaste of the uttermost solitude of death; yet our fear of death is
itself based upon our fear of abandonment. And *that* fear is based
upon the fact that we are already, in some important sense, abandoned. This is nowhere better illustrated than in the existentialist
philosophy of Martin Heidegger.

Human existence, or *Dasein*—being-there—is, to Heidegger,
zum Tode sein—being toward-death; for it is only the resolute anticipation of one's unutterably unique and nonrelational death
that individualizes *Dasein* down to its own potentiality and frees it
from the power of *das Man*—the "They" of ambiguity, curiosity,
and idle talk. Granting that our anticipation of our death is a
present reality that enters into every moment of our existence, I
would nonetheless hold that Heidegger seems at times to forget
that what is given to us, hence what is *existentially* of importance,
is not the actual *future* moment of death but the *present* moment of
anticipation. Putting it another way, Heidegger takes the half-
truth of separation that the knowledge of our unique and individual death imparts to each of us and makes it into the specious
whole truth of our existence being "ultimately nonrelational." But
this nonrelational quality of our existence is, above all, a fact of
our isolation, our estrangement, our inability to live in organic
community with nature and our fellow men. T. S. Eliot's Gerontion has lost the possibility of contact through the failure of those
senses that once enabled him to reach out to others, but the
fundamental reality, as he recognizes, is that there was already

little possibility of real contact even when his senses were fully empowered.

What can we do in the face of this situation? Medical science has not yet reached the stage where it can indefinitely postpone old age and death. Nor is there sense in railing at the modern person for *not* being organically connected with nature and the human community. We must ask, rather, what resources, if any, are left to us to accept age as the best that is yet to be, "the last of life for which the first is made." This is only possible if we can attain a new and active relation to aging which no longer makes it merely a time of renunciation, resignation, and purgation—à la "Ash Wednesday"—but sees it, instead, as the ground for a new beginning.

In "Sailing to Byzantium," W. B. Yeats had pointed to that new beginning in a spirit close to Eliot's *Four Quartets*, namely as a renunciation of the physical in favor of the spiritual, the flux of life in favor of the timeless and the eternal:

I

That is no country for old men. The young
In one another's arms, birds in the trees
—Those dying generations—at their song,
The salmon-falls, the mackerel-crowded seas,
Fish, flesh, or fowl, commend all summer long
Whatever is begotten, born, and dies.
Caught in that sensual music all neglect
Monuments of unageing intellect.

II

An aged man is but a paltry thing,
A tattered coat upon a stick, unless
Soul clap its hands and sing, and louder sing
For every tatter in its mortal dress, . . .

III

O sages standing in God's holy fire
    .   .   .
. . . be the singing masters of my soul.
Consume my heart away; sick with desire
And fastened to a dying animal
It knows not what it is; and gather me
Into the artifice of eternity.

How sublimely Yeats himself contradicts this sublime and rarefied spirituality in his final poems on "Crazy Jane" where the full reality of mortal and sensual life is given its due!

We should like to know something more and better than this trading of physical life for spiritual life; for that was always open to us, and to reserve it for old age is obviously a *pis aller*, making the best of a bad bargain.

Martin Buber tells of how his concern with folk-schools brought him together with the noble old thinker Hans Natorp in the years immediately following the First World War, and in so doing he gives us a hint of a fuller understanding of what it might mean to begin anew:

> At that time I was happily surprised at how the man with the steel-grey locks asked us at the beginning of his talk to forget all that we believed we knew about his philosophy from his books. In the last years, which had been war years, reality had been brought so close to him that he saw everything with new eyes and had to think in a new way. To be old is a glorious thing when one has not unlearned what it means *to begin;* this old man had even perhaps first learned it thoroughly in old age. He was not at all young, but he was old in a young way, knowing how to begin.[2]

What Natorp achieved, from Buber's report, was clearly not the renunciation of one of his functions or powers for another but a new integration, a new totality, a new and greater wholeness than any he had previously achieved.

Carl G. Jung has the virtue of having been the first to call to our attention the midlife crisis in which the contraction of body and psyche can lead not to despair or simple renunciation but a new integration and individuation in which the deeper goals of the person are fulfilled. There are many existential crises in life and they come at different times. The midlife crisis might be described as an existential crisis that is an organic and inevitable part of adult development. This does not mean that it comes at the same time or in the same way for all persons who are growing older, much less that they respond to it in any similar fashion. However, what Adrian Van Kaam says of existential crises can be applied to the crisis of aging, namely, that it involves the three phases of psychological death, decision, and rebirth, that it entails the frustration of facing one's growing limitations, and that, if the person does not fall into illusion or despair, it means seeking new, more realistic goals, renouncing old dreams in order to be free to pursue new ones, giving up old unrealistic self-images but also creating new, more mature ones.

To the Protestant theologian Paul Tillich, the nonbeing that threatens us in the existentialist crisis must be transcended through an essentialist faith which enables us to receive the grace that accepts us despite our being unacceptable. I believe, in contrast, that an existential crisis must be met by an existential response. Mystic experience and religious faith may give us an *essential* trust, but they cannot give *existential* trust. Yet only existential trust makes accessible to us both the "courage to address and the courage to respond." An essential part of this courage to address and respond is the willingness to begin anew. Without existential trust one cannot make a new beginning, and without it being old cannot be "a glorious thing." As I have written in *Touchstones of Reality:*

> The trust in existence that enables us to live from moment to moment and to go out to meet what the new moment brings is the trust that makes it possible that in new meeting we again become whole, alive, present. If I trust in a person, a relationship, this means that despite what may and will happen, I shall enter into relationship again and bring all the past moments of meeting into present meeting. The particular person who is my partner may die, become sick, disturbed; he may betray me, rupture the relationship, or simply turn away and fail to respond. Sooner or later something of this does happen for most of us. When it does, it is trust which enables us to remain open and respond to the new address of the new situation. If we lose our trust in existence, conversely, we are no longer able to enter anew into real dialogue.[3]

The existential mistrust that gets in the way of our beginning anew is probably with us from our earliest childhood experiences of separation and betrayal, and it is enormously heightened by the smog of existential mistrust that pollutes our culture. But surely it is in the time of aging that it is most difficult to begin anew for all but the exceptional few. It is in this time that we experience the attrition of our energy and powers, the loss of our hope, *and* the loss of confirmation by significant others and by the broader community. At the age of sixty the enormously prolific and creative Austrian novelist Stefan Zweig joined with his wife in what the Germans call *Freitod*, a joint suicide in which they carried out their resolution to leave life at the height of their powers rather than experience the waning into age. Zweig did not think that old age was the time of serenity and wisdom. It was, for him, the time of the loss of power and control. If we flowed with the Tao, we would not, to be sure, be so concerned with power and control. But it is precisely *this* existential trust which is largely lacking in our culture. Old age is like sleep in that it means, in the language of Peter Koestenbaum, a *deconstitution* of the ego, a letting go, a trust in others, a willingness to be dependent. We begin with such a dependence and trust in childhood, but to end with it in our "second childhood" is more than some of us can contemplate; for we doubt with good reason that there is much to depend upon.

My mother actually drew up a legal document in which she stated her insistence that she not be put into a nursing home, or what used to be called an "old folks' home" when she grew old. My sister with whom she lived nonetheless found it necessary to put my mother into such a home for the last four years of her life. The last time I saw my mother alive was in the home of my sister in Wichita where we all celebrated the sixtieth birthday of my older sister who had come from Florida for the occasion. We were all enormously gratified at how lucid my mother was. She spoke of how strange it was to her to have a daughter of sixty, made a beautiful little speech, and presented each of her three children a check. To me this was especially wonderful because when I had seen my mother two years before she had just had a stroke and did not even recognize me. My younger sister and I took my mother back to the nursing home fifteen miles outside Wichita. When she got out of the car, my mother stumbled. By the time we got her into the nursing home, she no longer recognized me. Two years after my mother's death, this same sister broke down weeping at lunch and told me how racked with guilt she was for having put our mother in the nursing home even though it seemed, at the time, the only possible thing to do, given my mother's penchant for lighting fires under pots with nothing in them while no one was at home. She also told me how afraid she was that some similar fate may await her when she gets to be my mother's age.

Perhaps because I was not so closely tied to my mother as my sister was and did not have the responsibility for the decision to put her in a nursing home, I have not dwelled much on thoughts of guilt or fears of my own approaching old age. On the other hand, at a much younger age than my mother did, I have acquired a habit of losing things and frantically searching for them! I have always rather looked forward to my retirement as a time when I can write without outside impediments. But I have occasionally asked myself whether there will not be by that time *inside* impediments by way of loss of energy, anxiety, illness, or whatever other ravages age may bring. I suspect that the answer to this question depends upon my own ability to begin anew. Can I live in closer tune with my body? Can I take up the writing of a novel where I left off thirty years ago and launch a whole new direction in my writing? Or is such creativity reserved for the intensity of youth which makes up for its lack of perspective and direction with an overabundance of energy?

Carl Jung was certainly not concerned with an essentialist answer to the existential question of aging but wished, rather, to find a wholly existential one. His own life, as we encounter it in *Memories, Dreams, Reflections* and in the films taken of him in his old age, is impressive testimony to his having achieved an existential wholeness and strength greater than his more youthful ones. What is more, Jung has supplied us with a rich literature of myth and symbol that serves as a useful counterpoise to the undue emphasis of our culture upon youth.

Yet there is one aspect that Jung and the other explorers of the midlife crisis and the crisis of aging have ignored or underplayed. That is the aspect of community. Most of Jung's myths and symbols are drawn from earlier, more organic communities than any that exist now. What is more, they represent the communal *confirmation* of the individual who is going through these rites of passage. Such a confirmation is largely absent in today's culture, and no amount of Jungian therapy and books richly studded with the myths and symbols of the past can make up for this lack. The existential crisis of the person who is aging in our culture is neither an entirely individual one nor is it simply an affair of one's inner life and one's dreams.

Overcoming the crisis of aging depends, we have suggested, upon beginning anew, and the ability to begin anew is a function of existential trust. But existential trust is not something that is subject to our will nor is it entirely a function of our spiritual life in detachment from the whole of our existence. It is what makes possible the courage to address and to respond anew even when "the conditions are no longer propitious" and those we have formerly addressed and responded to in our lives have long since fallen away. The dread of old age is inextricably bound up with our sense of alienation and isolation from real community. After the death of one Hasidic rebbe, a friend of his said that if he had had someone to talk to, he would still be alive. The dread is also bound up with the fact that our culture does not confirm the powers of age but only those of youth. We do not look to the Confucian scholar, the rabbinic sage, the aged *staretz,* or the wise old man as our sources for communal wisdom but to the successful young executives, the bright young governors, and the movie stars who are still in their prime. When John Fitzgerald Kennedy became President of the United States, everyone ws impressed by the fact that youth was at last at the helm. The shock that reverberated through the nation and the world on the day of his assassination was in no small measure connected with the destruction of precisely that symbol.

On that very day I went to a celebration in New York in which Loren Eisely and my own professor and member of my dissertation committee Charles Hartshorne were awarded the Le Comte du Noüy Prize for their work on bringing together religion and science. I had not seen Hartshorne in some years, but I had been in correspondence with him in my role as co-editor of the *Philosophy of Martin Buber* volume of *The Library of Living Philosophers.* Hartshorne wrote the essay for our volume on Buber's metaphysics, and he began it with the statement, "Buber is no metaphysician, Buber is one of the greatest metaphysicians." Then, as one would expect of the greatest disciple of Alfred North Whitehead, he remade Buber's philosophy in the image of a "Process and Reality" approach to metaphysics. When Buber replied, he wrote, "Dear Hartshorne, I have read your essay attentively several times. I am afraid that we can only agree on the first of your two propositions, that I am no metaphysician." In the short paragraph that followed, Buber rejected the metaphysician's insistence that one must choose between a God that is absolute and a God that is in relation. Buber spoke of God as the "Absolute Person" who is in relation with man and the world. When I spoke with Hartshorne during the reception following the presentations, this invariably mild-mannered man expressed an anger that I had never witnessed in him. This did not bother me, but I was disturbed by his statement, "Buber must be getting senile!" Instead of considering that there might be a real difference of approach here worthy of understanding, however much he might disagree with it, Hartshorne, himself already in his seventies, wished to lay what angered him at the doorstep of Buber's advancing years.

Buber was not senile then or even later. Despite the failure of his eyesight and repeated illness, he continued his work on revising the fourth edition of his translation of the Hebrew Bible into German until he entered his final coma at the age of eighty-seven. In the summer of 1946, when he was sixty-eight years old, Buber attested in the preface to his new collection of Hasidic tales that by far the greater part of it was written since his arrival in Palestine in 1938. Buber attributed his ability to begin anew to his relationship to his new homeland:

> Along with much else, I owe the urge to this new and more comprehensive composition to the air of this land. Our sages say that it makes one wise; to me it has granted a different gift: the strength to make a new beginning. I had regarded my work on the Hasidic legends as completed. This book is the outcome of a beginning.[4]

Buber did not, to be sure, receive the confirmation in Palestine, later Israel, that he had in Central Europe. Still, for all his controversial stances and the relative isolation that they brought, he knew there too the meaning of connection with community.

No person is so totally self-sufficient that he or she can live without this confirmation, much less make a new beginning. Kierkegaard's "knight of faith" who knows the solitary relationship of the Single One to his divine Thou cannot be a model for us, for he ignores the existential trust that cannot be totally divorced from one's relations to one's fellow men. Dostoevsky's Prince Myshkin is a more realistic portrait. There is something genuinely terrifying about the ending of Dostoevsky's novel *The Idiot* that cannot be resolved or alleviated. Prince Myshkin's suffering points us to the dreadful question of whether a person can find the highest meaning in a lonely suffering in which he is not only abandoned but unconfirmed; whether he can continue *as a person* to follow a path in "fear and trembling" without the grace received from others that enables him to be human. Socrates, to be sure, was able to persevere in his life-stance at the age of seventy even when the majority of Athenians disconfirmed him. But he had a large minority that backed him and a group of faithful disciples who remained with him until the end. Jung too, for all his great individual strength, was deeply confirmed by a large community of disciples. Without the confirmation by others in community one can make no meaningful new beginning in response to the crisis of old age.

Yet we have already stressed the lack of the organic community of the past in our present culture. My sister's guilt about my mother was triggered, in part, by her hearing of the way in which old people are treated in other cultures, such as the Netherlands. This treatment depends upon the existence of extended families, which are more and more becoming rare in this culture, or upon a community consciousness of shared responsibility which we are almost totally lacking. The old, like the insane, the retarded, and the criminal, are to be put out of sight so as not to disturb that pleasant idyll in which the rest of us choose to live. Relatively few grown children today consider it their responsibility to take their aging parents into their homes and care for them as they were once cared for by these same parents when they were children. Reciprocity between the generations is largely understood as passing on to our children the advantages that our parents passed on to us.

We cannot go backward to the organic community of the Middle Ages or even to the extended family systems of a few generations ago. But we can, we *must* go forward to a new type of community if the "gray panthers" are to have their day in court. This new community is what I have called the "community of otherness." What makes community is people finding themselves in a common situation—a situation which they approach in different ways, yet one which calls each of them out. The very existence in community is already a common concern, a caring for one another. But part of the problem of aging, we have already seen, is the reluctance of the rest of the community to acknowledge that the old *are* in a common situation with them or that they are properly objects of a communal concern which is not pity or charity but a vital aspect of community itself.

"When people age they lose the sense of the I-boundary in which they are invested," the Gestalt therapists Erving and Miriam Polster have said. This is because aging necessarily means a *contraction* of the boundary of the self. But is that undermining of the very self that is a contributing factor to so much senility and gerontic insanity really necessary? A program for senior citizens in San Diego concerned with educational growth opportunities has as its acronym, "EGO." It is clearly an attempt to create a community of otherness that will help to confirm the self of the senior citizen that the ordinary structures and cultures of our society disconfirm. Abraham Joshua Heschel suggested at a White House conference on aging that there should be senior universities where the old could learn for the sake of learning. Another program for the aged in San Diego is appropriately called "Lifeline."

When we encounter one another beyond terminologies and beyond differences in age, social position, and culture, the lived reality of "the community of otherness" can come into being. If we tell the aging, by word or glance or action, that their day is past, that they have nothing essential to contribute to the culture, that they are no longer really a part of the ongoing community, then we have hastened the spiritual death that so often precedes the physical one. The distinguished family psychiatrist Ivan Boszormenyi-Nagy has shown that our connection with our parents and grandparents is not only an organic and inescapable one but is also the only real avenue open to us for reestablishing trust in our society and healing the breaches in relationship and in self that we carry with us and impart to our own children and grandchildren. Even if aging people are not wise sages, they are still inalienable members of our community, and we cannot be careless of their voices without losing our own humanity.

The building of true community is the building of a community of otherness. It is not requisite upon a community to turn itself inside out for the sake of the old people in its midst. But much depends upon whether it takes action as a real community which listens to the voices of all or just as a majority which is able to override those whose voices are no longer heard at all or are heard and discounted because they are the voices of the aged. Sometimes our dialogue can only mean standing our ground in opposition to the aged; yet it can never mean being unconcerned for how the aged see the world or careless of the validity of their standing where they do. The reality of community is polyphonic, it is many-voiced. In a community of otherness the voice of the aged is heard because real community creates an atmosphere of trust which enables them to make their witness. I have been in very few groups in my life, including the finest, where real community has not been violated day after day by a few "weighty" persons imposing their will upon the less sure and the less articulate in the name of what *should* be done.

When Martin Buber was seventy-six years old he wrote a statement about the "specifically modern apocalyptic" that undoubtedly betrays something of how he felt about being an old man who wanted to begin anew in a world that wishes to fix the aged in their places and is not ready to confirm them in a new beginning. The irremediable old age of our world is accepted as self-understood, Buber contended. The modern apocalyptic no longer says that one cannot swim against the stream since this image of the stream, to which an outlet belongs, already appears too full of pathos. Rather it says, "An old period must behave like an old period if it does not wish to be laughed at." In an aged world one knows exactly what is legitimate and what is not.

> If one comes and rebels against the indirectness that has penetrated all human relationships, . . . he is upbraided by his critics as a romantic beset by illusions. If he resists the flagging dialogical relationship between men, he is forthwith reproached with failing to recognize the fated solitude of present-day living, as if the fundamental meaning of each new solitude were not that it must be overcome on a more comprehensive level than any earlier one. If one declares that one of the main reasons why the crisis in the life of the peoples appears hopeless is the fact that the existential mistrust of all against all prevents any meaningful negotiation over the real differences of interest, he is set right by a smile of the shrewd: an "old" world is necessarily shrewd.[5]

In opposition to this specifically modern apocalyptic, Buber called for a dialogical openness that would not limit any person or group in advance on the basis of fixed objective calculations of their resources—a caution that applies in particular to the aged in our culture who tend to be written off more readily than any other group:

> As in the life of a single person, so also in the life of the human race: what is possible in a certain hour and what is impossible cannot be adequately ascertained by any foreknowledge. It goes without saying that in the one sphere as in the other, one must start at any given time from the nature of the situation insofar as

it is at all recognizable. But one does not learn the measure and limit of what is attainable in a desired direction otherwise than through going in this direction. The forces of the soul allow themselves to be measured only through one's using them. In the most important moments of our existence neither planning nor surprise rules alone: in the midst of the faithful execution of a plan we are surprised by secret openings and insertions. Room must be left for such surprises, however; planning as though they were impossible renders them impossible. One cannot strive for immediacy, but one can hold oneself free and open for it. One cannot produce genuine dialogue, but one can be at its disposal. Existential mistrust cannot be replaced by trust, but it can be replaced by a reborn candour.[6]

If we can overcome existential mistrust with candor and the community of affinity with the community of otherness, we may, even as we age, be able to begin anew.

A fiddler once played Rabbi Hanok a tune. He said: "Even melodies that grow old lose their savor. When we heard this one at Rabbi Bunam's long ago, it made our hearts leap. Now it has lost its savor. And that is how it really is. We must be very well prepared and ready for old age. We pray: 'Cast me not off in the time of old age!' For when I see that after all I have done I am nothing at all, I must start my work over again. And it is said of God: 'Who reneweth the creation every day continually.' "[7]

It is this beginning anew that I should like to achieve in my own life as I enter old age, and it is this that I hope for and would point to as a realistic hope for the lives of others. Obeying an impulse of the heart, I recently tracked down and wrote to a friend with whom I had not been in touch for forty years, not knowing whether I would get a response at all or, if I did, what response I might expect. In a few weeks a letter came back which heartened me enormously, because it shows so concretely the joy of beginning anew. I am sure that my friend too is "not at all young," but she is "old in a young way."

After all these years, after graduating from the sculpture department at Yale, after showing for the first time at the age of twenty-three, after marrying a painter, and after raising three daughters, I am now happily divorced and living in New York. I am still a sculptor with twenty-some solo shows and my share of recognition. In January, after thirty years of teaching, I quit to concentrate on being the kind of sculptor I always felt I would be when I could give it my full attention. This is a glorious time for me. I wake up every morning delighted not to have to go to the college. My work is expanding and taking new directions with a great burst of energy.

To be old is a glorious thing if one knows how to begin anew.

Chapter 19

TRANSCULTURAL NURSING AND THE CARING COMMUNITY

A CREATIVE contribution to the confirmation of otherness in community and society is being made today by Madeleine Leininger, Dean of the University of Utah's College of Nursing, through her Association for Transcultural Nursing. The Third National Transcultural Nursing Conference in 1977 used the comparative method of anthropology and transcultural nursing to explore cross-cultural health and illness, and lifestyles of the adolescent and middle years. This conference explored physical anthropology and transcultural nursing, sex role assumptions of adolescents, and health and care systems among Chinese, Vietnamese, and American and Mexican Indians. Nursing already implies in itself an attempt at the confirmation of otherness. Transcultural nursing adds a second dimension to this attempt and the concern for adolescence and middle age a third. My own concern is to try to give a foundation to this three-dimensional attempt through the perspective of confirmation and the community of otherness.[1]

*　　*　　*　　*

What do I as a philosopher have to say of value concerning transcultural nursing? In our culture, philosophy is regarded as one of the most impractical and nursing as one of the most practical activities; philosophy as one of the most useless, nursing as one of the most useful, contributions to society. To the extent that this is so, if you and I succeed in having a genuine dialogue, that will already teach us something about transcultural communication. For today most so-called "cultures" are really conglomerates of cultures and quite as much effort is involved in establishing communication between one class, sex, age, or social role and another within our culture as in communicating with people of similar class, sex, age, or social role in another culture.

My particular concern as a philosopher, however, may not be altogether useless or impractical. This concern is for the wholeness and uniqueness of the human—what is called in the technical jargon "philosophical anthropology." Unlike cultural anthropology or any of the other social and human studies such as sociology, psychology, and economics, philosophical anthropology is the one discipline which asks about man as a totality rather than some particular abstraction. It is not concerned merely with describing nor is it concerned only with values and ideals. It wants to know what makes the human human, what is essential to our existence as human persons in direct and indirect relationship with one another and with the environments in which we are set.

Starting from that standpoint, we can say at the outset some interesting and significant things about nursing. Although the registered nurse is not found everywhere and always in human societies, nursing is. The closer knit the extended family and tribe is, the more the function of nursing is likely to be taken care of by a mother, a grandmother, an aunt, a father. But even in the most tightly knit cultures there always have been special figures particularly concerned with nursing in one or another of its aspects— midwife, wetnurse, shaman, medicine man, witch doctor, herbal healer, *baal-shem*.

To nurse means to care for, often in time of crisis and/or transition—sickness, accident, childbirth, infancy, puberty, old age, death. One paradox of this caring aspect of nursing is given us by the words themselves. A "nursery" is a place where young children or young plants are cared for so that they may grow and thrive. Yet a nurse is often associated with the needs of those who are not thriving but hurting, who are not growing toward maturity and health but who are aging and dying, or with nursing those who are sick and wounded back to that health in which they shall need no nursing.

This paradox is already present in the two age groups that the Third National Transcultural Nursing Conference is focusing on—adolescence and middle age. In the Middle Ages there was no adolescence as we know it. Adolescence, like childhood, is of relatively recent vintage, and the prolonged adolescence that we know in our culture (one of my science colleagues at Sarah Lawrence College once remarked at lunch that by the time a child is thirty or at least thirty-five she should stop blaming her parents and take some responsibility herself!) is certainly rare in the history and in the cultures of the world. But it is assumed that this is the great opportunity to grow and change, mature and develop in order to come into the legacy of adulthood that our culture bequeaths us. Practically speaking, of course, adolescence often appears not so close to heaven as to hell—both for the adolescents themselves and their parents—and many of the physical, mental, and emotional problems of society center in this age.

If some persons remain adolescent into middle age, there are many others, in our culture at least, who throw off the seriousness and even responsibilities of middle age to enjoy a second adolescence. The caricatures of Esalen Institute and the Human Potential Movement, such as the movie *Bob and Carol and Ted and Alice*, may make this seem a fad easily to be dismissed. But actually today it is increasingly being recognized that middle age too is a time of transition not unlike adolescence, even though it is not moving toward the prime of adulthood but toward old age and death. Many years ago the psychologist Carl Jung recognized what is beginning to find acceptance and understanding today: that one does not become adult once and for all, that every time of life has its tasks and crises, its passages and its *rites de passage*, and that middle age in particular is a gateway to meaning for which the more practical concerns of "making it" in the adult world leave little time.

Nursing is essentially a caring role. Twenty-five hundred years ago the great Chinese sage Laotzu spoke of himself as a person who cherished three things: to care, to be fair, and to be humble:

. . .

> *When a man cares he is unafraid,*
> *When he is fair he leaves enough for others,*
> *When he is humble he can grow;*
> *Whereas if, like men of today, he be bold without caring,*

Self-indulgent without sharing,
Self-important without shame,
He is dead.
The invincible shield
Of caring
Is a weapon from the sky
Against being dead.[2]

There is an even deeper paradox connected with the phenomenon of caring than with that of the similarities and contrasts between adolescence and middle age. Put at its simplest, caring brings into close but unequal relation two persons who have no intrinsic reason to be in relation unless they are in some sense equal. The asymmetry of roles is inevitable in caring and is structured into the caring professions as it is practiced in hospitals, clinics, nursing homes, or any similar institution. One person cares for and one is cared for. One person is active and the other is "patient." One person, presumably, is in health, the other is sick or in some other way in need. There is nothing new in all this and nothing significant except when the very role of caring gets in the way of caring because the one cared for no longer appears as a person on the same level as the one who cares. An author of a book on T-groups that I recently looked at reported that the groups of nurses that he worked with tended to be less aware of the real needs and problems of their patients precisely because they saw them as "sick people." Perhaps this is why Laotzu joined being humble and being fair to caring as the three qualities he cherished.

The very existence of social roles means inequality of some sort, and the helping professions represent a built-in inequality of helper and helped in contrast to the unstructured and informal mutual give-and-take of some friends and some families. This inequality does not in itself prevent mutual respect and mutual trust as long as the attitude remains that of a person-to-person partnership. When the social role denotes some superiority of one person over another, this is no longer so, and when persons of whatever helping profession receive their own personal confirmation through feeling that *they* are the helpers and the others are the helped, the "patients," this mutuality is endangered.

In his famous story *Metamorphosis*, Franz Kafka tells of how Gregor Samsa, an altogether ordinary traveling salesman, wakes up one morning transformed into a gigantic insect. As long as he is still capable of human speech, his family reluctantly see him as their son and brother upon whom some monstrous calamity has fallen, even though they shut him in one room of the house which they use as the storeroom for all the things they do not want. Once he is no longer able to speak, they assume that he cannot understand them and soon convince themselves that he is not really Gregor at all. When the charwoman comes to tell them that the "thing" has died and she has thrown it into the trash can, they all breathe a sigh of relief and continue life as normal.

This cruel story concerns the family, but how often is it also true of the terminally ill, the deaf, the dumb, the blind, those who cannot speak or move due to a stroke, those who are transfigured by accident or disease so we do not recognize our own humanity in them? Whenever a nurse or doctor sees anyone first and foremost as a "patient," a member of the class of the sick, to be "helped" but not to be related to, there is the danger of that progressive decay of communication which may transform that person too, like Gregor Samsa, into a "thing."

If this paradox is present in the relation of the well nurse to the sick patient, it is particularly so in the relation to persons of other cultures. The instinctive tendency of the American to raise his voice when talking to a "foreigner," as if shouting louder would enable the other to understand English, is indicative of our tendency to lose sight of the common humanity of those with whom we cannot easily communicate. Nor is this paradox to be overcome simply by diligent study of the language and culture of other peoples or by the field trips of the anthropologist. For our very "knowledge" of other cultures may lead us to stereotypes and caricatures that get in the way of meeting the other in her or his uniqueness. It would be equally fatal to approach a person of another culture as if that person thought and felt the way you did *and* as if that person mechanically responded to cultural stimuli the way some textbook or field report said they did.

Many years ago Martin Buber expressed the paradox of caring in the contrast between "pity" and "compassion":

> The helping man, in a certain sense, does not concern himself about the other, but does what he does . . . through the seemingly isolated, seemingly unconcerned, seemingly unconnected action that each performs out of himself. . . . To help one another is no task, but a matter of course, the reality on which

life-together is founded. Help is no virtue, but an artery of existence. . . . not to help out of pity, that is, out of a sharp, quick pain which one wishes to expel, but out of love, that is, out of living with the other. He who pities does not live with the suffering of the sufferer, he does not bear it in his heart as one bears the life of a tree with all its drinking in and shooting forth and with the dream of its roots and the craving of its trunk and the thousand journeys of its branches, or as one bears the life of an animal with all its gliding, stretching, and grasping and all the joy of its sinews and its joints and the dull tension of its brain. He does not bear in his heart this special essence, the suffering of the other; rather he receives from the most external features of this suffering a sharp, quick, pain, unbridgeably dissimilar to the original pain of the sufferer. . . . But the helper must live with the other. . . . Thus it is told of one [Hasidic rabbi] that when a poor person had excited his pity, he provided first for all his pressing need, but then, when he looked inward and perceived that the wound of pity was healed, he plunged with great, restful, and devoted love into the life and needs of the other, took hold of them as if they were his own life and needs and began in reality to help.[3]

For many years I worked closely with the Quakers, or Friends, and taught at Pendle Hill, the Quaker study center at Wallingford, Pennsylvania. Noting that they were fond of turning George Fox's answering "that of God in his enemies" into an affirmation of the goodness of man, I occasionally teased them by saying, "I love that of God in you. I just can't stand you!" What I meant, of course, is that such universal love is not love at all. Rabbi Moshe Leib of Sasov said that he learned to love when he went to an inn where he witnessed the conversation of two drunken peasants. "Do you love me?" the first peasant asked the second. "I love you like a brother!" the second peasant answered. "You don't love me," rejoined the first peasant. "You don't know what I lack. You don't know what I need." The second peasant fell into a sullen silence. "But I understood," said Moshe Leib. "To love another is to understand his need and bear the burden of his suffering." This is not human need in general. It is not even the need that one can deduce from the knowledge of a particular culture. It is the need of this concrete, other person in all her or his uniqueness, including all those things that shame her or burden him.

The great existentialist philosopher Martin Heidegger affirms what I have called the "partnership of existence" by saying that

"Dasein ist Mitsein"—to be in the world means to be together with others in the world. Yet he sees the essential relationship between persons in the world as one of solicitude. Solicitude, as Martin Buber points out in his critique of Heidegger, cannot *as such* be an essential relation since it does not set a person's life in direct relation with the life of another, but only one person's solicitous help in relation with another person's lack and need of it. True solicitude does not come from mere coexistence with others, as Heidegger thinks, but from essential, direct, whole relations between person and person.

> In mere solicitude man remains essentially with himself, even if he is moved with extreme pity; in action and help he inclines toward the other, but the barriers of his own being are not thereby breached; he makes his assistance, not his self, accessible to the other; nor does he expect any mutuality, in fact he probably shuns it; he "is concerned with the other," but he is not anxious for the other to be concerned with him. In an essential relation, on the other hand, . . . the other becomes present not merely in the imagination or feeling, but in the depths of one's substance, so that one experiences the mystery of the other being in the mystery of one's own. The two participate in one another's lives in very fact.[4]

The paradox of the caring relation is captured *par excellence* in a Hasidic story entitled "Climbing Down": "If you want to help another," one Hasidic rabbi said, "it is not enough to stand above and throw down a rope. Rather you must descend yourself into the mud and filth and then with strong arms pull yourself and the other up to the light." If you content yourself with standing above, you will not be able really to care for the other. You will not understand his need from within but only in terms of one category or another that you impose upon the situation. On the other hand, if you go down into the "mud and filth," you risk being caught yourself, in which case you will only succeed in dragging the other still further down. Really to care means to be able to enter into the situation of the other yet to bring with you some resources that the other does not have so that you may not cause but facilitate the healing that may come to pass in the meeting between you.

Recently I attended "grand rounds" at the family medicine center of a great university hospital. In preparation for these grand rounds and my participation in them, I had viewed a forty-five minute interview between a family medicine resident and a thirty-two-year-old woman suffering from "lupus," that disease of the tissues that produces antibodies that attack the very organs they are meant to protect. The doctor was a middle-class American man who described himself as an atheist. The young woman was a Spanish-American, or Chicana, from a very religious Catholic background. The doctor was sympathetic and helpful and moved with great facility from one topic to another. The more he leaned forward in his chair, the more she settled back with her feet outstretched and her hands clasped in her lap. The more he elicited from her statements about her anger, temper, irritability, impatience, the more totally lacking in affect was her voice. The more he moved from topic to topic, the more sketchy were her answers and the less she volunteered on her own.

Among the many things that struck me about this interview and which I commented on during my part of the "grand rounds," two in particular stand out for me now as a paradigm of the problem of transcultural nursing and the paradox of caring. One was the very sensitive way in which he pointed out to her that, although she took many medicines, none of them were miracle drugs which promised any effectiveness. As a result, to use his own words, he "became complacent" about her pain. He did not mean by this that he would not relieve her pain if he could or that he did not care about her pain. In a sense, he cared too much. Knowing that her illness was chronic and that its prognosis was ever greater pain, systematic malfunction, and early death, he could only protect himself from his overcaring by ceasing to make her pain present to himself. It would have relieved him if she had expressed anger at him for this. Instead she only said of him, as of God, that she wondered sometimes if they were aware of her limits and of how much she could be expected to bear. Her real anger she claimed to be directed at the disease itself, and at the same time she complained that she could not "fight back." God and religion, which she described as a personal search for a meaning which seemed to be more in the future than in the present, had given her, she asserted, "peace of mind." Yet it was clear that this surrender of hers to the divine will was a very partial one which did not overcome for very long that temper and impatience which she saw as her heritage from her father.

The other event that struck me in particular in the interview seems to fall rather on the side of insensitivity to her culture, to her position in her family, and to her religious feelings and concerns. Almost ten years before, she left her tight-knit family in Arizona to come live and work in San Diego. Now as the result of her lupus, she found herself, not without obvious resentment, drawn more closely to ties with and dependence on her mother, though she still made no move to go home. Although she succeeded in holding for a while a bilingual job that gave her status, salary, and independence such as her domestic work had never afforded, she had little social life and little to save her from the growing isolation and fear of her sickness. Yet the doctor did not trouble to find out whether she had, through a church or any other group, any sort of support system that she might turn to as her pain grew more and more unbearable and his medicines less and less effective. A question about birth control pills he turned off as medically contraindicated, and he returned to the subject of her possible sexual activity only at a time when she was in such great pain that she responded, "Where am I supposed to do it? In my ear?!"

Instead of seeing her religious search as an integral part of her battle to achieve some workable balance in the tension of dependence and independence of her family, the resident treated it as an isolated curiosity. When she said that she might go to a certain church, which she left unnamed, if she did not find satisfaction in another which someone (I assume her family) wanted her to try out first, he inquired no further. Nor did his questions about whether she prayed and what she prayed for show any greater understanding of her situation from within. Finally, he advanced the entirely hypothetical question of what she would do about the religious education of her children if she had children. "I would want them to go to church when they were young and then decide for themselves later," she replied. "Why not the other way around?" he asked. "Let them have no religious upbringing and then decide for themselves." "Because I believe they should have some religious training when young," she said. "First toilet training, then the church," he retorted and, catching himself, added, "Strike that from the tape."

Confronted with her immediate pain, he was afraid of getting stuck in the mud and the filth. Confronted with her fear of isolation and death, he remained above and threw down a badly frayed rope!

But what else can you expect of a doctor or nurse who has to deal with a great many patients from all ways and walks of life, you may ask. I do not expect any particular behavior from them for I am well aware of the limitations of our understanding and resources. But our calling as helpers and carers does ask of us what our existence itself asks of us: to hold the tension between our personal uniqueness and our social role in the way in which we bring ourselves to others and in the way in which we let others come to us. To hold this tension means that we do not relegate our existence as persons in person-to-person relationships to after work hours and weekends but move toward genuine dialogue in and through our social roles. This tension is of especial importance for the transition stages of life, such as adolescence and middle age. In understanding this tension we may come to understand in greater depth confirmation and the community of otherness as an approach to transcultural nursing.

That confirmation which we need to exist as human beings and to become the unique persons that we are called to become cannot be identified simply with our confirmation in our social roles. This is something that all societies have known in their emphasis upon providing rites of passage for those individuals who must separate themselves from the tribe during puberty, childbirth, sickness, ecstasy, danger, or death. This is also something we are beginning to rediscover in our contemporary concern with "passages," though this discovery itself is dulled by our wish to pin down precise life-tasks that go with every age and to reassure ourselves that our life-crises are "normal," thus losing sight of our personal uniqueness and the dreadful isolation that may accompany it.

We cannot be confirmed merely by insisting, any more than we can confirm others merely by willing to do so. True confirmation is only possible in a caring community, a community in which each really cares for the other in her or his otherness. Our ordinary notion of community is one based upon affinity, commonness—having the same customs, tastes, opinions, faith, or family. If there is to be such a thing as transcultural nursing and transcultural caring, we must work in the direction of a very different sort of community—one in which it is precisely the otherness of each person, family, and subgroup which is valued and confirmed. How else will we be able to understand and help those of different cultures, ages, sexes, and social backgrounds than ourselves?

Thus the paradox of caring and of transcultural nursing is the paradox of our human existence itself. We do not exist as self-sufficient monads that only secondarily come into relationship with each other, any more than we are mere cells in a social organism. We exist as persons who need to be confirmed in our uniqueness by persons essentially other than ourselves. To be confirmed we must be made present by the other as the persons we are. This confirmation takes place neither out of selfishness—because it is in the interest of the other to do so—nor out of altruism—because the other selflessly sets her or his self aside to minister to our needs—but out of the fundamental reality of the partnership of existence. We do not have to choose between the individual and society, solitude and togetherness. Rather we have to hold the tension of being at one and the same time separate and together, ever more deeply in dialogue and, just as a result, ever more fully unique.

If transcultural nursing is to be real and effective, it must include an openness, a flexibility, a willingness to withstand the concrete situation. Genuine dialogue means the recognition of real limits and real tragedy, as in the case of lupus. But it also means hope because it does not assume that what was true this moment will necessarily be true the moment after—hope, not as idealism, therefore, but as a readiness to assess the new moment in its concreteness. This also means, of course, the readiness to know the needs of the other. Dialogue has to include the hope that will enable you to enter again, both actively and imaginatively, into the concrete situation of the other—to risk and involve yourself and to discover in that situation what your resources are. We respond to what calls us with our actions and our lives—out of a concern as deep as the human, as real as the situation that faces us, as whole as we are able to be.

Such dialogue flowers into the "community of otherness" when our openness becomes a way of responding and response. A psychiatric nurse who is the head of a community health project devoted to maternal and child care has just hired a paraprofessional midwife of American Indian background to work in her project. "I am hopeful of learning more of the art of childbirth—all along the same path," the psychiatric nurse writes. This is a step toward the "community of otherness."

The reality of community is polyphonic, it is many-voiced. In real community, the voice of the minority culture is heard because real community creates an atmosphere of trust which cares about this voice and enables it to be heard. Dialogue means the meeting with the other person, the other group, the other culture—a meeting that confirms the other yet does not deny oneself and the ground on which one stands. Our choice is not *between* ourselves and the other; for genuine dialogue is at once a confirmation of community *and* of otherness. The community of otherness means the willingness to live and work even with those who are not "like-minded," those who do not share our cultures and our worldviews. We have to confirm others in their uniqueness and in their need. We have to confirm the common ground of communal existence as a meaning larger than that of the individual but inclusive of it. Communal existence does not mean harmony or obedience to authority, but building together—each from where he or she is and from what she or he is—the community of otherness. The community must set limits where necessary, but, if it has real communal concern, it can never just cut off the person and cease to be responsible for her or him. We must get beyond techniques and theories and be ready to meet one another as persons and groups building together in a common concern. In the medical world this implies the readiness for that sort of interdisciplinary cooperation between doctor, nurse, psychiatrist, social worker, and even philosopher, in which I took part at the "grand rounds" of the family medicine center. Dr. Elizabeth Kubler-Ross reports that at one hospital where she worked, a black woman orderly—herself from a large poverty-stricken family—was the only one who was able to talk with the patients and help them with their fear. What makes community real is people finding themselves in a common situation which they approach in different ways, yet which calls each of them out. Wherever persons meet in a spirit of common concern, ready to encounter each other through and beyond their cultural differences, the lived reality of the community of otherness can come into being.

Chapter 20

THE HUMAN COSTS OF UN- AND UNDEREMPLOYMENT

THE CONFIRMATION of otherness in society means above all the confirmation of the workers who make up the primary economic units of the society. The workers are also, of course, consumers, and the consumer too must be seen in his or her otherness if a confirming community is to exist. But the essential problematic of the confirmation of otherness in society arises most pressingly with the worker because it is precisely here that exploitation and with it the non- and disconfirmation of the other most often appears. Nowhere perhaps does this problem attain clearer focus than in those combined evils of any large-scale economic system—unemployment and underemployment. Here the questions both of the quantity and the quality of work converge.

Studs Terkel, in his justly famous book *Working* (subtitled *People Talk About What They Do All Day and How They Feel About What They Do*) has given us penetrating insight and concrete illustration of the need of the worker for confirmation, and of the disconfirmation and confirmation that an enormous range and variety of workers experience in working. In his introduction he says of *Working:*

> It is about a search, too, for daily meaning as well as daily bread, for recognition as well as cash, for astonishment rather than

torpor; in short, for a sort of life rather than a Monday through Friday sort of dying. Perhaps immortality, too, is part of the quest. To be remembered was the wish, spoken and unspoken, of the heroes and heroines of this book.[1]

The question implicit in all daily work is: ought it not earn "an acknowledgment of man's *being*"? Since this acknowledgment must come from employers and fellow workers it is, essentially, a confirmation of otherness. Most workers are looking for a calling, not a job; yet most have jobs that are too small for their spirits. Even the most "ordinary" person is aware of a sense of personal worth—or more often a lack of it—in the work s/he does. The president of a United Automobile Workers local describes the members of his local as not happy in their work at a General Motors plant and indifferent to how good the product is and to running the plant. But they do want to have some say about what *they* do, and they want to be treated with dignity. On the other hand, a woman with an independent income testifies strongly to how important it is to be occupied and to find some joy in one's occupation. Work is essential to human life, yet "much of what we call work is dehumanizing and brutalizing." Without work one cannot maintain one's balance or sanity or create any coherence in life. One needs to have a place in the world, to be needed, to create something new.[2]

Sadly enough, what is often reflected in the pages of *Working* is the way in which the worker's uniqueness and otherness is *dis*confirmed. Speaking of TV commercial casting, an actor tells of the rudeness of the people who do the hiring: "If you're not a star, there is humiliation and degradation—if you allow it to happen to you." Even the actor whom younger actors respect because he has not sold out, says that to pay the rent he has sold out lots of times and done jobs he was not particularly proud of. In fact, he sees what has changed in the nature of work in this country as "the lack of pride in the work itself. A man's life is his work." One of the testimonies that is made over and over again in *Working* is that the worker sees herself as a machine and that the actual machines are treated better than the workers. If the machine breaks down, there is someone there to fix it, but if the worker breaks down, he is pushed aside to keep the assembly line running. An ex-president of a business conglomerate jeers at the notion of loyalty to a corporation and points out the way in which executives suddenly lose their humanity and their personhood as soon as they are laid off. The ego is crushed when the person who is busy and sought after finds himself without friends and without function. "The warm personal touch *never* existed in corporations." Many family-held companies have gone broke and been "taken over by the cold hand of the corporation."[3]

On the other hand, *Working* contains a few eloquent testimonies of the confirmation to be found when one's work is not merely a job but also a personal calling. Although housewives in movies and on television are pictured as mindless, a woman film critic recognizes that "being involved with kids may be much more creative than what their husbands do at drudge jobs. It takes a lot of intelligence to handle children and it's a fascinating process watching kids grow up." An interstate truck driver who has become active in a small new truckers' union speaks of being catapulted into levels of decision making he never dreamed of before and of finding his own sense of self-respect. A housewife speaks of the satisfaction she gets from seeing her pie eaten by the family because she knows she is needed. "I think it's the greatest satisfaction in the world to know you've pleased somebody." The ex-president of the conglomerate says that money was not as important to him as the power, status, and prestige. But he also says that suddenly it all became empty and that now that he has become a consultant he recognizes that what he is doing is much more fun than going back into "that jungle" even if it does mean giving up status. The carpenter-poet Nick Lindsay (son of the American poet Vachel Lindsay) tells of how things fall into place when one brings one's whole universe into each nail that one hits. In remarkable consistency with his life-philosophy when I knew him more than thirty-five years ago, Lindsay stresses the meaning that is found in each unique task if one brings one's whole self to that task. Although the carpenter may be working fast, he does not hurry from one nail to the other but treats each lick of the hammer as a separate person or friend of that one moment—"Unique, all by itself. Pow!" And the fireman who used to be a bank clerk states with pride that now he is really saving somebody as opposed to the unreal paperwork he did in the past. "When you see the firemen come out with babies in their hands or give mouth-to-mouth to a guy who is dying, you know that is something real that you can't get around."[4]

As an undergraduate at Harvard, I majored in Labor Economics and Social Reform to prepare for a career as a labor organizer or educator. In the Harvard of my day were such notable professors of Economics as Alvin Hansen, Gustav Haberler, and Paul Sweezy, as a result of which I immersed myself fully in the economics of John Maynard Keynes and of Karl Marx, two economic systems which differ chiefly in their basic assumptions but not, I saw then and still hold, in their economic workings. Today I call myself a philosophical anthropologist, i.e., a philosopher concerned with the wholeness and uniqueness of the human. As such, I can no longer restrict my focus to the economic but must see the problem of the worker in the broader context of the *human* cost of un- and underemployment. There are, of course, incredible economic, social, political and other costs, and all of these are human. But I mean the costs to our full humanity. The economic approach to unemployment is an essential one; yet we shall overlook equally important matters if we limit ourselves to this approach.

What are the philosophical-anthropological assumptions underlying classical economics? Adam Smith was one of the first economists to talk about the *specialization of labor*. That is a basic economic assumption, but it is an equally basic anthropological one. Specialization of labor is how we do live in society. Yet this very foundation of civilization regularly results in a situation in which persons are treated in terms of the functions they serve in the economic machine.

Classical economics postulated the *profit motive* as the self-understood axiom of the economic system. Even John Maynard Keynes, for all his innovations, accepted the profit motive as the basis of his theory. The profit motive assumes individualism in which everyone is only out for him or herself alone. This assumption tends to become a self-fulfilling prophecy. Yet it is not anthropologically sound, as I shall endeavor to show.

Even Karl Marx with his theory of "surplus value" was still following the classical economics version of the profit motive. Only he saw the underside of this "prime mover." In the capitalist system the laborer becomes a commodity, to be bought and sold like any other commodity. In this connection, Marx gave us the classic portrayal of another anthropological assumption of his economics, the *alienation of labor*. The worker becomes alienated from him or herself, from nature, from other persons, from his work, and from life in general.

How can we put these economic-anthropological assumptions into a fully human perspective? The economic costs of the profit motive during times of depression are very obvious. But there is also a terrible human cost to both the laborer and the entrepreneur because the result is that everyone, in fact, becomes a commodity. Everyone becomes a function of the economic system; everyone becomes less than human. The possibilities of the interhuman, of community, that remain among us are systematically and organizationally unrealized. When a recent Secretary of the Treasury answered a question about the role of labor by saying that management will manage and labor will work, he indicated the assumption that labor participation in decision making will be economically costly. This has been shown to be untrue, but more important still, it is *humanly* costly to deny such participation. Studies of AT&T in the 1920s and the statistics cited by Charles Hampden-Turner in his book *Radical Man*[5] demonstrate the fact that the more workers participate in decisions and innovations, the more meaningfully they work with each other, the greater production can be, and the more it is a human process.

What further anthropological assumptions do we need in order to understand un- and underemployment? The most meaningful one that I know is the dual concept of "distance and relation" that underlies Martin Buber's philosophy of dialogue. What distinguishes man from the animals is that we become human through a double process—the distancing from the environment and from one another that makes a world over against us that we can perceive as whole and one, and the overcoming of distance through relating that gives us personal existence within interhuman, interpersonal, communal, and social contexts. This double process gives us insight into the paradox that to be human we need to be confirmed by others as the unique persons that we are meant to become. Our becoming is not just that of the species in which the little tiger grows up to be a big tiger. We need, paradoxically, to be confirmed as the persons that we can become, and yet we need to be confirmed by other people. We cannot simply confirm ourselves.

This paradox lays the groundwork for a joker, a "Catch 22." In our desperate need to be confirmed by others, we sacrifice real confirmation for a "contract." In order to win the confirmation of those persons who are significant to us we become "seeming persons," trying to appear to be the way we imagine they want us to be. Nowhere are we under such pressure to assume an appearance as in our work. We are afraid of losing our jobs or of not getting jobs because we do not appear the way that a particular industry or office wants us to be, whether it be wearing hats or not wearing beards, having or not having certain opinions, values, life-styles, or tastes. This, of course, is particularly true for women. But it is also true for everyone in some way or another, even for the topmost executive. A project coordinator comments in *Working* that by economically intimidating and threatening people, our reward system makes them into "apple polishers and ass kissers." A commercial artist and designer, who has given up commercialism because he finds it "degrading," admits that he "may have to pimp again for survival's sake" but protests that he will not give up sane work and that he will work on a road crew and cut lumber rather than play again "the full-time lying dishonest role I've done most of my life." A teacher of adult education relates that when he was a salesman, there was never a day in which he felt he could be absolutely honest. Playing the role on somebody else's trip, he felt that he had to wear a mask every minute on the job.[6]

I believe the anthropology of distance and relation and of confirmation gives us a more inclusive way of understanding the specialization of labor. Specialization of labor is not only economically necessary, it is necessary for us to become and remain human within society. It carries within it a possibility of cooperation among us that can lead us to become more fully human. But it also carries the opposite possibility when it is approached only from the functional standpoint. This happens regularly when we are given an aptitude or skills test and are told on the basis of it to select one type of employment rather than another. Recently a nurse said to me, "I am a skilled nurse; I am thirty-five years old; and I have wanted for some years to change my vocation. I want to work in personal relations, but I can't do it because everybody says to me, 'You're skilled in nursing so you remain a nurse. You haven't got typing, bookkeeping, or an M.S.W.' " Even a person in a highly skilled job is underemployed if that person no longer wishes to do that type of work. We are imprisoned in underemployment by a specialization of labor that functionalizes us. This is true of most socialist states quite as much as capitalist states. We need specialization of labor; yet we need to have it in a more human way.

"For large numbers of men, the conditions of work in early adulthood are oppressive, alienating and inimical to development," writes Daniel J. Levinson. This is, in the first place, because they work in institutional structures of all kinds which give the aims of productivity and profit making top priority. We have not yet learned "how to create organizations that work productively, humanely and in ways that support the adult development of their employees and clients." Levinson also points to the need of improving the quantity and quality of mentoring in the work world in order to give young men some degree of emotional support, guidance, and sponsorship. There is little mentoring in the work world and what there is is generally of poor quality, with the result that the young man's entry into the adult world is greatly hampered.

Still a third change that is necessary to humanize the work world, according to Levinson, is to give an adequate place to women so that not only women but also men can integrate the Masculine/Feminine polarity:

> The freer participation of women in the work world is an important step toward the liberation of men from their one-sided masculinity and their anxiety about the feminine. Men need women as colleagues, bosses and mentors. These relationships enable them to form richer identities, to live out more aspects of the self, and to reduce the burdens created by the excessive masculinization of work. Changes of this kind will also free women from the constraints imposed by the excessive feminization of parenting and by the discrimination that restricts their participation in most of our institutions.[7]

Levinson also offers us an insight into the underemployment that arises from the fact that most occupations are defined and understood from the perspective of early adulthood. Recognizing that the nature of a man's work changes appreciably in middle adulthood, he asks how jobs and careers should evolve during this period of a man's life. "What can be done to provide for greater learning and rejuvenation within the same occupation, for shifting to a 'second career,' or for early retirement and change to new forms of work in middle adulthood?"[8]

The understanding of our becoming human through being confirmed by others also illuminates the fact that our human existence must be understood as a dialogue with others in person-to-person, family, and communal relations. This insight into human existence entails the radical rejection of the assumption of individualism that underlies the profit motive. It is simply not true that individual gain is the primary moving force of our existence, for we do not exist primarily as isolated individuals relating to all others only in terms of how we can exploit them for our benefit. Yet in a system that operates primarily in terms of the profit motive, people are pressed into this sort of behavior.

An example of how this dialogue with others is corrupted by the competition for work is the situation of a skilled social worker with whom I recently talked. Three days per week she works through her lunch hour because she knows that there is a group of unemployed social workers who are waiting for her job. This is not just an economic matter. Here is a woman who is already overworked. What it does to her not to have one break in her whole day of seeing clients, what it does to the quality of her work, of her human performance, of her existence as a human being, is beyond thinking. Even if she were not correct about her assumptions, it would not matter. The presence of thousands of unemployed social workers forces the quality of work lower and lower. This is true, of course, not only of social workers but all through society, especially today when there really is what Marx called an "army of the unemployed."

I see the community of otherness as a direction of movement toward a community in which we shall certainly still be concerned about economic, political, and social factors yet will also remain concerned for the confirmation of every particular person, group, and community. I do not mean confirmation merely as good workers but as *persons* who are also workers, as workers who do not cease to be persons during the time they work. This confirmation must be understood in terms of a necessary and fruitful tension between our personal uniqueness and our social role. No one can live without a social role. Yet it is of vital importance for our full humanity, that, insofar as possible, we hold this social function in tension with our personal uniqueness. Precisely through our social role we develop into the persons we can become. One economic system can vitally weaken this fruitful tension, whereas another economic system can vitally strengthen it.

Working again offers abundant evidence of how essential it is to hold the tension between personal uniqueness and social role and of the price that is paid when one does not hold it. A writer/producer tells how deep down she feels demeaned when she produces a successful commercial. She sees herself and the other people in the business as hustlers who have to be witty and glib. "I've never pretended this is the best writing I can do. Every advertising writer has a novel in his drawer. Few of them ever do it." A woman film critic says she considers herself really lucky because she loves her occupation. But most of her life she spent working at boring jobs that she hated, jobs that exhausted her energy and spirit. "Most people work at jobs that mechanize them and depersonalize them." This is something that I too have felt strongly since my study of labor economics at Harvard. My three-and-a-half years of doing largely "made" work in Civilian Public Service camps for conscientious objectors during the Second World War has left me with little tolerance for meaningless work even in the groves of academe and has greatly intensified my feeling for the vast majority of humanity who are condemned to do boring, routine, and dehumanizing labor.

A spot-welder complains in *Working* that there is no time for the human side of his work because he cannot proceed at his own pace, and he looks forward to another type of work which will be not a job but a career. An editor who is a staff writer for an institution publishing health care literature describes the very work where she had expected to put her energy, enthusiasm, and gifts as "token labor":

> It's so demeaning to be there and not be challenged. It's humiliation because I feel I'm being forced into doing something I would never do of my own free will. . . . I'm vegetating and being paid to do exactly that. . . . Somebody has bought the right to you for eight hours a day. The manner in which they use you is completely at their discretion.

The teacher of adult education finds the key to his own life in the meaninglessness he sensed in his father's job and his father's success. Witnessing the way in which the corporation took over the whole of his father's life, he finds himself unwilling and afraid to settle into a groove. In his own work he can imagine being fired or being criticized for his teaching methods. But there is no way that the administrator of his college can deprive him of the satisfaction of doing his job well. A lawyer who has given up working for established business to become a "poor people's lawyer" complains of being overcommitted and overextended and of being depressed and overwhelmed by his sense of powerlessness. But he sees his battles as meaningful in contrast to the meaningless hassles of the insurance company. He is aware now of what is going on in our society and of what the system does to people. "I have no regrets. . . . I would have died on the other job. I would have become an alcoholic or a drug addict."[9]

The direction of movement of the "community of otherness" is toward a society in which we are not unconcerned with *any* person, no matter where or who. It is a movement toward a community of communities, one in which there is communal structuring and communal power and communal life all the way through. Marx spoke of overcoming the alienation of labor through the ownership of the means of production. But as we have seen in the Soviet Union and elsewhere, the mere fact that the socialist state owns the means of production does not in itself change the quality of community life. Only a movement in the direction of a community of otherness can do this.

In our present situation the people who are already least confirmed by society—the youth, the blacks, Chicanos, women, former homemakers—are also the ones who are the first to be disconfirmed by being unemployed. This situation is considered to be economically practical because of the notion that whoever has seniority or has been employed longer ought to be the last to be dismissed. This situation not only creates a vast army of unemployed threatening the salaries and quality of life of those employed; it is also a cancer in our midst that is enormously disconfirming of what it means to be a human being. Anyone who has been unemployed for any length of time and has tried to find a position knows that very soon one ceases to see one's situation objectively as simply a matter of statistics. Instead one sees it as a demoralizing commentary on one's own inadequacy. One sees it as a disconfirmation of oneself as a person, and one more and more feels that one has no place in society. That is also true if one is stuck in a meaningless job.

The sense of worthlessness that was reported by the unemployed during the Great Depression of the 1930s has been echoed by those on welfare in more recent times, even though they know that as mothers working at home they are, in fact, making their contribution to society. Today, when more Americans are out of work than at any time since 1939, there are not only material costs in lost education, autos, homes, and businesses but also deep emotional wounds—threats to the worker's sense of identity and self-esteem and to his sense of the future. The job loss is often only mildly traumatic compared to the rebuffs and dashing of hopes which follow. As Freud already recognized, a job is an individual's strongest link to reality and his most essential means of defining himself in relation to the rest of society. A study done for Congress showed that over thirty years, "increases in the unemployment rate were accompanied by increases in suicide, mental illness, homicide and deaths from strokes and heart and kidney disease." Adding to the burden of unemployment is the shame many feel at their predicament. Not only in the Great Depression but even during the 1975 recession, many persons stayed off the street during the day because of the embarrassment they felt at having lost status. The emotional and physical toll of unemployment makes it harder for some victims to find jobs later, forces others into a dead-end street of lower paying and less-skilled work, and leads still others to develop "unemployment careers" that last a substantial part of their lives.[10]

This situation points to our need to use the blacks, Chicanos, women, and youth as a touchstone for the fully human approach necessary to overcome it. This means taking whatever economic, political, social, and communal measures that might help our society move in the direction of giving people jobs. It also means taking those measures that will enable us to be aware of and concerned about the quality of the job and the relation of the person to the job and of persons to each other within the job. If I am elaborating the obvious, it is because what is obvious when we think in human terms tends to drop out of sight when we see things only in economic terms. Every person who has been un-employed or underemployed knows deep down in his or her heart how essential it is to look at our employment situation in anthropological, or fully human terms. This means above all look-ing at it from the standpoint of the humanity of all the "others" that make up that community of otherness toward which we strive.

Chapter 21

THE COMMUNITY OF OTHERNESS AND THE COVENANT OF PEACE

THE "COMMUNITY of otherness" implies a relationship that takes place *between* persons and cannot be counted on as a social technique at our disposal. Our whole notion of action—that we use *this* means to *that* end—is a plain violation of the concrete reality, which is that we do not know what the consequences are going to be of almost any action that we perform. We must have social planning and social action, but we cannot string together events in such fashion that they become links in a chain of cause and effect or moves in a chess game. We think that we know what will happen because we imagine it happens *through* us. Yet we do not even know our own resources, much less the situation that will confront us. If we are so well "prepared" that we carry the situation off the way we expected, we may be sure that we have not really been present, that we have not heard the real address of the situation. We have to founder and flounder before we can discover what is asked of us. What we have said of encounter groups is true of social planning in general: We can plan the *structure* within which social events will take place, but we cannot plan the events themselves.

This is something John Friedmann has understood clearly in placing "the life of dialogue" at the heart of his book *Retracking*

249

America, and he has understood it within the context of the "community of otherness." Through his experience as director of urban planning at the University of California at Los Angeles, Friedmann has recognized that genuine dialogue begins with the acceptance of "otherness" as a basis for meaningful communication, and that this means in turn the acceptance of the reality of conflict and of the possibility of overcoming conflict "by a mutual desire to continue in the life of dialogue." "Dialogue presumes a relation of shared interests and commitments," "of reciprocity and mutual obligation," "a relationship that unfolds in real time." "Transactive planning is carried on the ground swell of dialogue," writes Friedmann.

> In mutual learning, planner and client each learns from the other—the planner from the client's personal knowledge, the client from the planner's technical expertise. In this process, the knowledge of both undergoes a major change. A common image of the situation evolves through dialogue; a new understanding of the possibilities for change is discovered. And in accord with this new knowledge, the client will be predisposed to act.[1]

It is particularly in a large and wealthy society like America that Friedmann sees the possibility of building a community of otherness, for it "is quite capable of accommodating a multiplicity of life styles and the simultaneous pursuit of many different interests." Planning for the community of otherness means openness to surprise. Friedmann argues for "the recognition and acceptance of a class of actions that, rather than being goal-oriented, is *exploratory* in nature." Such "non-directed actions" are "increasingly important in a society where we can know relatively little about the probable consequences of actions, except in certain restricted areas of behavior." This open-ended approach leads Friedmann to the recognition of the historically limited validity of social theories in contrast to the claim of general validity:

> The return of theory to practice in the fullness of historical situations, with none of the variables held constant as in a laboratory, will either confirm or deny the theory's practical value in these specific situations. It will not say anything about the potential applicability of the theory in other situations that, however similar in some respects, will have different overall contexts.[2]

This distinction is almost identical with the one that I have made between the testing of "touchstones of reality" and scientific testing:

> However true our touchstone, it will cease to be true if we do not make it real again by testing it in each new situation. This testing is nothing more nor less than bringing our life-stance into the moment of present reality. In contrast to the scientist who is only interested in particulars insofar as they yield generalizations, we can derive valid insights from the unique situations in which we find ourselves without having to claim that they apply to all situations. We take these insights with us into other situations and test the limits of their validity. Sometimes we find that these insights do hold for a particular situation and sometimes that they do not or that they have to be modified. Yet that does not mean that they cannot be valid insights for other situations.[3]

Calling for networks of communication links relating clusters of task-oriented working groups, or cells, Friedmann envisages a spirit of mutual trust, self-criticism, and collective evaluation within these cells that make each separately and the network in general into communities of otherness. He recognizes that modern man's capacity for dialogue is stunted, that, as I have put it, "much of our sharing is pseudosharing because we lift it to a plane of objective discourse" and abstract what the other says from the personal and existential ground from which he says it. Because our relations are determined by roles and utility, we hear without listening and speak without responding. "Extremely skillful in exchanging functional bits of information," writes Friedmann, modern man "fails in assessing the underlying meanings because he assumes, incorrectly, that information has a reality independent of the persons through whom it becomes available and to whom it is addressed." But this failure of the life of dialogue may be overcome, Friedmann holds, through the mutual participation of small, irreducible cells of a learning society, cells which can easily be formed anywhere at any time.

> Task-oriented working groups may be spontaneously created in a variety of environments—in factories, offices, neighborhoods, clubs, schools, and universities. Their actions will have an experimental character; the ingenuity of working group members

will lead to innovations and discoveries. The life of dialogue will be encouraged, simply because it is the most natural way to approach a problem solution that asks of every member a commitment to the total effort and, above all, to the group's continued existence so long as the challenge of a task remains. The group has no means of survival but for the strength of its internal dialogue.[4]

Friedmann believes that there is an even chance of a learning society coming into existence in America, though it would entail "social innovations on a scale unheard of until now." "But so long as the root remains healthy . . . and life is celebrated in dialogue," he concludes, "even the topmost branches will be vigorous and bear new shoots."

Reconciliation depends upon each of us doing his share to build the "community of otherness." Reality is not given in me alone or in some part of reality with which I identify myself. Among primitive tribes, the members of other tribes were often not even considered human beings. Even the civilized Greeks saw the rest of the non-Greek world as "barbarians" and therefore by nature unequal to them and properly forced into permanent slavery when conquered. On the coast of Africa there are still great castles in which for four hundred years the Portuguese, the Dutch, and the English vied with one another as to who could get the most profit out of shipping fifty million slaves to America for sale there. The ravaging of the American frontier and the ravages of the whaling industry, similarly, show that a good deal of what has characterized modern man, long before the Nazi exterminations, has been a lack of respect for the otherness of creation, including the nonhuman.

Giles Gunn has placed this loss of the sense of otherness at the heart of his understanding of the American mind in his book, *The Interpretation of Otherness:*

There is no blinking the distance which separates most contemporary Americans from all talk of "other" minds, "other" selves, indeed, of "otherness" itself. For in a world bounded on the one side by the agonies and atrocities of Vietnam or the American urban ghetto and on the other by televised moon landings and cloning experiments, it would appear that we wonder, if at all, only about what is left to wonder at or wonder about. The imaginative capacity for wonder—whether it takes the primitive form of awed and passive astonishment before the unexpected, *or* the more sophisticated form of active, imaginative penetration into modes of being other than our own—requires a special openness to the unanticipated, a certain susceptibility to surprise, and most of us can no longer allow ourselves to be so vulnerable. Instead of remaining receptive to novelty, we have become rotten-ripe with knowingness as the imagination's last defense in a world which, if experienced directly, might stun us back into the Stone Age. . . .

. . . When the environment has become but an extension of man himself, there is no way of telling the difference between what Robert Frost calls "counter-love, original response" and "our own voice back in copy speech." Thus one is left yearning, as Americans have always been, for "a world elsewhere" beyond the self and independent and even other than the self, yet suspicious that whatever traces of it are left constitute evidence of nothing so much as our own delusion or paranoia. In such circumstances as these, wonder gives way all too easily either to cynicism or ecstatic frenzy, yearning to submission or resentment, and hope to the madness of boredom.[5]

The respect for the otherness of the other does not mean that I love everyone or even that I have the resources to meet everyone in genuine dialogue. But it does mean that everything that confronts me demands my attention and response—whether of love or hate, agreement or opposition, confirmation or merely letting be. There is a growing tendency today, on both sides of the generation gap, on both extremes of the political spectrum, and on both sides of every militant social and racial confrontation, to regard some people as totally irrelevant because they are not "where it is at." The "community of otherness" stands in uncompromising opposition to this tendency. I have freedom, but I am not the whole of reality, and I find my existence in going out to meet what is not myself.

The greatest task of contemporary man is not to build "enlightened" utopias but to build peace in the context in which he finds himself. The true peacemakers are those who take upon themselves, in the most concrete manner conceivable, the task of discovering what can be done in each situation of tension and struggle by way of facing the real conflicts and working toward genuine reconciliation.

"A peace without truth is a false peace," said Rabbi Mendel of Kotzk. What "truth" means here is made clear by the Talmudic statement the Hasidic master partly quoted: Controversies for the sake of heaven endure. This is completely contrary to Aristotelian logic with its assumption that a statement and its opposite cannot both be true. If controversies take place for the sake of heaven, then *both* sides will endure. It does not mean that eventually one will be proved right and the other wrong. The knowledge that the other also witnesses for his "touchstone of reality" from where he stands can enable us to confirm the other in his truth even while opposing him. We do not have to liberate the world from those who have different witnesses from us. The converse of this also holds, namely, that each must hold his ground and witness for his truth even while at the same time affirming the ground and the truth of the other. This imaginative task of comprehending a relationship from the other side as well as one's own is essential to the goal of overcoming war, for every war justifies itself by turning the enemy into a Manichaean figure of pure evil.

If the present crises lead us to succumb to the merely political, we shall have reinforced the mistrust between nations that makes them deal with each other not in social or human terms but in terms of political abstractions and catchwords. "Our work is for education," one of the leaders of an organized protest against atomic bombs said to me. If this is so, then this work cannot afford to be purely political, purely external. It must start from some organic base. It must build on social reality and find its roots in the community already there. It must be concerned about real communication with the people whom it approaches. For the distinction between propaganda and education does not lie in whether one is a Communist or a pacifist but in whether one approaches another wishing to impose one's truth on him or whether one cares enough for him to enter into dialogue with him, see the situation from his point of view, and communicate what truth one has to communicate to him within that dialogue. Sometimes that dialogue can only mean standing one's ground in opposition to him, witnessing for what one believes in the face of his hostile rejection of it. Yet it can never mean being unconcerned for how he sees it or careless of the validity of his standing where he does. We must confirm him even as we oppose him, not in his "error" but in his right to oppose us, in his existence as a human being whom we value even in opposing.

The truth opposite of this imposition is that trust through which the "other voice" is elicited of the person who will speak only in an atmosphere that weighs every voice equally no matter how hesitant or how much in the minority it may be. From 1921 until his death in 1965 Martin Buber continued to insist that Jews live *with* the Arabs in Palestine and later Israel and not just *next* to them and to warn that the way must be like the goal—*Zion bmishpat* ("Zion with justice")—that the humanity of our existence begins just where we become responsible to the concrete situation by saying: "We shall do no more injustice than we must to live," and by drawing the "demarcation line" in each hour anew in fear and trembling. The covenant of peace—between person and person, between community and community, and between nation and nation—means dialogue.

Dialogue means the meeting with the other person, the other group, the other people—a meeting that confirms the other yet does not deny oneself and the ground on which one stands. The choice is not *between* oneself and the other, nor is there some objective ground to which one can rise above the opposing sides, the conflicting claims. Rather genuine dialogue is at once a confirmation of community *and* of otherness, and the acceptance of the fact that one cannot rise above that situation. "In a genuine dialogue," writes Buber, "each of the partners, even when he stands in opposition to the other, heeds, affirms, and confirms his opponent as an existing other. Only so can conflict certainly not be eliminated from the world, but be humanly arbitrated and led towards its overcoming."

During three years of work as chairman of the American Friends of Ichud (the Israeli association for Israel-Arab rapprochement led by Judah Magnes and Martin Buber), I was again and again surprised to encounter among men of good will, including men working for reconciliation of the conflict, either an attitude which simply did not take into account the real problems to be reconciled, one that saw these problems from one point of view only, or one that proceeded from some pseudo-objective, quasi-universal point of view above the conflict. Every conflict has at least two sides. Even if one of the two sides is "dead wrong" in its opinion or stand, it represents something real that cannot be done away with, namely, its existence itself. In that sense it literally has a different point of view which must be recognized quite apart from the question of the rightness or wrongness of the position it takes. All too often, the word "reconciliation" becomes associated with a sentimental good will that looks away from the very conflict that is to be reconciled or assumes that with this or that action or approach a tragic situation can be transformed into a harmonious one. Genuine reconciliation must begin with a fully realistic and fully honest recognition of real differences and points of conflict, and it must move from this recognition to the task of discovering the standpoint from which some real meeting may take place, a meeting which will include *both* of the conflicting points of view and will seek new and creative ways of reconciling them.

Almost a quarter of a century after my own work for Israeli-Arab rapprochement the necessity for the confirmation of otherness as the only practical approach to conflict has become startlingly clear through the excesses of the Israeli Lebanon war. In the second part of his "Journal of the Longest War" the Argentinian journalist and victim of police torture Jacobo Timerman has repeatedly called for the perception of otherness and the response to it as the way forward for Israel:

> The soldiers returning from the front . . . speak to us of the existence of the Other: the Palestinian. . . . The soldiers came to know that region which is so difficult to penetrate: the affective world of the Other. . . . The soldiers met Palestinian youths who serve as volunteers in hospitals, who have friends, who want to have children someday, and who, like the Israelis, dream of a motorcycle, of a girl; youths who are also proud of being unafraid of death and who also mourn the death of others. They brought back stories of nurses who remained with the wounded, of doctors who did not flee, of Palestinian youths who, like them, did not ask for mercy and did not humble themselves.

Timerman tells of a play entitled "Imagining the Other" at Tel Aviv University in which the three Arab actors intone an Israeli patriotic song, making the Israelis aware of the Arabs' presence as "others" in their lives. What is surprising about this play, Timerman quotes a critic, is not its evident sincerity and honesty but its lack of hate. Timerman comments:

> To understand the existence of the Other and then to admit his existence without hatred is something new for Israel as a whole, even though some democratic sectors of Israel have always lived this way. This widespread mood—even if it has not yet become a state of consciousness—has never existed before. A new real-

ity is taking shape as dispersed links from the most disparate places are joining together. Unexpected attractions have come into play, as the two peoples of this region grow ever more conscious of the horrors we have forced each other to live through. . . .

It is extraordinary for us, the Palestinian and Israeli peoples, to reach that culminating moment in the encounter of two enemies when they mutually confess their mistakes, their crimes, their terrors, and their inevitable need for each other.

When the Israeli takes in the fact that the United States no longer feels inextricably tied to Israel, then what remains, says Timerman, is "the eternal and immovable presence of the Other—the irreducible Palestinian." The crimes and the mistakes of the Palestinians do not mean that the Israelis can safely ignore their existence or deny the rightness and justice of their claim. "If we could learn to accept their human identity, as we did in the case of the Germans after the Second World War, we would know how to accept their national identity." All the machinations and manipulations of the parties to the Middle East conflict can produce nothing other than variations on the endless butchery unless the opportunity is seized for the mutual recognition of the two peoples, Israelis and Palestinians. The alternative to this opportunity that Timerman sees the Begin government taking is the return "to the mood that prevailed in the ghetto, where survival meant knowing that the Other hated us, meant defeating the Other." Timerman recognizes that what makes the situation difficult is a conflict between equal rights. This conflict cannot be resolved by a peace agreement but only by constructive action, including "a decision by the Israeli people to reconstruct in Lebanon what our Army has destroyed."

> It will be one more way to allow us to establish a dialogue with the outside world. To renounce impunity, to take responsibility for what was destroyed, is a part of this dialogue. To ask the world's cooperation for the reconstruction we owe the world is another part of this dialogue. All reparation is an act of civilization.

"For quite a long time, if we want to live in peace," Timerman concludes, "understanding the Other is going to be as necessary as understanding oneself." "Psalm 137 tells me that I must never forget Jerusalem," he movingly adds. "I have not forgotten her. With the same fervor and tenderness, I will never forget Beirut."[6]

The covenant of peace is neither technique nor formula and still less is it a universal principle which needs only be applied by deduction to the particular situation. It takes its start from the concrete situation, including all of its tensions—tensions which we can never hope or even desire to remove entirely since they belong to the very heart of the community of otherness. The covenant of peace is no ideal that one holds above the situation, but a patient and never-finished working toward some points of mutual contact, mutual understanding, and mutual trust. It builds community by way of the mutual confirmation of otherness, and when this community shipwrecks, as it again and again tends to do, it takes up the task anew. The covenant of peace means a movement *in the direction of* the community of otherness, such movement as each new hour allows.

The community of otherness grows out of conflict within mutual cooperation, mutual understanding, and ultimately mutual trust. But in bedrock situations even a negative protest may be a positive step toward dialogue if it is done in the spirit of dialogue. The covenant of peace implies a "fellowship of reconciliation"; yet it is precisely here that we have fallen short. We have tended to turn "reconciliation" into a platform to expound, a program to put over, and have not recognized the cruel opposition and the real otherness that underlie conflict. We have been loath to admit that there are tragic conflicts in which no way toward reconciliation is at present possible. We have been insufficiently tough-minded in our attitude toward love, turning it into an abstract love for mankind or a feeling within ourselves rather than a meeting between us and others. We cannot really love unless we first know the other, and we cannot know her until we have entered into relationship with her.

Only a real listening—a listening witness—can plumb the abyss of that universal existential mistrust that stands in the way of genuine dialogue and peace. The Peace Movement has not adequately recognized the power of violence in our day nor that its roots are not just in human nature in general or in the stupidity of individuals but in the special malaise of modern man—his lack of a meaningful personal and social direction; his lack of an image of the human; his loss of community; his basic loss of trust in himself and others and in the world in which he lives; his fear of real confrontation with otherness; his tendency to cling to the shores of institutionalized injustice and discrimination, rather than set out upon the open seas of creating new and more meaningful structures within which the "wretched of the earth," the dispossessed and the systematically ignored, can find their voice too. The true heart of the covenant of peace is the community of otherness.[7]

Chapter 22

CONFIRMATION/DISCONFIRMATION THROUGH VIOLENCE/NONVIOLENCE

ALTHOUGH IN general nonviolence confirms otherness and violence disconfirms it, nonviolence may disconfirm otherness when it is used as a tool of monologue and, in a limited sense at least, violence may confirm it. Nonviolence may be, and sometimes is, covert violence, congealed violence, suppressed violence, apocalyptic rage, perfectionist intolerance. It was not these things in Gandhi, A. J. Muste, and Martin Luther King; for in them it was grounded in personal existence and in genuine relation to other persons, rather than objectified into an omnicompetent technique. If we make the distinction that should be made between the force that sets necessary limits and the violence that destroys its object, we shall not imagine that violence ever confirms the otherness and uniqueness of the persons on whom it is used. But we can, in an age of terrorism, recognize the paradoxical fact that occasionally the terrorist's acts of violence, like the acting out of the child within the family system, are an attempt to call attention to the otherness of a minority group or people that has been ignored and passed over in the "general harmony," the violence of the status quo. To understand the confirmation of otherness in community and society we must examine both violence and nonviolence in some depth.

Two of the great social theorists of all time, Thomas Hobbes and Jean-Jacques Rousseau, had completely opposite conceptions of violence. To Hobbes violence was the natural state of man and only a strong central authoritarian government could do anything about it, since in this state of nature man's life was nasty, raw, brutish, and short, a war of all against all. Rousseau, in contrast, imagined man in the state of nature as a good, spontaneous, loving creature. Only the chains of civilization turned him into the predatory animal that he now is. The English poet Alexander Pope was able to accept all social evil in terms of the "great chain of being," and to tell us that whatever is, is right: "We are but parts of one tremendous whole, whose body nature is, and God the soul" (*An Essay on Man*). William Blake, also an eighteenth-century Englishman, had exactly the opposite view of violence: "A Robin Redbreast in a cage/Puts all Heaven in a rage." Confinement, imprisonment, destruction, mutilation are already violence and will produce more violence. "The Harlot's cry from street to street/Shall weave Old England's winding sheet" ("Auguries of Innocence"). As Blake walks down the "chartered streets" of London and sees the "mind-forged manacles" of woe, he understands that the tigers of wrath are wiser than the horses of instruction, and he cries out against "the human abstract," the deceit, mystery, humility, and pseudocharity, where "mutual fear brings peace, till the selfish loves increase," and he protests against the violence done to the chimney sweep, who says in Blake's poem, "And because I am happy, & dance & sing,/They think they have done me no injury:/And are gone to praise God & his Priest & King,/Who make up a heaven of our misery."

From Karl Marx to Herbert Marcuse, violence has been explained in terms of the economic system. The humanistic ideals of liberty, equality, fraternity, says Marx, Lenin, Marcuse, cannot be transformed into reality under a capitalist system the very nature of which is the exploitation of those below by those who control the means of production. Since the state in the capitalist system is there for the express purpose of keeping the control of these means of production in the hands of the capitalists, the entrepreneurs, and the managers, there can be no hope of gradual social change. One of the terrible ironies of this theory is that Marx believed that a socialist state would make unnecessary a police force and an army, that socialism would be followed by an automatic withering away of the state. Regrettably, that has not happened: capitalists and communists can claim equal honors in violence.

There really is a double standard, as Herbert Marcuse says, when you condemn the violence that it takes to produce or perhaps merely to carry along or conduct social change, and when you do not even count the far greater daily violence that is used to preserve and maintain the *status quo*. According to such an outlook, violence is the monopoly of the *status quo*. Laotzu put it very beautifully a long time ago: "However a man with a kind heart proceed,/He forgets what it may profit him;/However a man with a just mind proceed,/He remembers what it may profit him;/However a man of conventional conduct proceed, if he be not complied with,/Out goes his fist to enforce compliance." Our genteel society has that fist hidden just beneath the surface to enforce compliance. In Émile Zola's novel *Germinal*, in the French town where the people lived in great poverty, the grocery storekeeper would take out the credit that people owed him by sleeping with the men's wives. When finally rebellion came, this static violence produced actual violence. Not only was the grocery man killed, but the organ with which he had collected his credit was displayed on high.

In his essay "Violence: A Mirror for Americans," Ivan Illich suggests that violence is less likely to arise from purely economic or military causes than from the symbols that middle-class America is trying to sell to Latin America and to the black man in the American ghetto. Starting as "a healthy though angry and turbulent rejection of alienating symbols," violence is hardened through exploitation into hatred and crime, riots and vandalism. Violence is not caused by the American way of life but by the insistence that the superiority of this way of life be accepted by the billions of underdogs. Against this demand spontaneous violence always breaks out, and it is met in turn by planned violence that is "justified by the need to reduce a man or people to the service of the idol they threaten to reject." Nor is there any hope to be found in putting weapons into the hands of the people, for these will always be used against them. But the worldwide growth of two societies, separate and unequal—the immensely rich economy of the United States and the capital-starved economies of Latin America, the Third World, and the black ghettos—should make clear the dynamics that provoke violence between them.[1]

Violence is the product of frustration, rage, shame, envy, the product of all those things that Rainer Maria Rilke called "unlived life." Unlived life itself is something more than the failure to express yourself or to dominate others, though that is what the romantic often thinks. It is the failure to give our passions direction by bring-ing them into the dialogue with the other human beings with whom we live—in our family, in the community, in the neighborhood, in the city, and in the country. The failure to give our passions direc-tion has to do with the fact that we do not take our stand, that we do not make our objection when we must, that we allow a pseudohar-mony to continue to exist. Often we cannot do otherwise, for we do not even consciously know that we have another point of view from that of the dominant group. Or if we do know it, we know the consequences of not staying "in our place." This goes right through our society—not just among the poor and underprivileged, but in the worlds of business, commerce, and government. It is this that leads many young rebels not only to "drop out" but to adopt every way possible of not conforming and of showing "disrespect for their elders."

Rollo May has cast a profound light on the sources of violence in general and in America in particular in his book *Power and Innocence*. He sees violence as the response, provoked by the sense of powerlessness and apathy, to a situation which is felt to block off all other ways of response. Thus deeds of violence, despite their negative form, are potentially constructive in that they are a way in which people who feel impotent try "to estab-lish their self-esteem, to defend their self-image, and to demon-strate that they, too, are significant." Curiously enough, even when as in America there actually is power, the denial of power in the name of a pseudoinnocence may lead to a feeling of power-lessness which produces an "explosion of impotence" as violent as real powerlessness. Violence also arises from mutual mistrust, including the mistrust of language: "When the bond between human beings is destroyed—i.e., when the possibilities for com-munication break down—aggression and violence occur." Vio-lence unites the self on a level below the human one, says May. It may also be the only way to wrench social reforms from the dominant group. If this is true of the blacks in Africa, says May following Frantz Fanon, it is also true of the proletarian class who, unable to communicate with the tongue, may find in violence a necessary and appropriate form of communication.[2]

Simone Weil defined violence as reducing a person to a thing, the ultimate of which is killing, i.e., reducing a person to a corpse.[3] If that is so, then violence can no more be avoided in our culture or any culture than we can avoid what Martin Buber calls the "I-It relation," that is, the relation in which we use, and know, classify, and categorize one another; for this is an enormous part of our culture and becomes more so every day. It is these very categories, indeed, which lead us in the first place to prejudice, racism, and violence. But if violence means converting the human Thou into an It, then violence is no more always inevitable than the domination of the It. We live in an age, God knows, in which the machine, the corporation, and the technocrat dominate to an incredible degree. Yet a real possibility remains, through fighting and standing one's ground, of bringing these back into human dialogue. It remains with us and cannot be removed by the fist of any number of economic, psychological, social, military, or political realists who say, "This is the way it is." But if we are going to take this possibility seriously, then in each concrete situation we have to discover the hard way what the resources are for dialogue and for creating something human, to bring the passion which explodes into violence into a real interchange.

Our recognition that the true heart of the covenant of peace is the community of otherness is similar to the link to which Martin Buber pointed between genuine dialogue and the possibilities of peace. Gandhi with his *satyagraha*, as V. V. Ramana Murti suggested, was establishing dialogue with the British in Buber's sense of the term because he was confronting them with respect as an equal and bringing India stage by stage to the place where there could be a real dialogue.

> The way of violence works as a monologue, but the nature of nonviolence is a dialogue. . . . The technique of Gandhi's *satyagraha* is capable of creating the conditions that are necessary for the fulfillment of Buber's concept of dialogue. The history of nonviolent resistance as it was practised by the Indian National Congress under Gandhi's leadership eminently proved this. . . . If Gandhi was able to carry on *dialogue* with England, it was only because of *satyagraha*. . . . The old relationship between master and slave was changed thereby into a new partnership between equals in a "dialogue." . . . Gandhi was able to win by his nonviolent technique a progressive response from the British government that led to the development of a "dialogue." Each of the major campaigns of nonviolent resistance evoked the necessary recognition of India's emerging nationalism by Great Britain at successive stages of the struggle. . . . There has not been a greater example of a genuine *dialogue* between two nations in recent times than that between India and Great Britain through Gandhi's *satyagraha*.[4]

Buber would not have agreed that invariably *"satyagraha* is the answer to the basic question that is inherent in the *dialogue,"* as Murti states, or that "the methods of *satyagraha* such as nonviolent noncooperation, genuine self-sacrifice, and voluntary suffering" invariably "fulfill the great end of the *dialogue."* On the contrary, in his famous "Letter to Gandhi" Buber rejected Gandhi's suggestion that the Jews in Germany could use *satyagraha* effectively against the Nazis, since death in the concentration camps was anonymous martyrdom, not political witness.[5] But he did see nonviolent civil disobedience as something that was more and more likely to be the demand of the particular situation upon those contemporary persons who are concerned not only for justice but for man as man. He also knew the meaning of tragedy where "each is as he is" and oppositeness crystallizes into unbridgeable opposition. This is a tragedy that Gandhi and Martin Luther King knew too—long before either was assassinated. There are tragic limitations to nonviolence, situations such as South Africa where the polarization has gone too far. Perhaps it has gone too far already in America—and even more ominously so in the Middle East. Much of what is happening today cannot be called either violence or nonviolence, and certainly it cannot be called dialogue—whether it is a climbing aboard the Polaris submarine or the occupation of the Pentagon, or spilling blood on or burning draft files. It is very hard, moreover, for any man in our time to make a personal or social witness that cannot be immediately corrupted and distorted by television and by the press.

Genuine dialogue, whether between persons, groups, or nations, means holding your ground, but also, in opposing the other, confirming his right to stand where he is. This approach is more fruitful than the one of violence versus nonviolence. Nonviolence often is not dialogue at all, but just monologue—an attempt to use a technique to impose something on someone else, underneath which there is often real hatred and congealed violence. Violence, on the other hand, is not always monologue. It usually is; for, as Camus says, it silences the other man. It reduces him to the place where he has to submit, where he cannot stand his ground. But there are situations in which violence too expresses a caring not just about yourself but about the relationship, about our society, about America, about the world. The danger today, though, is that violence too is politicized so that people set out to use it merely as a technique.

It is important to contrast dialogue with a word that has become very popular in our times, "confrontation." The notion of confrontation as real when the other is a caricature and you are a caricature and there is mutual mistrust—this is the thing we have to fight. Confrontation will come when people will not listen in any other way. But to turn confrontation into a slogan and a political technique, to say, as many who never understood the meaning of "dialogue" in the first place say, that the time for "dialogue" is over, the time for "confrontation" is here, means to politicize real polarity into a false Either/Or.

What we need for our time is an openness, a flexibility, a willingness to resist and withstand the concrete situation. If dialogue means the recognition of real limits and real tragedy, it also means hope because it does not assume that what was true this moment will necessarily be true the moment after—hope, not as an idealism, therefore, but as a readiness to assess the new moment in its concreteness. This also means, of course, the readiness to know the needs of the other. A failure to recognize his needs is what the black man properly accuses the white man of: How can you say you are for brotherhood, peace, integration, progress, when you don't even hear me, when you don't imagine concretely what it means to live in the ghetto, to be black? Dialogue, therefore, has to include not just hope of something happening but hope that will enable you to enter again, both actively and imaginatively, into the concrete situation of the other—to witness, to risk yourself, to involve yourself, to stand there and discover in that situation what the resources are.

We have been deluded by the notion that political power is the only power. Of course, political power is great power, and usually behind it are economic power and military power. Yet a large part of what we call politics is only the facade—a facade of catchwords, slogans, pretenses, nuances, innuendos, and downright lies. I believe with Martin Buber that the reality is in fact more basically social, even though the political always tries to get more power and domination than it needs. In 1954 the Supreme Court struck down the "separate but equal" clause of the Interstate Commerce Act. We have learned to our great cost that this decision was necessary but not sufficient, that it has to become a social reality in every neighborhood, and it is not just law enforcement alone that is going to do that.

Concrete reality is found first of all in actual social living. This reality of our actual human and social life takes a while to manifest itself. But it is there beneath the surface, awaiting the day when social suffering will transform itself into unmistakable social movement. If you lose sight of the concrete and everything becomes tactics, then you also lose sight of the actual goal you are working toward.

This recognition of the human factor in the confrontations of our age can lead us to a new and deepened appreciation of Gandhi's *satyagraha*. This "soul-force," or "truth-force," should not be understood as a universal metaphysical, political, or ethical theory but as an image of the relations between person and person and between person and society.

Gandhi was very clear in his teachings that *satyagraha* is not a technique to be applied in miscellaneous acts but a way of life that has to arise out of the deepest human attitudes. Gandhi saw *ahimsa* not only as nonkilling but also as boundless love that "crosses all boundaries and frontiers" and envelops the whole world. "A little true non-violence acts in a silent, subtle, unseen way and leavens the whole society." He knew too that the taking of life is sometimes benevolent compared to slow torture, starvation, exploitation, wanton humiliation and oppression, and the killing of the self-respect of the weak and the poor. *Ahimsa* demands bravery and fearlessness. If the only choice is between violence and cowardice, then violence is preferable. If we do not know how to defend ourselves by the force of nonviolence, we must do so by fighting. But the force of nonviolence is no method that can be taught, like judo or karate. It is the quality of the life that takes place between person and person: "The very first step in non-violence is that we cultivate in our daily life, as between ourselves, truthfulness, humility, tolerance, loving-kindness. One who hooks his fortunes to *ahimsa*, the law of love, daily lessens the circle of destruction and to that extent promotes life and love."[6]

Gandhi's *satyagraha* cannot be applied to all situations regardless of who is applying it. It is a direction of movement within the interhuman, the social, and the political which brings persons away from the vicious circle of violence and toward cooperation and mutual respect. *Satyagraha* is not possible, said Gandhi, unless others have assurance of safety. The only way to conduct campaigns of noncooperation, Gandhi asserted, is that the crowds behave like disciplined soldiers so that the opponents might feel as safe as in their own home "by reason of our living creed of non-violence." Only insofar as *satyagraha* is permeated by the life of dialogue and concretely embodied in the meeting between person and person will it be able to fulfill the claims that Gandhi made for it.

Martin Luther King was close in spirit to both Gandhi and Buber in his fight for true community and his confirmation of otherness through nonviolence. Recognizing with Reinhold Niebuhr man's potential for evil as well as good, the complexity of man's social involvement, and the glaring reality of collective evil, King nonetheless upheld true pacifism as "a courageous confrontation of evil by the power of love." Nonviolence "does not seek to defeat or humiliate the opponent, but to win his friendship and understanding." Its goal is the "creation of the beloved community." The love about which nonviolence centers is not affectionate emotion but "understanding, redemptive good will." *Agape*, to King, "is love seeking to preserve and create community. It is insistence on community even when one seeks to break it. *Agape* is a willingness to sacrifice in the interests of mutuality. *Agape* is a willingness to go to any length to restore community." Personality, to King, can only be fulfilled in the context of community. To meet hate with love closes the gap in broken community. To meet love with hate is to become depersonalized oneself and to intensify the cleavage in broken community. But there can be no split here between love and the demands of justice. "When I am commanded to love, I am commanded to restore community, to resist injustice, and to meet the needs of my brothers." Nonviolent resistance, to King, is the narrow ridge between acquiescence and violence. "With non-violent resistance, no individual or group need submit to any wrong, nor need anyone resort to violence in order to right a wrong." The black man "must convince the white man that all he seeks is justice, *for both himself and the white man.*"[7]

Our best defense against Communism, says King in *Strength to Love*, is not anti-Communism but positive action "to remove those conditions of poverty, insecurity, injustice, and racial discrimination which are the fertile soil in which the seed of Communism grows and develops." In his famous letter from the Birmingham jail, King expresses his disappointment in the white moderate and liberal who prefers the negative peace of absence of tension to the positive peace of the presence of justice and "who paternalistically believes he can set the timetable for another man's freedom." "We who engage in non-violent direct action are not the creators of tension," King points out. "We merely bring to the surface the hidden tension that is already alive" so that it can be seen and dealt with. "Segregation, to use the terminology of the Jewish philosopher Martin Buber, substitutes an 'I-it' relationship for an 'I-thou' relationship and ends up relegating persons to the status of things." To stand, as King did, for the I-Thou relationship is to stand for the other as well as oneself, for the dialogue between person and person. "Eventually," King writes, "the civil-rights movement will have contributed infinitely more to the nation than the eradication of racial injustice. It will have enlarged the concept of brotherhood to a vision of total interrelatedness."[8]

While asserting that riots are indefensible and sympathizing with the whites who feel menaced by them, King insists that the white person recognize that the main culpability lies with municipal, state, and national governments from whom reforms must be demanded if the white (and black) citizens are to be protected. "Negroes hold only one key to the double lock of peaceful change. The other is in the hands of the white community." Although King was not in favor of the Black Power slogan, he recognized that it arose as a psychological reaction to the indoctrination that created the perfect slave whose selfhood was forfeit to his unconditional submission. The black man "must stand up amid a system that still oppresses him and develop an unassailable and majestic sense of his own value."[9]

"Society needs nonviolent gadflies to bring its tensions into the open and force its citizens to confront the ugliness of their prejudices and the tragedy of their racism." Through such gadflies the liberal will finally "see that the oppressed person who agitates for his rights is not the creator of tension" but merely brings out the hidden tension that is already alive.[10]

Recognizing that power is not evil in itself but is the ability to achieve purpose, King deplores the common tendency to contrast the concepts of love and justice as polar opposites so that love becomes the resignation of power, power the denial of love. The major crisis of our time is this collision of immoral power with powerless morality.

What is needed is a realization that power without love is reckless and abusive and that love without power is sentimental and anemic. Power at its best is love implementing the demands of justice. Justice at its best is love correcting everything that stands against love.[11]

This statement is almost identical with Martin Buber's 1926 poem, "Power and Love":

I

Our hope is too new and too old—
I do not know what would remain to us
Were love not transfigured power
And power not straying love.

II

Do not protest: "Let love alone rule!"
Can you prove it true?
But resolve: Every morning
I shall concern myself anew about the boundary
Between the love-deed-Yes and the power-deed-No
And pressing forward honor reality.

III

We cannot avoid
Using power,
Cannot escape the compulsion
To afflict the world,
So let us, cautious in diction
And mighty in contradiction,
Love powerfully.[12]

To be afraid to stand up for justice is to be dead already. To take a stand for what is right, though the whole world criticize and misunderstand you, is to be a majority of one with God. For, says King, you are never alone.

We cannot conclude this chapter without speaking of the ultimate violence that hangs heavily over our heads and that is becoming in our time the one issue that is bringing large groups of people into concerted social action as at no time since the Vietnam war: the threat of extinction by nuclear war. In 1952 in his farewell speech in America, "Hope for This Hour," Martin Buber called for the overcoming of the massive mistrust that divided the two hostile camps in the "cold war" and the renewal of dialogical immediacy between human beings. The first task to accomplish this he saw as the drawing of demarcation lines for the validity of those general theses—Marxian, Freudian, or any other—that so easily get turned into instruments of unmasking to show the views of one's opponents as merely "ideologies." The second task was the meeting of true representatives of the peoples who "must have overcome in themselves the basic mistrust and be capable of recognizing in their partner in dialogue the reality of his being." Acquainted with the true needs of their own and other peoples, they "will unrelentingly distinguish between truth and propaganda within what is called the opposition of interests" thus making it possible for beginning the settlement of the real conflicts between genuine needs.

> For if the globe is not to burst asunder, every man must be given what he needs for a really human life. Coming together out of hostile camps, those who stand in the authority of the spirit will dare to think with one another in terms of the whole planet.[13]

The success of these representatives, Buber added, "will depend on those represented, on their unreserved honesty, their goodwill with its scorn of empty phrases, their courageous personal engagement."

When I submitted this essay at Buber's request to *Partisan Review* for possible publication, its editor William Phillips rejected it on the ground that it did not take into consideration the realities of the "cold war," dealing with them as an "abstract philosophical" question instead of a "concrete political" one. When I informed Martin Buber of Phillips' response, he wrote a postscript to "Hope for This Hour" entitled "Abstract and Concrete." Characterizing the "concrete political" treatment of the "cold war" as "helping swell the literature of invective piling up in both camps," Buber insisted that he had appealed from the political not to any kind of philosophy but to what was, in fact, far more concrete than politics:

> I appealed directly to the genuine concrete, to the actual life of actual men which has become smeared over and crusted with the varnish of political fictitiousness. The representatives of one side and of the other insist that the reproaches that they hurl at their opponents make up the only reality of the situation worth considering. Many of these reproaches on both sides are, in fact, realistic enough; but in order for this reality to be regarded *in*

concreto, it too must first be freed from its encrustation of catch-words. . . . Enclosed in the sphere of the exclusively political, we can find no means to relieve the present situation; its "natural end" is *the technically perfect suicide of the human race*.[14] (italics added)

In 1953 when Martin Buber accepted the Peace Prize of the German Book Trade against universal criticism in Israel and the Yiddish press in America—a criticism that extended to his closest personal friends who did not think the Jews, still sick from the Holocaust, were ready for *this* confirmation of otherness—he did so for the sake of helping those within each people, including the Germans, who carry on the battle against the anti-human. To "build the great unknown front across mankind" true representatives of each people are needed who can speak "unreservedly with one another, not overlooking what divides them but determined to bear this division in common." Here too, as in "Hope for This Hour," the heart of what Buber called for was the confirmation of otherness:

> I believe, despite all, that the peoples in this hour can enter into a genuine dialogue with one another. In a genuine dialogue each of the partners, even when he stands in opposition to the other, heeds, affirms, and confirms his opponent as an existing other. Only so can conflict certainly not be eliminated from the world, but be humanly arbitrated and led towards its overcoming.[15]

In 1954 Buber applied this approach specifically to the threat of nuclear war. Again calling for "an adjustment of interests providing for the real vital needs of the peoples on both sides," this time Buber inveighed against the politicians who gamble with the life of the human race in a game in which both partners must lose: "This time the war game will mean destruction of all the lands and peoples involved, till there remains nothing to be destroyed—and nobody to do the destruction." The choice before us is "mutual concessions on the basis of discernment and fairness, or the unwilled suicide of mankind." In 1961 when he was asked to predict what might happen in twenty years, Buber did not, in fact, anticipate that the technically perfect yet unwilled suicide of mankind would have taken place. But although Buber agreed "that by the joint efforts of the nations war will be averted and mankind will be able to develop in peaceful conditions," he stressed that "everything depends upon what the word peace signifies here: mere cessation of the cold war or real coexistence."

> If the way is not to lead to a new and still more dangerous cold war such as may be expected from further technical development, real coexistence can and may mean nothing less than real cooperation for the mastery of the common problems of the human race that are growing ever more critical.[16]

Today, just over twenty years later, we must affirm both parts of Buber's prophecy: nuclear war *has* been averted, yet in its place we have no real coexistence. We cannot even speak of a cessation of the cold war but only an uneasy jockeying for power in which half-hearted attempts at mutual disarmament alternate with ever more staggering arms outlays. A new factor has even been added to the mutual mistrust as each side sees the other's preparations for defense against nuclear war as evidence that it is prepared to make a first strike. At the same time, in a curious mixture of blindness and deceit, the governments expend great energy to convince their peoples that there *is* some realistic civil defense when, in fact, no remote possibility exists of there being either the time or the means for the mass removal of populations from cities that the governments envisage.

Listening to Dr. Jonas Salk, Helen Caldicott, and Senator Alan Cranston speak at a mass rally against nuclear armament sponsored by Physicians for Social Responsibility in San Diego in June 1982, I was struck once again that the *only* alternative to these preparations for the unwilled but technically perfect suicide of mankind is precisely that genuine dialogue for which Martin Buber called twenty and thirty years ago. Only such dialogue contains the possibility of the confirmation of otherness that is not based on any sentimental overlooking of conflict but upon the readiness humanly to arbitrate the conflict through each of the partners, even when it stands in opposition to the other, heeding, affirming, and confirming its opponent as an existing other.

Part VI

TOWARD
A COMMUNITY
OF
COMMUNITIES

Chapter 23

RESTORING RELATIONAL TRUST

THERE HAS been no attempt in this book to present a comprehensive or systematic social theory nor to deal at any length with the political and economic realities that would need to be included in such a theory. *The Confirmation of Otherness* rather is meant as a pointer, an indicator, a helpful hint of the direction in which we must move on all levels if we are to remain a human society. The community of otherness is not an ideal or a specific goal. It is a direction of movement. Or rather it is a twofold direction of movement—a movement within each particular structure of family, community, and society to discover the maximum possibilities of the confirmation of otherness within that structure, and a movement from structure to structure until it reaches, hopefully, the structure that does not yet exist—a community of communities.

Despite these necessary disclaimers as to what this book has tried to do, its aim is not modest. It proposes nothing less than that the old and tired polarities of individual versus society, individualism versus collectivism, competition versus cooperation, free enterprise versus socialism, capitalism versus communism, freedom versus social welfare be replaced by the confirmation of otherness as the *only* meaningful direction of movement for friendship, marriage, family, community, and society within a democracy.

We have already spoken of the community of otherness as a "caring community" in connection with transcultural nursing. A caring community is one in which each shares with and cares about the other members of the community and the community as a whole. So far in our society caring communities have been few and far between. Yet if the understanding and making real of caring community were extended and deepened sufficiently, it might no longer be a contradiction in terms to speak of a "caring society." It is the fear of otherness—of allowing otherness a voice and even acknowledging its existence—which stands in the way of the movement toward a community of otherness. By the same token, there must be a restoring of relational trust for this direction of movement to acquire significant strength in our time. "Restoring Relational Trust" is the title of the national conference on "Leverages in Individual and Family Therapy" that the Human Systems Council sponsored in Massachusetts in 1980. It must be evident to the reader of this book that the restoration of relational trust is necessary not only for the one-on-one relations of friendship, love, and marriage, as well as the family, but for every aspect of the community and society with which we have dealt and many more with which we have not.

One cannot legislate relational trust nor can one make it the goal of planned social action. Yet there are things that we can do at every level to help bring it about. One of these is the recognition of its centrality for therapy, education, family life, community, and the fellowship that holds society together. Another is the movement to build climates of trust insofar as the situation, the structure, and our resources allow. Naturally a "climate of trust" too cannot be made into a specific goal without destroying the spontaneity and the "betweenness" which are essential to such a climate. Yet we can become more aware of what genuine listening and responding is; we can become more sensitive to the voices that are not ordinarily heard within the family, community, and society; and we can overcome that mistrust founded on hysteria that imagines that something dreadful will happen if we allow such voices to express points of view that may not accord with our own or even with the dominant structure of the group. Obviously here too we are limited by the severe grace of the situation, for trust and trustworthiness are not ultimately personality characteristics that inhere *in* particular persons. They are realities of the "between," and the between cannot be willed or manipulated, however much we may work toward it as a general direction of movement.

Originally, I had thought of devoting the last part of this book to the scaffolding of a general social theory, a sort of revisioning of socialism to update the Marxist-Keynesian socialism of my undergraduate days. I have never given up my socialism, despite the attacks on it in the name of freedom by my famous namesake Milton Friedman. But neither do I consider myself a socialist in the active way that I once was when I was working toward becoming a labor economist, educator, and organizer.

One of the books that I had intended to read for this last part is entitled *Le Socialisme Difficile*, a title which intrigued me so much that it even entered into my dreams. Although the socialism that I earlier espoused was based upon a sophisticated understanding of economics, politics, and history, it was still an easy socialism in that it looked toward the establishment of a new economic regime from the top. My sympathies during the years since have been much more with the federalistic or decentralized socialism of Gustav Landauer, Martin Buber, Erich Fromm, and Carlo Levi. If what I espouse in *The Confirmation of Otherness* is not precisely socialism, any more than it is capitalism, cooperatives, or any other specific economic ism, it nonetheless points the way to what might indeed be a "difficult socialism": one built up from the realization of the community of otherness in family, community, and society.

In our discussion of the confirmation of otherness in society, we have dealt with specific aspects, such as women's liberation, aging, transcultural nursing, un- and underemployment, as well as more general questions of the covenant of peace and of the relative confirmation of otherness to be found in violence and nonviolence. What has been implied in all this but has not been spelled out with sufficient explicitness is the fact that a community of otherness cannot be a closed one. To continue to grow in its otherness it must have its own ground and center, to be sure, but it must also be in open dialogue with individuals and communities outside itself. The search for the "blessed community" is ultimately an illusion, whether it expresses itself in the form of a community of affinity, or like-mindedness, a church or cult, or a commune that shuts itself off from the rest of society. The dialogue among communities of otherness can only sustain itself if there is a steady movement from casual and desultory contacts to regular, fruitful dialogue and interaction and from there to what we have called the "community of communities."

The community of communities is a term I have taken from Martin Buber's *Paths in Utopia*, that classic study of utopian socialism which we discussed, briefly, in "Reflections on Intentional Community." What Buber offers in his conclusion to *Paths in Utopia* is not a decentralistic as opposed to a state socialism but a movement in the direction of fellowship and social spontaneity and a limitation of the dominance of the "political principle" of government to only what is necessary at any given time to preserve the unity of society. In his concluding chapter, "In the Midst of Crisis," Buber claims that the primary aspiration of all history is a genuine community of human beings. By *genuine* community he means *community all through,* a community based "on the actual and communal life of big and little groups living and working together, and on their mutual relationships." For such a communal life to exist, the collectivity into which the control of the means of production passes must facilitate and promote in its very structure and in all its institutions the genuine common life of the various groups composing it.

A community does not need to be "founded," Buber asserts. Wherever historical destiny has brought a group of people together in a common fold, a living togetherness, constantly renewing itself, can already be there, and all that needs strengthening is the immediacy of relationships. The communal spirit has always been able to overcome the danger of seclusion by breaking windows for itself so that it may look out onto people, mankind, and the world. But a community of communities does have to be built, and this can be done only if the process of community building runs all through the relations of the communes with one another.

> Whether a rebirth of the commune will ensue from the "water and spirit" of the social transformation that is imminent—on this, it seems to me, hangs the whole fate of the human race. An organic commonwealth—and only such commonwealths can join together to form a shapely and articulated race of men—will never build itself up out of individuals but only out of small and ever smaller communities: *a nation is a community to the degree that it is a community of communities.*[1]

Our very pointing to the ultimate goal of a community of communities brings us back to the general and specific barriers to the confirmation of otherness that we have discovered at every level through our discussion of family, community, and society. Once the community of communities is envisaged as a nation and still more as a community of nations, as we have glimpsed it in our chapter on "The Community of Otherness and the Covenant of Peace," we must add to the limits we have already looked at, the worldwide barriers of communication that are caused by custom, language, nationality, traditional enmity, suspicion, and mutual mistrust. These are not so easily overcome through the new computer age as communications experts like Marshall McLuhan and Alvin Toffler seem to expect. Even the advent of the age of the computer and the possibility of simultaneous translation and instant worldwide transmission cannot in themselves overcome the interhuman, international, and existential mistrust which dogs our every step. Yet these things *can* be used to move in that direction, as can television, travel, education, and a thousand other innovations that the ocean of progress has thrown up on our shores.

We concluded our chapter "Reflections on Intentional Community" by quoting Buber's strange statement from the end of his essay "On the Psychologizing of the World" that "community in our time must ever again miscarry." Why must it miscarry? Some of the reasons are the general limits to the confirmation of otherness that we have discussed—fear of otherness, mistrust, self-involvement, mutual exploitation, categorization and fixing people in social roles, anxiety about disconfirmation, "seeming," and a host of others. Other reasons can be found in the specific obstacles that arise at any given time in any specific situation and structure, obstacles that can only be known, wrestled with, and, we hope, in some cases overcome, as we encounter them in the field and not through any social or psychological theory that might give us adequate foreknowledge of them.

Over and above these there is the phenomenon of psychologism to which Buber points in this essay. It is psychologism, with its tendency to remove the events that take place between persons into the isolated psyches of separate individuals, that eclipses the image of the human and the reality of the "between" in our age. "The monstrous, the dreadful phenomenon of psychologism so prevails that one cannot simply bring about healing, rescue with a single blow," writes Buber immediately after his statement that community in our time must ever again miscarry.

There is another, deeper reason why community must miscarry, one that Buber does not even hint at in this essay yet does touch on here and there in other of his works. This has to do with the paradox of confirmation itself which we have already discussed in Part Two, "The Problematic of Confirmation." Confirmation, as we have seen, is something that is essential to human existence yet cannot be aimed at as a specific goal. We cannot properly either will to confirm or will to be confirmed; for confirmation is a reality of the between. When we go from the consideration of the confirmation of the individual person in person-to-person relationships to the confirmation of otherness in community and society, we begin to glimpse tragedy in the deepest sense of the term. This is the tragedy of the limits of our resources, which make each of us what we are and which stand in the way of our turning conflict and contradiction into fruitful tension and meaningful dialogue. It is in this deepest sense of the term that we must speak also of the limits of the confirmation of otherness and the destiny of community in our time to miscarry.

But it is also in this deepest sense that we can understand Buber's further statement: "The disappointments belong to the way. There is no other way than that of this miscarrying." If confirmation of otherness is an affair of the between, then it is, in the existential meaning of the term to which I have pointed, a "grace." The reason we cannot will to confirm or to be confirmed is that we cannot handle both sides of the dialogue. But it is also that a dialogue is more than a sum of the two sides. It is a manifestation of the "between" that comes into being in that dialogue. If this is so then the real confirmation of otherness is not identifiable with social and political effectiveness or with historical success. These latter may be thought of in terms of cause and effect, plan and execution, effort and victory. Confirmation of otherness cannot. It is a reality that takes shape in the depths of history and retreats to those depths when it is obscured, manipulated, or overridden, as seems to be increasingly the case in the age we have now entered.

One could speak of this confirmation in the depths of history, as Buber himself has, in terms of the Taoist notion of *wei-wu-wei*, the doing through not-doing, the action through non-action that appears to be "passivity" only because it is done with the whole being. In a speech on "China and Us" at a conference in Germany five years before the Nazi accession to power, Buber pointed to this Taoist understanding of action ("The way to do is to be") as a commentary on a time that identifies historical reality with success. This pointing was a somber, negative, prophetic hint but one whose meaning should not be lost on us who stand in not too different a place more than half a century later:

> We have begun to doubt the significance of historical success, i.e., the validity of the man who sets an end for himself, carries this end into effect, accumulates the necessary means of power and succeeds with these means of power: the typical modern Western man. . . . Genuine effecting is not interfering, not giving vent to power, but remaining with one's self. This is the powerful existence that does not yield historical success, i.e., the success that can be exploited and registered in this hour, but only yields that effecting that at first appears insignificant, indeed invisible, yet endures across generations and there at times becomes perceptible in another form. At the core of each historical success hides the turning away from what the man who accomplished it really had in mind. Not realization, but the hidden nonrealization that has been disguised or masked just through success is the essence of historical success. Opposed to it stands the changing of men that takes place in the absence of success, the changing of men that takes place through the fact that one effects without interfering. . . . With us this knowledge does not originate as wisdom but as foolishness. We have obtained a taste of it in the bitterest manner; indeed, in a downright foolish manner.[2]

Curiously enough Buber speaks in very similar terms of biblical history, the history that is recorded in the Hebrew Bible, the so-called "Old Testament." Outer history sees only success. Inner history knows that "the way, the real way, from the Creation to the Kingdom is trod not on the surface of success but in the deep of failure." It is the unrecorded and anonymous work of the secret leadership, the work which leads to the final messianic overcoming of history in which outer history and inner history will fuse. Real biblical history, to Buber, is not the history of success but of failure. This failure is not the refusal to enter into dialogue which history records but the unrecorded failure in dialogue—in our terms, the movements to the limits of the confirmation of otherness in any given situation and the acceptance of these often tragic limits.

Buber traces this failure in the dialogue between people and God from one stage to another: As the failure of the judge leads to the king and the failure of the king to the prophet, so the failure of the prophet in his opposition to the king leads to the conception of two new types of leaders who will set the dialogue aright—the Messiah of Isaiah and the "suffering servant of the Lord" of Deutero-Isaiah. In connection with this figure of the "suffering servant," Buber again hints at a confirmation that comes in the depths of history, the confirmation by God of the man who is afflicted and despised in the eyes of his fellow men, not because he is, as Christianity claims, the incarnation of God but because God is with him in his sufferings and shares in the fate of his witness for the community of otherness. The suffering servant is like the arrow that is hidden in the quiver; yet it is he and not the successful men—Nebuchadnezzar, Alexander, Caesar, Napoleon, and Hitler—who does the *real* work of history:

> The way, the real way, from the Creation to the Kingdom is trod not on the surface of success, but in the deep of failure. The real work, from the Biblical point of view, is the late-recorded, the unrecorded, the anonymous work. The real work is done in the shadow, in the quiver.[3]

At this point I can imagine Joe Hill asking me if I am offering my readers "pie in the sky by and by." Is this seeming excursus into theology at the end of *The Confirmation of Otherness* a smoke screen to hide the otherwise undeniable fact that the "community of otherness" is one more utopian dream destined to fail or not even be tried like all the others? I do not think so; for the community of otherness, as we have said, is not an ideal but a direction of movement and one, moreover, that we must take if we are to move at all toward the restoration of relational trust and toward bringing the hidden human image out of its hiding. What is more, what I at least am pointing to here is not theological at all, but the mystery and grace of the "between" which resides in our midst, in the depths of history, and needs no divine name or transcendent referent for us to point to it.

An autobiographical fragment which Buber wrote in 1928, the same year as his essay on "China and Us," gives us our deepest insight into this hidden confirmation in the depths of history through which we can understand the miscarrying of community and the way that leads from one such miscarrying to another in our times. In this fragment Buber tells of his last meeting in person with Theodor Herzl, the great founder of Zionism for whom Buber worked in his youth and to whom he looked up as a Jewish embodiment of the Nietzschean hero. Buber belonged to a group of young cultural Zionists which called itself the "Democratic Fraction" and which found itself, from one Zionist Congress to the next, in ever greater opposition to their beloved leader Herzl. At the Sixth Zionist Congress in 1902 this conflict took the form of a personal attack by Herzl on Davis Trietsch, one of the leaders of the Democratic Fraction, for his colonizing activities in Cyprus.

When Buber and his close friend Berthold Feiwel went in to see Herzl to protest against the personal and unjust nature of this attack, Buber found his faith in Herzl wavering for the first time in a revolt of the soul so violent that he still had a physical recollection of it more than a quarter of a century later. When they entered Herzl's chamber, however, his pounding heart suddenly grew numb at the sight of the ordinarily composed and masterly Herzl striding up and down like a caged lion, breathing wildly, with flashing and burning eyes, and a pallor that Buber only noticed later. (Herzl succumbed within two years to a heart attack.) Buber testified that here, at the age of twenty-four, he set foot for the first time on the soil of tragedy, where there is no longer such a thing as being in the right:

> It became at once compellingly clear to me that here it was impossible to remain inwardly the representative of one side. Outside, in the hall, was a man, my friend and ally, who had been hurt, who had suffered a public injustice. But here was the author of the injustice, whose blow had dealt the wound—a man who, though misled, was still my leader, sick with zeal; a man consumed with zeal for his faith: his faith in his cause and in himself, the two inextricably bound together.[4]

This experience and Herzl's confession that he had spoken as personally as he did because Trietsch's fiancée, a "splendid" young woman with flashing eyes, had stood directly opposite him as he spoke, led Buber to reflect in the years to come on the identification of cause and leader to which all history up till now has attested. No one could have called Herzl to account, for he identified the Zionist movement with himself. Only if they could have placed his *charisma*, his personal power, in question could they have questioned his claim. The hope for a dialogical relationship between leader and follower—a true community of otherness—alone could give us any grounds for contesting this identification between the cause and the leader.

Yet Buber also reflected in 1928 that the fiancée with the flashing eyes might have brought home to Herzl that his opponent had at least one human being who would take his part *thus*. Through this realization Herzl might also have been gripped by the question of a very different confirmation in the depths of history from that which he had taken for granted in his lifetime of striving for political success:

> . . . whether there might not be yet another reality, different from that of obvious world history—a reality hidden and powerless because it has not come into power; whether there might not be, therefore, men with a mission who have not been called to power and yet are, in essence, men who have been summoned; whether excessive significance has not perhaps been ascribed to the circumstances that separate the one class of men from the other; whether success is the only criterion; whether the unsuccessful man is not destined at times to gain a belated, perhaps posthumous, perhaps even anonymous victory which even history refuses to record: whether, indeed, when even this does not happen, a blessing is not spoken, nonetheless, to these abandoned ones, a word that confirms them. . . .[5]

To make out of this the assertion that God enters into a history as a *deus ex machina*, like the ancient Greek deities who entered into the great plays at the last moment to save the situation, would be too easy and too untrue to history as we know it. The heart of this confirmation lies rather in the social, historical, and political effectiveness of every step in the direction of the confirmation of otherness in family, community, and society. This is a different philosophy of action, one which sees effectiveness not in political success but in the restoring of relational trust, in healing through meeting, in bringing the hidden human image out of its hiding.

When Senator McGovern conceded defeat in the 1972 elections he quoted the verse from Deutero-Isaiah, "Those who wait upon the Lord shall run and not be weary, shall walk and not be faint" (Isaiah 40:31). Though this allusion to the suffering servant of the

Lord did not prevent McGovern from following Senator Eugene McCarthy into the oblivion of those candidates who do not get elected, it touched me deeply at the time. After my book *The Hidden Human Image* was published in 1974, I was struck by how quickly some of its major concerns—from education and encounter groups to social witness and nonviolent action—seemed to go out of date. Suddenly few persons cared about these matters or about communes or any of the other breakthroughs of the '60s except for liberalized sex and women's liberation. Yet of this witness I shall say what I said in *The Hidden Human Image* of the much more lonely witness that I made many years ago as a Jewish conscientious objector in the Second World War. Looking back on it from the standpoint of the late 1960s, I welcomed company when I had it, but I was ready to go my way alone again when necessary, *after* that company as *before*:

> When I came to teach at Sarah Lawrence College in 1951, I was dismayed by the utter lack of social concern on the part of the students even when their own boyfriends were risking their lives in the Korean War. By 1958 this situation had decisively changed with the Civil Rights Movement, the Northern Student Movement, SNCC, and the beginnings of the "freedom rides" in the South. This change has proved a lasting one [sic!], even when the emphasis has shifted from integration to the Vietnam War and from nonviolent direct action to the New politics. It has done my heart good to see the "silent generation" of the late forties and early fifties turn into the rebellious generation of the late fifties and sixties. It is a gladdening experience, in particular, to find so many young people walking with me in their support of the Peace Movement and their opposition to the war in Indochina. *But the joy of finding unknown comrades walking beside one must also include the courage to walk alone again if it should prove necessary.*[6]

NOTES

CHAPTER 1

1. Martin Buber, *Between Man and Man*, trans. Ronald Gregor Smith (New York: Macmillan, 1965), p. 168. See also pp. 175, 202–204.
2. Ibid., p. 179.
3. Martin Buber, *The Knowledge of Man: A Philosophy of the Interhuman*, ed. Maurice Friedman (New York: Harper Torchbooks, 1966), p. 149.

CHAPTER 2

1. William James, *Essays in Pragmatism*, ed. Aubrey Castell (New York: Hafner Publishing, 1949), p. 157.
2. John Dewey, *Reconstruction in Philosophy*, enl. ed. (Boston: Beacon Press, 1948), pp. 163–64.
3. Martin Buber, *The Legend of the Baal-Shem*, trans. Maurice Friedman (New York: Schocken Books [paperback], 1969), p. 41.

CHAPTER 3

1. Buber, *Between Man and Man*, pp. 61–62.
2. Ibid., pp. 96–97.
3. Ibid., p. 98.
4. Buber, *The Knowledge of Man*, pp. 80–81.
5. Buber, *Between Man and Man*, pp. 196–97.
6. These ideas are more fully developed in Maurice Friedman, *Touchstones of Reality: Existential Trust and the Community of Peace* (New York: E. P. Dutton, 1972; Dutton Books [paperback], 1974).

CHAPTER 4

1. Buber, *Between Man and Man*, p. 16.
2. Ibid., p. 114.
3. Buber, *The Knowledge of Man*, pp. 67–68.
4. Ibid., p. 71.
5. Ibid., p. 107.
6. Ibid., p. 108.
7. Ibid., pp. 121–48.

CHAPTER 5

1. Buber, *The Knowledge of Man*, pp. 180–83.

CHAPTER 6

1. Sidney Jourard, *Disclosing Man to Himself* (New York: D. Van Nostrand Co., 1968), pp. 86, 88.
2. R. D. Laing, *The Politics of Experience* (New York: Ballantine Books, 1967), pp. 42–43.
3. Ivan Boszormenyi-Nagy and Geraldine Spark, *Invisible Loyalties: Reciprocity in Intergenerational Family Therapy* (New York: Harper and Row, Medical Division, 1973), p. 248.

CHAPTER 7

1. *The Collected Poems of W. B. Yeats*, definitive ed. (New York: Macmillan, 1956), p. 240.
2. R. D. Laing, *Self and Others* (Hamondsworth, England, and Baltimore, Maryland: Penguin Books, 1971), p. 136.
3. Laing, *The Politics of Experience*, p. 97.
4. On this aspect of the problematic of confirmation, see my discussion of Kafka in Maurice Friedman, *Problematic Rebel: Melville, Dostoievsky, Kafka, Camus*, 2nd ed., rev. and enl. (Chicago: University of Chicago Press and Phoenix Books [paperback], 1970), pp. 374–99, 476–83.
5. Carl R. Rogers, *Carl Rogers on Personal Power* (New York: Delacorte Press, 1977), pp. 51, 55.
6. Carl R. Rogers, *Becoming Partners: Marriage and Its Alternatives* (New York: Delacorte Press, 1972).
7. Kate Millett, *Sexual Politics* (Garden City, New York: Doubleday, 1970), pp. 25–26, 28–29, 31–35, 54, 58, 179, 189, 196.
8. Robin Morgan, ed., *Sisterhood Is Powerful: An Anthology of Writings from the Women's Liberation Movement* (New York: Vintage Books, 1970), pp. 45, 94, 181, 246, 278, 290–91, 172, 174–75.
9. Quoted in Morgan, *Sisterhood Is Powerful*, p. 564.
10. Marya Mannes, "The Roots of Anxiety in Modern Woman," *Journal*

of Neuropsychiatry, Vol. V (1964), p. 412, quoted in Morgan, *Sisterhood Is Powerful*, p. 244.

11. Daniel J. Levinson et al., *The Seasons of a Man's Life* (New York: Alfred A. Knopf, 1978), p. 144.

12. Ibid., pp. 153–54.

13. Ibid., p. 323 and footnote.

CHAPTER 8

1. Friedman, *Problematic Rebel*, p. 456.

2. Albert Camus, *The Myth of Sisyphus and Other Essays*, trans. Justin O'Brien (New York: Alfred A. Knopf, 1955), p. 6.

3. A number of passages in this chapter are based upon Friedman, *Problematic Rebel*, pp. 456–59, 477–82.

CHAPTER 9

1. *The Analects of Confucius*, annotated and trans. Arthur Waley (1938; reprint ed., New York: Vintage Books, n.d.), Book I, #2, p. 83.

2. *The Way of Life According to Laotzu*, trans. Witter Bynner (New York: Capricorn Books, 1962), #18, p. 35.

3. Ibid., #38, p. 49.

4. Ibid., #49, p. 56.

5. Ibid., #35, p. 47.

6. Ibid., #7, p. 28; #81, p. 76; #54, p. 59.

CHAPTER 10

1. Martin Buber, *Pointing the Way*, ed. and trans. Maurice Friedman (New York: Schocken Books, 1974), pp. 65–66.

2. Viktor E. Frankl, *Das Menschenbild der Seelenheilkunde: Kritik des dynamischen Psychologismus* (Stuttgart: Hippokrates Verlag, 1959), p. 91. My translation.

3. Rogers, *Carl Rogers on Personal Power*, p. 43.

4. Germaine Greer, *The Female Eunuch* (New York: McGraw-Hill, 1971), pp. 52, 59–60, 69, 86, 108.

5. Pamela Kangas, "The Single Professional Woman: A Phenomenological Study" (Ph.D. dissertation, California School of Professional Psychology, San Diego, 1976).

6. Beverly Jones, "The Dynamics of Marriage and Motherhood," in Morgan, *Sisterhood Is Powerful*, p. 52.

7. Leslie H. Farber, *lying, despair, jealousy, envy, sex, suicide, drugs, and the good life* (New York: Harper Colophon Books, 1978), Chapter 8.

8. Rogers, *Carl Rogers on Personal Power*, pp. 68, 230.

9. Ibid., pp. 55, 232–33.
10. Blair Justice and Rita Justice, *The Broken Taboo: Sex in the Family* (New York: Human Sciences Press, 1979), p. 29.
11. Ibid., p. 32.
12. Ibid., p. 65.
13. Ibid., p. 78.
14. Ibid., p. 95.
15. Ibid., p. 97.
16. Ibid., p. 143.
17. See Maurice Friedman, *Healing Through Meeting: Dialogue and Psychotherapy* (forthcoming), Chapter 13, "Disconfirmation and 'Mental Illness'" and Chapter 22, "Contextual Therapy: Ivan Boszormenyi-Nagy."
18. Warren Farrell, *The Family Sex Problem* (New York: Bantam Books, 1984).
19. Ibid.
20. Ibid.
21. Ibid.

Chapter 11

1. Linda Leonard, *The Wounded Woman: Healing the Father–Daughter Relationship* (Athens, Ohio: The Swallow Press, 1982).
2. Ibid.
3. Ibid.
4. Ibid.
5. Erich Fromm, *The Art of Loving* (New York: Bantam Books, 1963), p. 86.
6. Doris Agnes Crisler, "New Family Constellations: Dimensions and Effects of Systemic Culture Shock" (Ph.D. dissertation, California School of Professional Psychology, San Diego, 1977), pp. 1–4.
7. Ibid., p. 12. The words are Crisler's, not Mead's. Crisler is paraphrasing statements on this subject from Margaret Mead, *Male and Female: A Study of the Sexes in a Changing World* (New York: Morrow, 1967).

Chapter 12

1. Nagy and Spark, *Invisible Loyalties*, p. 184.
2. Martin Buber, *Meetings*, ed. and trans. Maurice Friedman (LaSalle, Illinois: Open Court Publishing, 1973), pp. 18–19. Italics mine.
3. Richard D. Stanton, "Dialogue in Psychotherapy: Martin Buber, Maurice Friedman and Therapists of Dialogue," (Ph.D. dissertation for Union Graduate School/West, April 30, 1978), p. 181.
4. Nagy and Spark, *Invisible Loyalties*, pp. 128–31, 134–35.

5. Ibid., p. 20.
6. Ibid., pp. 20–21.
7. Ibid., pp. 134, 224, 245, 376. The last quotation is from p. 105.
8. Ivan Boszormenyi-Nagy, "Contextual Therapy: Therapeutic Leverages in Mobilizing Trust," in Robert T. Green and James L. Framo, eds., *Family Therapy: Major Contributions* (New York: International Universities Press, 1981), pp. 393–415.
9. Ibid., pp. 18–21.
10. Ivan Boszormenyi-Nagy and Barbara R. Krasner, "Trust-Based Therapy: A Contextual Approach," *American Journal of Psychiatry*, July 1980.
11. Letter from Ivan Boszormenyi-Nagy to Maurice Friedman, June 17, 1980.
12. Ivan Boszormenyi-Nagy and David N. Ulrich, "Contextual Family Therapy" in A. S. Gurman and D. P. Kniskern, eds., *The Handbook of Family Therapy* (New York: Brunner/Mazel, 1981), pp. 159–86.
13. Helm Stierlin, *Separating Parents and Adolescents: A Perspective on Running Away, Schizophrenia, and Waywardness* (New York: Quadrangle, 1974).
14. Buber, *The Knowledge of Man*, p. 136.
15. Rogers, *Carl Rogers on Personal Power* pp. 29–31, 37.

CHAPTER 13

1. Martin Buber, *A Believing Humanism: Gleanings*, trans. Maurice Friedman (New York: Simon & Schuster, 1969), pp. 94–95.
2. Erving Goffman, *Stigma: Notes on the Management of Spoiled Identity* (Englewood Cliffs, New Jersey: Prentice-Hall, A Spectrum Book, 1963), pp. 32–33, 38, 121–24, 133.
3. William R. Coulson, *Groups, Gimmicks, and Instant Gurus: An Examination of Encounter Groups and Their Distortions* (New York: Harper & Row, 1972), pp. 18, 20. The quotation is from Buber, *Between Man and Man*, p. 114.
4. Louis Paul, "Some Ethical Principles for Facilitators," *Journal of Humanistic Psychology*, Vol. XIII, No. 1 (Winter 1973), pp. 43–46.
5. Thomas C. Greening, "Encounter Groups from the Perspective of Existential Humanism," in *Existential Humanistic Psychology*, ed. Thomas C. Greening (Belmont, California: Brooks/Cole Publishing [paperback], 1971), p. 86.
6. Walter Tubbs, "Beyond Perls," *Journal of Humanistic Psychology*, Vol. XII, No. 2 (Fall 1972), p. 5. The original, set in verse form, was fittingly placed by Thomas Greening, editor of the JHP, as a prelude to my own article on "Dialogue and the Unique in Humanistic Psychology." For a reply to Tubbs that makes the

equally essential point that an I-Thou relationship cannot be aimed at or willed, see Don Horne, "Response to Tubbs' 'Beyond Perls,'" *Journal of Humanistic Psychology*, Vol. XIV, No. 1 (1974), pp. 73–75, and for a social satire of Perls' Gestalt Prayer, see p. 76, "The Getsmärt Prayer."

7. Carl R. Rogers, *Carl Rogers on Encounter Groups* (New York: Harper & Row [paperback], 1970), p. 46.
8. Coulson, *Groups, Gimmicks, and Instant Gurus*, pp. 53–55.
9. Vin and Pat Rosenthal, "With Leon (and Laing) in London: An Interview with Leon Redler," *Voices* (Winter 1973/74), pp. 47, 49.
10. Ibid., p. 49.
11. Ibid., pp. 51–52.
12. Carl R. Rogers, *A Way of Being* (Boston: Houghton Mifflin, 1980), p. 187.
13. Ibid., pp. 200–201.
14. Ibid., pp. 183, 194, 203–205; Rogers, *Carl Rogers on Personal Power*, pp. 175, 180.
15. Rogers, *A Way of Being*, pp. 184–85, 199–200, 204–205.

CHAPTER 14

1. Buber, *Pointing the Way*, pp. 98–105; Maurice Friedman, *Martin Buber's Life and Work: The Middle Years—1923–1945* (New York: E. P. Dutton, 1983), Chapter 11.
2. Friedman, *Touchstones of Reality*, p. 26. I have dealt at greater length in this book with much of the material in the present chapter.

CHAPTER 15

1. Levinson, *The Seasons of a Man's Life*, pp. 333–34.
2. Ibid., p. 334.
3. *Catalogue for the College for the Year 1981*, International College, 1019 Gayley Avenue, Los Angeles, California 90024/(213)208-6761.
4. Levinson, *The Seasons of a Man's Life*, p. 154.
5. For a highly significant study of the mentoring relationship which, so far as I know, is unique of its kind, see David S. Zucker, "The Mentor/Protégé Relationship: A Phenomenological Inquiry," The Professional School for Humanistic Studies, San Diego, 1981.

CHAPTER 16

1. Martin Buber, *Paths in Utopia*, trans. R. F. C. Hull (Boston: Beacon Press [paperback], 1958).
2. B. F. Skinner, *Walden Two*, 2nd ed. (New York: Macmillan, 1976).

3. Linda Savage, "A Fantasy," unpublished paper dated October 2, 1971.

4. Linda Savage and Jerry Spiegel, *On Becoming High: An Introduction to the Aquarian Age,* artwork by Edward Phelps, Jr., privately printed and distributed, p. 141. Italics mine.

5. Ibid., p. 150.

6. Ibid.

7. Ibid.

8. Friedman, *Touchstones of Reality,* pp. 210–15.

9. *Inside the Door—A Center of Alternatives for Youth,* written and produced through the collective efforts of Herschel Kaminsky, Irving Wexler, and the Staff of The Door (New York: 1982), pp. 3–5, 8, 17, 22, 25, 31.

10. Buber, *A Believing Humanism,* p. 152.

CHAPTER 17

1. John Stuart Mill, *The Subjection of Women* (1869), reprinted in *Three Essays by J. S. Mill,* World's Classics Series (London: Oxford University Press, 1966), pp. 523–24, quoted in Kate Millett, *Sexual Politics* (Garden City, New York: Doubleday, 1970), p. 103.

2. Morgan, *Sisterhood Is Powerful,* pp. 565, 233, 306, 219, 128–29, 165, 171, 373.

3. Ibid., pp. 486, 451–52, 465, xxxii, 28, 54, 357.

4. Shulamith Firestone, *The Dialectic of Sex: The Case for Feminist Revolution* (New York: Bantam Books [paperback], 1971), pp. 127, 139, 149, 152, 157.

5. Morgan, *Sisterhood Is Powerful,* pp. 107, 257.

6. Ibid., pp. xxvi, 260–61, 559, 341–43, 350–52.

7. Mattie L. Humphrey, "The Black Woman's Survival Kit," *Trends,* Vol. III, No. 2 (October 1970), p. 21.

8. Greer, *The Female Eunuch,* pp. 112–13.

9. Morgan, *Sisterhood Is Powerful,* pp. xxvii, 37–40, 43, 94, 96, 99, 115, 118, 422, 424, 428, 431, 436, 462, 562.

10. Paraphrased in Miriam Carroll, "Female Rebels Chart Their Course," *Catholic Sun Herald,* March 26, 1971.

11. Florence Bryant, "A Liberated Woman Looks at Woman's Liberation," *Trends,* Vol. 3, No. 2, October 1970, p. 14; Mary Daly, "Women and the Catholic Church," in Morgan, *Sisterhood Is Powerful,* pp. 131–32.

12. Firestone, *The Dialectic of Sex,* pp. 38, 210, 104, 227.

13. Greer, *The Female Eunuch,* pp. 10–11, 303, 313, 315, 325–29, 85, 109. The Rilke quotation can be found in context in Rainer Maria Rilke, *Letters to a Young Poet,* trans. M. D. Herter Norton, rev.

ed. (New York: W. W. Norton, 1954), Letter No. 4, pp. 38–39. Greer left out the significant end: " . . . in order simply, seriously and patiently to bear in common the difficult sex that has been laid upon them."

14. Morgan, *Sisterhood Is Powerful*, p. 131.
15. For a full-scale discussion of women's liberation, see Maurice Friedman, *The Hidden Human Image* (New York: Delacorte Press, Delta Books [paperback], 1974), pp. 183–223, on which this chapter and some passages in Chapters 7 and 10 of this book are based.

CHAPTER 18

1. Friedman, *The Hidden Human Image*, pp. 149–51.
2. Martin Buber, *Eclipse of God: Studies in the Relation Between Religion and Philosophy* (New York: Harper Torchbooks, 1957), "Prelude: Report on Two Talks," trans. Maurice Friedman, p. 6.
3. Friedman, *Touchstones of Reality*, p. 319.
4. Martin Buber, *Tales of the Hasidim: The Early Masters*, trans. Olga Marx (New York: Schocken Books, 1978), p. xii.
5. Buber, *Pointing the Way*, p. 205.
6. Ibid., p. 206.
7. Martin Buber, *Tales of the Hasidim: The Later Masters*, trans. Olga Marx (New York: Schocken Books, 1978), p. 318.

CHAPTER 19

1. The remainder of the present chapter consists of an address, delivered by the author to the Transcultural Nursing Conference in 1977. No attempt has been made to remove the signs of oral delivery, or of its being directed to a specific audience.
2. *The Way of Life According to Lao-tzu*, # 67, pp. 68–69.
3. Buber, *The Legend of the Baal-Shem*, pp. 48–49.
4. Buber, *Between Man and Man*, pp. 169–70.

CHAPTER 20

1. Studs (Louis) Terkel, *Working: People Talk About What They Do All Day and How They Feel About What They Do* (New York: Pantheon Books, 1974), p. xi.
2. Ibid., pp. xiii, xxiv, 84, 193, 422–24.
3. Ibid., pp. 81, 84, 160–61, 409–11.
4. Ibid., pp. 156, 218, 303, 411–13, 519, 589.
5. Charles Hampden-Turner, *Radical Man: The Process of Psychosocial Development* (Cambridge, Massachusetts: Schenkman, 1970; reprinted as a Doubleday Anchor Book).
6. Terkel, *Working*, pp. 347, 527, 567.

7. Levinson, *The Seasons of a Man's Life*, p. 338.
8. Ibid., p. 339.
9. Terkel, *Working*, pp. 71–72, 155, 168, 523–24, 540, 565, 567–68.
10. Ibid., pp. 303–305; S. Zawadski and P. Lazarsfeld, "The Psychological Consequences of Unemployment," *Journal of Social Psychology* VI (1935), p. 239, quoted in Goffman, *Stigma*, p. 17; Robert Shogan, "Ghosts of Unemployment Haunt Victims for Years; Recession: Human Cost Includes Mental Illness, Suicide, Homicide," *Los Angeles Times*, January 11, 1982, Part I, pp. 1, 10.

CHAPTER 21

1. John Friedmann, *Retracking America: A Theory of Transactive Planning* (Garden City, New York: Doubleday Anchor Books, 1973), p. 185.
2. Ibid., p. 235.
3. Friedman, *Touchstones of Reality*, p. 24 f.
4. Friedmann, *Retracking America*, pp. 240–41.
5. Giles Gunn, *The Interpretation of Otherness: Literature, Religion, and the American Imagination* (New York: Oxford University Press, 1979), pp. 179–81.
6. Jacobo Timerman, "Journal of the Longest War–II," *The New Yorker*, October 25, 1982, pp. 55–64, 73f.
7. For a full-scale discussion of the "covenant of peace"—both its relationship to the biblical covenant and its implications for nonviolence and peace—see Friedman, *Touchstones of Reality*, Chapters 7 and 15. Chapter 21 of this present book is based upon the larger chapter of the same title in Friedman, *The Hidden Human Image*, pp. 358–71.

CHAPTER 22

1. Ivan Illich, *Celebration of Awareness: A Call for Institutional Revolution* (Garden City, New York: Doubleday, 1970), pp. 25–28.
2. Rollo May, *Power and Innocence: A Search for the Sources of Violence* (New York: W. W. Norton, 1972), pp. 23, 44, 52–53, 67, 192–93, 245–46.
3. Simone Weil, *The Illiad, or The Poem of Force* (Wallingford, Pennsylvania: Pendle Hill Pamphlets, n.d.).
4. V. V. Ramana Murti, "Buber's Dialogue and Gandhi's Satyagraha," *The Journal of the History of Ideas*, Vol. XXIX, No. 4 (October–December 1968), pp. 608–12.
5. Martin Buber, *Israel and the World: Essays in a Time of Crisis* (New York: Schocken Books [paperback], 1963), pp. 227–33.
6. *The Gandhi Sutras: The Basic Teachings of Mahatma Gandhi*, arranged by

D. S. Savna (New York: Adair Publishing, 1940), pp. 31, 36, 54, 58–60, 63, 66, 68.

7. Martin Luther King, Jr., *Stride Toward Freedom: The Montgomery Story* (New York: Ballantine Books, 1960), pp. 78–85, 174, 176.

8. Martin Luther King, Jr., *Strength to Love* (New York: Harper & Row, 1963), pp. 100, 123; Martin Luther King, Jr., *Why We Can't Wait* (New York: New American Library, Signet Books, 1964), pp. 84–85, 82, 152.

9. Martin Luther King, Jr., *Where Do We Go from Here: Chaos or Community?* (New York: Harper & Row, 1967), pp. 12–13, 18, 21–22, 40–41.

10. Ibid., pp. 46–49, 51 f., 60–61, 63–64, 66, 90–91.

11. Ibid., p. 37.

12. Buber, *A Believing Humanism*, p. 45.

13. Martin Buber, *Pointing the Way: Collected Essays,* ed. and trans. Maurice Friedman (New York: Schocken Books, 1974), "Hope for This Hour," p. 228.

14. Ibid., "Abstract and Concrete," p. 230.

15. Ibid., "Genuine Dialogue and the Possibilities of Peace," p. 238.

16. Buber, *A Believing Humanism*, "Stop!", pp. 203 f., "In Twenty Years," p. 180.

Chapter 23

1. Buber, *Paths in Utopia*, p. 136. Italics mine.

2. Buber, *Pointing the Way*, pp. 124–25.

3. Buber, *Israel and the World*, "Biblical Leadership," trans. Great Hort, p. 133.

4. Buber, *Meetings*, pp. 34–35.

5. Ibid., pp. 37–38.

6. Friedman, *The Hidden Human Image*, p. 334. Italics mine.

ACKNOWLEDGMENTS

Grateful acknowledgment is made for permission to reprint copyrighted material.

Excerpts from *A Believing Humanism: Gleanings* by Martin Buber, trans. by Maurice Friedman (New York: Simon & Schuster, 1967) are reprinted with permission of Rafael Buber.

Excerpts from *Carl Rogers on Personal Power* by Carl Rogers, copyright © 1977 by Carl Rogers, are reprinted by permission of Delacorte Press.

Excerpts from *Retracking America* by John Friedmann, copyright © 1973 by John Friedmann, are reprinted by permission of Doubleday & Company, Inc.

Excerpts from *The Myths of Incest* by Warren Farrell (New York: Bantam Books, 1984) are reprinted by permission of Warren Farrell.

Excerpts from "The Love Song of J. Alfred Prufrock," "Gerontion," and "Ash Wednesday" in *Collected Poems 1909–1962* by T. S. Eliot are reprinted by permission of Harcourt Brace Jovanovich, Inc.; copyright 1936 by Harcourt Brace Jovanovich, copyright © 1963, 1964 by T. S. Eliot.

Excerpts from *Four Quartets* by T. S. Eliot are reprinted by permission of Harcourt Brace Jovanovich, Inc.; copyright 1943 by T. S. Eliot, renewed 1971 by Esme Valerie Eliot.

Excerpts from *Invisible Loyalties: Reciprocity in Intergenerational Family Therapy* by Ivan Boszormenyi-Nagy and Geraldine Spark (New York: Harper & Row, Medical Division, 1973) are reprinted by permission of Harper & Row, Publishers, Inc.

Excerpts from *The Knowledge of Man* by Martin Buber, ed. by Maurice Friedman, trans. by Ronald Gregor Smith, copyright © 1965 by Martin Buber and Maurice Friedman, are reprinted by permission of Harper & Row, Publishers, Inc.

299

300 ACKNOWLEDGMENTS

Excerpts from *The Legend of Baal-Shem* by Martin Buber, trans. by Maurice Friedman, copyright © 1955 by Martin Buber, are reprinted by permission of Harper & Row, Publishers, Inc.

Excerpts from *Pointing the Way* by Martin Buber, ed. and trans. by Maurice Friedman, copyright © 1957 by Martin Buber, are reprinted by permission of Harper & Row, Publishers, Inc.

Excerpts (64 lines) from *The Way of Life* according to Laotzu, translated by Witter Bynner, (John Day) copyright 1944 by Witter Bynner, are reprinted by permission of Harper & Row, Publishers, Inc.

Excerpts from *The Broken Taboo: Sex in the Family* by Blair and Rita Justice (New York: Human Sciences Press, 1979) are reprinted by permission of Human Sciences Press, Inc.

Excerpts from *Inside the Door: A Center of Alternatives for Youth*, a project of the International Center for Integrative Studies, written in conjunction with Herschel Kaminski and Irving Wexler, are reprinted by permission of International Center for Integrative Studies, New York.

Excerpts from *Journal of the Longest War* by Jacobo Timerman (New York: Knopf, 1982) are reprinted by permission of Alfred A. Knopf, Inc.

Excerpts from *The Seasons of a Man's Life* by Daniel J. Levinson, et. al., copyright © 1978 by Daniel J. Levinson, are reprinted by permission of Alfred A. Knopf, Inc.

Excerpts from *The Female Eunuch* by Germaine Greer, copyright © 1970, 1971 by Germaine Greer, are reprinted by permission of McGraw-Hill Book Company.

Excerpts from *Between Man and Man* by Martin Buber, copyright © Macmillan Publishing Co., Inc. 1965, are reprinted with permission of Macmillan Publishing Company.

Excerpts from *Collected Poems* by William Butler Yeats, copyright © 1933 by Macmillan Publishing Co., Inc., renewed 1961 by Bertha Georgie Yeats, are reprinted by permission of Macmillan Publishing Co., Inc., Michael B. Yeats, Anne Yeats and Macmillan London Ltd.

Excerpts from *Meetings* by Martin Buber, ed. by Maurice Friedman (La Salle, IL: Open Court, 1973) are reprinted by permission of Open Court Publishing Co.

Excerpts from *The Interpretation of Otherness: Literature, Religion, and the American Imagination* by Giles Gunn (New York: Oxford University Press, 1979) are reprinted by permission of Oxford University Press.

Excerpts from *Sisterhood Is Powerful: An Anthology of Writings from the Women's Liberation Movement,* ed. by Robin Morgan (New York: Random House, 1970) are reprinted by permission of Random House, Inc.

Excerpts from *Working: People Talk About What They Do All Day and How They Feel About What They Do* by Studs Terkel, copyright © 1972, 1974 by Studs Terkel, are reprinted by permission of Random House, Inc.

Excerpts from *On Becoming High: An Introduction to the Aquarian Age* by Linda E. Savage and Jerry Spiegel are reprinted by permission of Linda Savage and Jerry Spiegel.

Excerpts from *Dialogue in Psychotherapy: Martin Buber, Maurice Friedman and Therapists of Dialogue* by Richard D. Stanton are reprinted by permission of Richard D. Stanton.

Excerpts from *Problematic Rebel: Melville, Dostoievsky, Kafka, Camus,* 2nd rev. edition, by Maurice Friedman, copyright © 1970 by the University of Chicago, are reprinted by permission of The University of Chicago Press.

Excerpts from "With Leon (and Laing) in London: An Interview with Leon Redler" by Vin and Pat Rosenthal, *Voices,* Winter 1973/74, are reprinted by permission of *Voices* magazine, New York.